Eclectic Psychotherapy
(PGPS-118)

Pergamon Titles of Related Interest

Anchin/Kiesler HANDBOOK OF INTERPERSONAL PSYCHOTHERAPY

Brenner THE EFFECTIVE PSYCHOTHERAPIST: Conclusions from Practice and Research

Kanfer/Goldstein HELPING PEOPLE CHANGE: A Textbook of Methods, 2nd Edition

Karoly/Kanfer SELF-MANAGEMENT AND BEHAVIOR CHANGE: From Theory to Practice

Papajohn INTENSIVE BEHAVIOR THERAPY: The Behavioral Treatment of Complex Emotional Disorders

Walker CLINICAL PRACTICE OF PSYCHOLOGY: A Guide for Mental Health Professionals

Related Journals*

BEHAVIORAL ASSESSMENT
CLINICAL PSYCHOLOGY REVIEW
JOURNAL OF PSYCHIATRIC TREATMENT AND EVALUATION
NEW IDEAS IN PSYCHOLOGY
PERSONALITY AND INDIVIDUAL DIFFERENCES

***Free specimen copies available upon request.**

Eclectic Psychotherapy
A Systematic Approach

Larry E. Beutler
University of Arizona

PERGAMON PRESS
New York · Oxford · Beijing · Frankfurt
São Paulo · Sydney · Tokyo · Toronto

Pergamon Press Offices:

U.S.A.	Pergamon Press, Maxwell House, Fairview Park, Elmsford, New York 10523, U.S.A.
U.K.	Pergamon Press, Headington Hill Hall, Oxford OX3 0BW, England
PEOPLE'S REPUBLIC OF CHINA	Pergamon Press, Room 4037, Qianmen Hotel, Beijing, People's Republic of China
FEDERAL REPUBLIC OF GERMANY	Pergamon Press, Hammerweg 6, D-6242 Kronberg, Federal Republic of Germany
BRAZIL	Pergamon Editora, Rua Eça de Queiros, 346, CEP 04011, Paraiso, São Paulo, Brazil
AUSTRALIA	Pergamon Press Australia, P.O. Box 544, Potts Point, N.S.W. 2011, Australia
JAPAN	Pergamon Press, 8th Floor, Matsuoka Central Building, 1-7-1 Nishishinjuku, Shinjuku-ku, Tokyo 160, Japan
CANADA	Pergamon Press Canada, Suite No 271, 253 College Street, Toronto, Ontario, Canada M5T 1R5

Reprinted 1988

Library of Congress Cataloging in Publication Data

Beutler, Larry E.

Eclectic psychotherapy.

(Pergamon general psychology series; 118)
Bibliography: p.
Includes index.
1. Psychotherapist and patient. 2. Psychotherapy.
I. Title II. Series. [DNLM: 1. Psychotherapy. WM 420 B569e]
RC480.8.B48 1983 616.89′14 82-22380
ISBN 0-08-028842-1

Printed in Great Britain by A. Wheaton & Co. Ltd, Exeter

To my wife, Maria Elena, with much love and appreciation.

Contents

Preface

This book began with a Ph.D. dissertation completed in January, 1970 at the University of Nebraska. From that initial work (published in 1971) I began to develop ideas and impressions about how to match therapists and patients. The initial paper on matching psychotherapy technique to patient type was originally presented at the Society for Psychotherapy Research in 1976 and later revised and published in the *Journal of Consulting and Clinical Psychology* in 1979. Allen E. Bergin stimulated me to develop the ideas then expressed beyond their initially limited scope. As a result, I now find a good deal in those early conclusions with which I disagree. I suppose that five years from now the concepts presented and refined in this book will also appear inadequate. The problem with publishing ideas is that one frequently feels compelled to defend them rather than allowing them to evolve. In the best of all possible worlds, the written word could be viewed as a developmental process rather than as a collection of sacred truths.

Collectively, this book is an effort both to define the ingredients present in good psychotherapy and to maximize their effective use by adding what we know about matching patients to both therapists and techniques. In this sense, the current volume is an effort to describe a systematic eclectic psychotherapy, one that can be applied in a relatively consistent and reliable fashion but which draws its strength from its variety and breadth. We live in a day of handbooks and psychotherapy manuals, each developed as an effort to describe how to apply the techniques of a given theory. This book is also a manual, but one that focuses on when to apply the many techniques that arise from multiple theories, rather than how to do so.

This book is roughly divided into seven sections. The first two chapters are primarily theoretical and outline, respectively, concepts and problems in the definition of eclectic psychotherapy and define the persuasion processes that constitute the therapeutic relationship. Chapters 3 and 4 are descriptive and review salient patient and therapist characteristics which influence both the therapy process and treatment outcome. Chapters 5 and 6 are devoted to the practical task of evaluating the patient on relevant dimensions as a prelude to developing a treatment program.

Chapters 7 and 8 consider the nonspecific and specific psychotherapy techniques that constitute the persuasive treatment process. While these latter chapters focus both upon the means of facilitating the treatment relationship and on descriptions of psychotherapy techniques, the real integration of treatment approaches comes together in Chapters 9 and 10. In these two chapters, specific guidelines are developed for matching patients to therapy procedures, taking into account the values and belief systems that characterize the patient-therapist relationship.

Finally, Chapters 11 through 15 describe various clinical applications. Five patients with whom I have had either direct or indirect treatment relationships have consented to provide critical descriptions of their own therapy. In approaching these individuals, I asked them to concentrate both upon positive and negative aspects of psychological treatment and to draw the readers' attention to those things that were helpful and not so helpful in facilitating therapeutic gain. I am indebted to those patients for their willingness to share so much of their lives. I hope that they will forgive my clinical approach to their stories, since I have interspersed their words with my own comments. In making these comments, it has been my effort to draw to the reader's attention the relationships among patient, therapist, and technique dimensions that are described in Chapters 1 through 10.

Finally, Chapter 16 provides a rough summary of the concepts presented and raises important questions, still to be answered. Answers to these questions are needed in order to gain greater clarification of ways in which the therapist and therapy technique can be matched to certain patients.

In undertaking this work, numerous authors and acquaintances have provided either guidance, motivation, or both. My original mentor, James K. Cole, provided the motivating force for me to initially study the dyadic relationship through what he called "dispositional assessment." Then and since I have been particularly influenced by the work of Jerome D. Frank and Arnold P. Goldstein. Both of these authors have taken a persuasion model of interpersonal change and applied it broadly and specifically to psychotherapy. I have tried to build upon their work in developing my own model of psychotherapy persuasion, but trust that the reader will not hold them accountable for my generalizations and interpretations. I have also found in the course of writing this book that I have been strongly influenced by the work of Hans H. Strupp. I observe this most in a review of the reference list wherein his name is prominent.

Finally, numerous individuals have provided support and help in the process of developing this manuscript and refining my ideas. My wife, Elena, has been particularly helpful in reviewing the manuscript, providing me with guidance and suggestions, and bearing with me through the process. Many students have both forced me to put my ideas into words and allowed me to usurp some of their own viewpoints, Maryruth Jones assumed the responsibility of typing and retyping the manuscript as well as pointing out grammatical and logical errors, Drs. Arnold P. Goldstein and Daniel Levinson were kind enough to review earlier drafts and to provide me with direct feedback about their value. Arnie's comments have been particularly helpful and provided the first real test of how another professional might see the ideas presented here. His positive response has been and is very much appreciated.

Finally, several individuals have assisted in processing the final manuscript. These people include Donna Vandenberg, Maria Felix, and Anne McCutchin. My thanks to each of them.

Eclectic Psychotherapy (PGPS-118)

1
Introduction

Psychotherapy is an activity that has successfully escaped a uniform definition. It is, perhaps, the only service provided by a highly trained professional where a substantial fee is charged, but the active ingredients remain both undefined and lacking in consistent agreement and the goals are usually unspecified. After 30 years of empirical investigation, we are only now able to say, with some degree of scientific credibility, that psychotherapy works. Yet as long as three decades ago the question of whether or not psychotherapy exerted a positive influence was already considered to be moot by most practitioners. To these clinicians, more relevant arguments regarded the manner in which psychotherapy worked, its specific consequences, the procedures or techniques that were most usable or useful, and the nature of the individuals to whom it should be offered. Indeed, psychotherapy research has always lagged far behind clinical practice in its effort to discriminatively evaluate the specific procedures advocated by a multitude of theories and clinical experiences. Only recently has research begun to investigate the complex but clinically relevant question of how, under what conditions, for whom, and to what end do given procedures work? However, such a question necessitates a reliable definition of practice and a philosophy of eclectic application.

THE PROBLEM OF ECLECTICISM

The value lag in scientific research has contributed to a communication barrier between practitioners and clinical researchers. Recent reviews of psychotherapy outcome literature (Bergin & Lambert, 1978; Bergin & Suinn, 1975; Gomes-Schwartz, Hadley & Strupp, 1978) conclude that early clinicians were right in assuming that psychotherapy is effective. This knowledge has allowed research to proceed in directions designed to close the gap between science and practice. Science has not proceeded sufficiently far along this path, however, to indicate a clear course for determining which treatment ap-

EP—B

proaches are better than others under given conditions. It is clear that a wide variety of treatment techniques or strategies have essentially equivalent impact when applied to a heterogenous group of patients. This finding has led research to shift from comparing the effectiveness of different treatments to largely examining their common ingredients (Frank, 1979; Gomes-Schwartz, Hadley & Strupp, 1978; Orlinsky & Howard, 1978; Strupp & Hadley, 1979). These common ingredients are the nonspecific (so-called) factors that exert an impact upon most therapeutic relationships and hence, upon treatment outcome. Nonetheless, this focus on nonspecific factors (which characterizes psychotherapy researchers) clashes with clinical practitioners who continue to develop new specific approaches to psychotherapy.

New psychotherapy theories are proliferating at an astounding rate, promulgated by enthusiastic practitioners and a willing, searching public. A recent count (Parloff, 1980) suggests that there are now over 250 conceptually distinct approaches to psychotherapy, all vying for honors as "the most effective treatment." This number represents a significant expansion over the estimated 130 reported by Parloff in 1978 and the 36 reported by Harper in 1963. A crude estimate based upon these figures suggests that an average of 13 "new" therapies are developed and packaged each year, and that the rate of growth is increasing. Assumably, the authors of these theories are convinced that their particular philosophy and orientation will both catch on and prove to be the breakthrough in a field that has defied breakthroughs for many years.

Perhaps the proliferation of theories is both a cause and symptom of a broader problem—that none of the theories or techniques which they spawn are adequate to deal with the complexity of the problems for which people seek help. While each theory operationally functions on the myth of therapy uniformity (Kiesler, 1976), reality demands an eclectic perspective. A theoretical system is needed that is sufficiently broad to encompass both the nonspecific and unique variables inherent in numerous theories and yet specific enough to ensure that these procedures can be applied in a reliable and maximally successful way.

For many years psychotherapists have become increasingly disenchanted with single theory formulations and have moved towards some form of eclecticism (Garfield & Kurtz, 1977). While there appears to be some movement back both to established traditionalism (Prochaska, in a personal communication based on a survey reported by Norcross and Prochaska, 1982), eclecticism still holds a great deal of conceptual appeal. As a result, an increasing number of both theoretical and empirical papers are appearing that advocate interactions among patient, therapist, and multitheory technique variables for inducing positive change.

Behavior theorists have been most successful in applying specific treatment techniques to patients with specific symptom patterns (e.g., Thompson & Dockens, 1975; Turner, Calhoun & Adams, 1981). These behavioral descriptions are often of such variety and detail that they at least seem to represent reliably different interventions for different patients or conditions. Unfortunately, such programs are usually based upon manifest symptom patterns and often do not suit treatment approaches that are not focused upon symptom removal alone. Goldstein, Heller, and Sechrest (1966) have systematically applied concepts of persuasion theory to various patient attributes in an effort to develop prescriptive rules for implementing more traditional psychotherapeutic activity. Goldstein and Stein (1976) have pursued this issue further in trying to outline specific approaches for specific types of patients or conditions. Nonetheless, while behavioral descriptions frequently fail to give due attention to the value of insight, expressive release, and cognitive change (Mahoney, 1980), prescriptive descriptions of psychotherapy are frequently too general and insufficiently attentive to patient variations (Kiesler, 1976).

While the current movement toward eclecticism is an improvement over earlier approaches to psychotherapy, it will still be some years before research can validate the many approaches advocated for working with specific clients. This observation is true, both because there are more individuals who write about the therapy process than there are those who research it, and because most writings do not conceptualize psychotherapy in a manner that facilitates research on these important issues.

THE PROBLEM OF ART VERSUS SCIENCE

Unlike others, this book does not advocate new techniques or theories. Instead, it is devoted primarily to the integration of existing theory and knowledge. While other books have been written on eclectic therapy, they have usually failed to integrate perspectives derived from research, the practicing clinician, and the patient who receives the treatment. It is no wonder that the practicing clinician has little appreciation of research findings (Barlow, 1981, Strupp, 1981a). Most books about psychotherapy are still written either from the standpoint of the therapist or with an eye toward reviewing clinical research. In the former case, information frequently contradicts empirical findings. In the latter case, research findings are seldom collected together and refined in a form that allows the clinician to make clear decisions based upon them.

More explicitly, most theoretical writers focus on techniques as the most powerful and influential forces in patient gain. In contrast, research evidence indicates that the power of techniques have been seriously overestimated (Lambert & DeJulio, 1978; Luborsky et al., 1975). Similarly, research evidence fails to represent the clinicians' understanding of the therapeutic process, and researchers are more pessimistic of therapeutic effects than can be justified by the subjective experience of practicing therapists.

Barlow (1981) has observed several differences between researchers and clinicians which might account for their failure to achieve a reciprocal influence. First, clinicians are interested in individual transactions, while researchers are more drawn to collective phenomenon as represented in large group designs. Hence, the clinician is often suspicious of collective phenomenon that might mask the unique changes or conflicts they see in their patients. It has been suggested (Beutler & Mitchell, 1981; Kiesler, 1971) that researchers might compensate for the blurring of individual differences by giving more credence to organismic variables. Nonetheless, even this relatively simple solution has not been often attempted.

A second controversy that separates the scientist and practitioner has to do with the effects of "no treatment." Because the researcher cannot ethically provide an interested, needy, and motivated patient with a satisfactory "no treatment condition," substitutes involving a variety of "nonspecific" therapeutic interventions have been made. This strategy tends to dilute the observed impact of the more complete treatment package, biasing the results in the direction of finding fewer gains than are actually there. Malan (1980), for example, suggests that meaningful analyses of group designs must keep control patients in an untreated condition for many years, not just through the duration of the study. This is an impossible requirement for both practical and ethical reasons. The use of subject analogue studies overcomes some of these difficulties, but their results are often disputed or ignored because of the incredulous assumption that college student volunteers are similar to seriously disturbed and emotionally distressed patients.

The rift between science and practice is also perpetuated by the age-old criterion problem for assessing treatment outcome. The scientists must objectively and reliably specify the dimensions being assessed and the areas of change. Yet clinicians know that the goals of therapy change during the course of treatment. What is initially a treatment objective may only be incidental by treatment's end. Moreover, the multiple perspectives by which outcome might be observed and measured are so broad that they seem to require individual analysis. While contemporary researchers have suggested the value of individually tailored criteria (Waskow & Parloff, 1975), such measures are almost impossible to consistently employ or interpret when groups are studied. A unit of change in one individually tailored target problem may not be equivalent to a unit of change in another. Since research designs typically rely upon large samples, such lack of equivalency is likely to obscure the significance of any observed effects (Beutler & Crago, in press).

Finally, another problem that separates the clinician and the scientist has to do with the power ascribed to statistical inference. Issues of statistical significance have little meaning to the clinician when the absolute difference is relatively small. A five percent level of statistical significance has limited social value when talking about one's mental health. Moreover, statistical inference often employs a single cause–single effect model of treatment change, a model which seems unduly simplistic to the therapist. Indeed, many philosophers of science (e.g., Bakan, 1967; Levine, 1974; Raush, 1974) question whether the rigid, "traditional" expectations of control can be appropriately employed on human subjects. On the other side of the issue, psychotherapy researchers are skeptical of phenomena that cannot be reliably measured, consistently employed by different therapists, or whose impact is unassessed. If psychotherapy is an undefined procedure applied to an unspecified population to produce indefinite results, it is incredulous to the thoughtful scientist.

AN EFFORT AT INTEGRATION

It is on the basis of the foregoing observations that the author has undertaken the effort to interpret some major findings in psychotherapy research in sufficiently practical language to allow their application. Patients' as well as therapists' perceptions of the therapeutic process will be explored in order to illustrate ways of both developing compatible treatment relationships and applying treatment techniques. Techniques and procedures will be discussed in a manner that allows their applications to be tailored for specific types of patients and problems. In this latter connection, the often wide disagreement between what patients describe as helpful, what therapists consider to be "therapeutic," and what research demonstrates as effective, leads one to wonder if theories and interventions have been constructed by listening to the wrong people. A glaring example is to be found in the almost universal tendency for patients to ask for direction, guidance, and support and for therapists to remain aloof and unresponsive to such requests (e.g., Storr, 1980). Efforts on the part of patients to have their wants or needs met in therapy have been typically interpreted as "resistance" or "transference"—terms that allow therapists to believe that the emotions expressed by the patient about the therapist are misdirected and infantile expressions of parental relationships. Hence, a patient's anger at not getting his "money's worth" is often interpreted as transference when it may, in fact, represent a realistic response to a nonsupportive therapist.

Perhaps, as therapists we have listened too little to both our patients and the scientists who investigate our methods. Yet it is unlikely that empirical findings and patients' views will avoid impacting clinical practice forever. Only when we understand the therapeutic process, its weaknesses and strengths, as perceived by the patient as well as the therapist, will we be able to optimally apply the numerous techniques available to us. It is necessary to be aware, however, that techniques are of secondary importance, and that patient and therapist characteristics are primary. Hence, before techniques can be introduced as a viable force in treatment, the practicing therapist must learn both to identify what patient characteristics contribute to beneficial outcome and to assess his/her own potential and actual impact on the patient as one human being to another.

From these considerations, it is not unreasonable to believe that in order to be effective, systematic psychotherapy must provide guidelines for matching a patient and a therapist along three dimensions:

1. *Personal compatibility.* Since the therapist's attractiveness and perceived credibility are fundamentally important to the enhancement of most positive relationships, the personal similarities and differences which facilitate these perceptions and characterize the treatment relationship must be considered. Moreover, the therapist must be able to enhance a view of his/her own capability, skill, and helpfulness when this is appropriate and to minimize such attributes when indicated. Research has provided clues to how perceptions of one's capability and helpfulness can be changed as well as the limitations of these perceptions in producing therapeutic movement.

2. *Treatment Technique.* Only after the patient is able to develop a personally compatible perception of the therapist will techniques have a major influence on treatment outcome. While there is scant evidence that one technique is better than another across a heterogeneous group of patients, some research (e.g., Beutler, 1979; Beutler & Mitchell, 1981; Gibbs & Flanagan, 1977; Luborsky & McLellan, 1981; McClatchon, 1972) suggests that certain types of patients may be more responsive to certain techniques than they are to others. Indeed, some patients may even respond negatively and others positively to a given technique (Frances & Clarkin, 1981a). Such mixed effects in a heterogeneous patient population may cancel out differential treatment responses. A truly integrative psychotherapeutic approach must address the issue of what treatment strategies to employ within a given patient population.

3. *Accommodating patient change.* The patient is not a static entity. The variables that initially indicate a particular approach for a particular patient by a given therapist may change over the course of time as the patient responds to the treatment. Hence, a third area of focus must be on the development of guidelines for determining when such shifts of strategy and technique need to be initiated, both within and across sessions. A central question involves determining when a change of focus is to be employed and what techniques should supplement or supplant those that have been previously used.

To those of us who have lived by the standard of eclecticism, the dictum to draw the most beneficial strategy from any theory available has been well-rehearsed. But do we all draw the same strategy with equal results? Obviously not! It is important to clarify the difference between eclecticism as subjective and as objective phenomenon. Most therapists believe that they draw from a variety of theoretical orientations those techniques that suit the patient. However, recent research (Strupp, 1981b; Strupp & Hadley, 1979) indicates that therapists are objectively quite unresponsive to patient differences in implementing changes of approach.

Even in pharmacotherapy, where subjective eclecticism is pervasive, recent evidence (Gillis, Lipkin & Moran, 1981; Gillis & Moran, 1981) indicates that prescription patterns of psychiatrists are more often influenced by nonpatient factors than by the patient's presentation. The type of institution where one works, the country where one lives, and previous prescription patterns predispose type and amount of medication prescribed. Whether drugs or psychotherapy, situational variables and predispositions of therapists are better predictors of treatment patterns than nuances of patient symptoms.

Competence, either in the use of medication or in the practice of psychotherapy might be more than simply a function of competence in the use of any particular set of procedures or "tools." Effective therapists might be distinguished from ineffective therapists not by their skill in the use of one or another technique, but in the timing, integration, and patterning of these strategies. Objective eclecticism, therefore, might be reliably applied if the cues or signals that indicate the use of a particular set of strategies can be determined. One might argue that this approach takes the "art" out of psychotherapy. However, I am not concerned with the truly artistic therapist whose intuitive approach is demonstrably effective but with the fact that all therapists assume that their methods of selecting the most effective procedures from among the variety available are without peer. Presumably, if some techniques are more effective than others for given patients and given situations, it would be well to find this out and to derive guidelines for their use.

In addressing these issues, this volume will extrapolate rather liberally from available research. While drawing upon the literature in this way, one should not consider this volume to represent an adequate review of knowledge. Indeed, the review presented is very selective and has attempted to distill the most clearly specified, relevant, and/or intriguing variables for consideration. Some of the primary sources presented in the bibliography will give the interested reader a grasp on the ambiguities and contradictions inherent in the present body of knowledge. Ignoring this common lack of specificity, however, the author's prerogative of overgeneralization will be exercised. Hopefully, practitioners will incorporate the findings of future researchers in making modifications in the guidelines suggested. At the current state of knowledge, the lack of specificity is a handicap in trying to apply research models to treatment relationships. Indeed, many will argue that integration is premature. Nonetheless, failure to make an effort to increase the specificity of applying research and clinical knowledge is, in the author's judgement, a serious breach of the faith which patients place upon their therapists when they enter into a treatment relationship.

SUMMARY

This chapter has addressed the problem of eclecticism and observed how the schism between art and science may have contributed to the wide variety of theories and therapies currently on the market. While eclecticism has intuitive appeal, it has not heretofore been applicable because it lacks a consistent definition and because clinicians and researchers have failed to attend to important patient variables. These observations establish some initial groundwork for identifying the patient, therapist, and therapeutic characteristics which facilitate patient growth and development.

The next four chapters will be devoted to clarifying, describing, and otherwise providing a reference point for understanding the contributions of patients, therapists, and contexts to psychotherapy. Obviously, however, these factors cannot be integrated without a suitable conceptual structure. In order to provide a consistent definition of psychotherapy under which a truly eclectic approach might find a haven, the broadest possible thesis must be employed. In selecting this fundamental thesis, one must keep in mind the objective of establishing a system which is empirically as well as theoretically based. By adopting such a viewpoint of psychotherapy it may be possible to redefine psychotherapy as a specific procedure directed at specific ends among distinct populations. This is *systematic eclectic psychotherapy.*

2

Description and Inference in Psychotherapy

THE ROLES OF THEORY

All humans have individual theories of change by which they struggle to predict and control their environments. However, these theories are seldom explicit, and people rarely hesitate to give thought to the assumptive models by which they assess change. This assumptive world consists of the perceptual sets, automatic thoughts, and cognitive maps collected since childhood (e.g., Beck et al., 1979). Yet most personal theories have intuitive validity, both in the sense that each individual believes his own assumptions even in the absence of objective validation and because these assumptions do a reasonable job of predicting and controlling one's personal world. From one perspective, a patient's psychopathology might be considered the consequence of his or her theory going awry. The patient's predictions of the world are no longer accurate and produce a state of anxiety and confusion. Out of this confusion, individuals respond either with anxiety and the associated neurotic defenses or by constructing an independent fantasy world which follows their idiosyncratic logic. By virtue of the fact that these many personal theories remain private, we have no way of knowing how closely they represent reality except by determing how well one is able to live in his environment.

Unfortunately (or fortunately, depending upon one's perspective), when people began to notice that certain behavior was frequently self-defeating and began to develop remediation strategies, theories were formalized in order to facilitate communication among helpers. At this level of *description,* inefficient and disturbed behavior was simply observed and catalogued. The process of descriptive theory development was largely one of constructing terms by which to label the interrelationships that were observed among behaviors. Even today, every theory has a descriptive substructure that is in fact a catalogue of terms describing commonly perceived relationships.

Most theories, however, also contain an *inferential* substructure by which the direction of causation among the described relationships is specified. It is usually at this inferential level that theories become contradictory. It is also at this inferential level that the validation of theories is most difficult. Skinner (1967) has aptly pointed out the pitfalls of extending beyond the observational to the inferential level in theory development. Not only are inferred constructs incapable of direct empirical validation, but their relationship to external events remains tied to the defining theory by the descriptive labels employed.

While a certain degree of inference is probably both desirable and necessary, the practicing therapist is well advised to consider such inferences as "working hypotheses" rather than realities. Yet even at the descriptive level, a surprisingly high degree of prediction can be achieved. Indeed, a high degree of sophistication has already been achieved in cataloguing and ordering the observations of human behavior. While one set of descriptive constructs is usually as good as another at this descriptive level, it is valuable to specify what constructs one is using in order to further communication.

Many of the behavioral classes that are labeled in the following pages can be equally well defined by a different set of theoretical structures. This point is illustrated in the early writings of Dollard and Miller (1950) who translated Freud's observations of psychological defense into behavioral terms. The relabeling process undertaken by Dollard and Miller had little implication for changing therapeutic procedures and certainly did not change the observations themselves. Moreover, they did not disagree with Freud's observations. They merely relabeled these observations in terms extracted from a differeint theoretical model. In so doing, however, they illustrated how labeling may mask similarities as well as differences between theories. Like a rose, a behavior pattern by any other name smells as sweet. Yet arguments frequently ensue about the label rather than about the phemenon. Hopefully, the reader will not become embroiled in the terminology employed here and will understand it as primarily a descriptive use of labels. These labels, in turn, are designed to catalogue relevant empirical observations and relationships among phenomenon which are groundwork for later efforts to specify how therapeutic strategies might be applied to different individuals.

THEORY AND TECHNIQUE IN PSYCHOTHERAPY

Theories of psychotherapeutic change are typically embedded within theories of psychopathology and personality development. However, there is not a consistent correspondence between the theories of personality and/or psychopathology which a therapist holds and the techniques which he or she employs. While a major purpose of psychotherapy theory is to understand the significance and meaning of an individual's behavior both within and outside of the therapy session, its avowed purpose is to direct the treatment behavior of the therapist. In reality, psychotherapy theory probably does not direct the application of specific therapy procedures as much as it determines the therapists' overall goals or objectives. It is through theory that the therapist attempts to recognize the meaning of patient behavior and then to guide the focus of his interventions in order to change the patient's experience of that behavior. Hence, while psychotherapy theories are usually associated with certain techniques and procedural rules, they probably exert their most profound impact by identifying the benchmarks by which one judges the patient's change (Glad, 1959).

Virtually all theories of psychotherapy are derived from a broad rather than a specific theory of psychopathology. That is, while all theories attempt to understand the fine nuances of individual behavior, they actually invoke a relatively small number of constructs. These constructs are derived from the dual beliefs that there are a few common variables through which all patients can be understood and that these variables predispose the ubiquitous use of a finite set of procedures. The myth of patient uniformity implicitly present in most theories of psychotherapeutic change is paradoxical, given the emphasis upon patient uniqueness which is also present (Kiesler, 1971). For example, Freud's early theories reduced the motivation of man to two basic instinctual drives which were assumed to be chronically frustrated in parental interactions. From these two common drives and the individual's efforts to defend against them, the fine nuances of personality were assumed to evolve. However, in spite of the elaborate interplay thought to occur between instinct and situation and the corresponding elaborate personality permutations that arose, the techniques advocated were relatively few. Free association and interpretative analysis of parent-therapist transference links were the predominant strategies with a somewhat lesser reliance upon dream interpretation.

While each new theory adds a set of procedures to the treatment armamentarium, each also encompasses many of the techniques proposed by prior theories. The primary differences among theories may be in the focus, objectives, or rationale applied by practitioners from different schools (see Chapter 8), rather than the techniques themselves. For Freud, for example, the goal of analysis was to assist in the development and maintenance of a stable ego in order to arbitrate between social expression and destructive drives. The therapeutic stance was most often that of a neutral, benign authority whose largely silent presence was assumed to force the emergence of projected feelings or images. Interpretations of these projections were designed to reinforce a realistic but not unduly stringent social reality. In contrast, the therapeutic focus of experiential therapists was to remove rather than arbitrate social constraints by encouraging patients to freely express their innate drives. Humanistic or personal growth theories incorporated many aspects of free association and dream work and added the tact of encouraging therapists to take increasingly active roles in confronting patients with the therapist's presence. This latter approach was, thereafter, readopted by proponents of short-term dynamic therapy (e.g., Davanloo, 1978; Sifneos, 1979).

Whereas fantasy and dream production were viewed as distorted attempts to either suppress or sublimate dangerous innate motives from a psychoanalytic perspective, an experiential approach viewed them as representations of healthy strivings. Free fantasy or association techniques in the first instance were designed to help distinguish "impulsive" from "desirable" behavior, while in the second instance they were themselves indicative of healthy efforts to reintegrate. Humanistic and experiential clinicans assume that the basic human drive is not a negative expression of sexual or aggressive instincts as Freud would have us think, but a positive and innately determined movement towards personal fulfillment. In turn, both psychoanalytic and experiential theories assume that their particular motivational conceptualizations are true of all individuals. Both theories come to dramatically different conclusions regarding the directional focus of their interventions, even though these interventions are more similar than different (Fiedler, 1950; Gomes-Schwartz, 1978).

A psychotherapeutic theory can be used to determine treatment objectives or focus when objective benchmarks are absent. As such, a theory assists the therapist to understand confusing elements of the relationship. But to the degree that one relies on rationally developed, formal theory for direction, a therapist may either be distracted from or misinterpret certain other aspects of the patient behavior and not confront the issue of the therapist's own uncertainty more directly.

THEORY AND PERSUASION IN PSYCHOTHERAPY

The proceding paragraphs have suggested that psychotherapy theories are more often distinguished by language and inferential labels than by therapeutic behaviors. It is mainly at the inferential level of theory that the therapist's perspective of personality and psychopathology can be expected to bear a strong relationship to fixed goals of psychotherapy process. For example, it is only when it is assumed that behavior is governed by a self-actualization drive rather than by destructive instincts that the therapist will decide to encourage impulse expression. Yet on a descriptive level, certain relationships between therapeutic behavior and positive therapy outcome can be observed and validated, irrespective of theoretical rationale.

Research accumulating over the past two decades indicates that psychotherapy can be considered to be a process in which the therapist attempts to persuade the patient to undergo certain behavioral, attitudinal, or value changes. The therapist teaches the patient his own assumptive system of beliefs, values, and attitudes. Accordingly, it is reasonably well documented

(Beutler, 1979b, 1981; Frank 1973; Strong, 1968) that: (1) patients' values and attitudes about the world change during successful psychotherapy; (2) this change is in a direction that makes patients become more similar to their therapist, even though therapists themselves vary widely in belief and value postures; (3) some beliefs about sex, attachment, and safety are more pertinent to psychotherapeutic change than other values or attitudes; and (4) these changes follow parameters of persuasion which are similar to those delineated in the social psychology laboratory.

These observations underline the therapy process as one in which a patient experiences relief when he or she changes certain attitudes or judgements about self or the world. The effectiveness of the therapeutic process is nearly a direct reflection of how skilled the therapist is in getting a patient to adopt his/her asusmptive world (Beutler, 1979b, 1981; Frank, 1973; Kessel & McBrearty, 1967).

The perspective of psychotherapy as persuasion process directly confronts an ethical and moral dilemma which is usually masked by psychotherapy theorizing. That is, it is the therapist's rather than the patient's beliefs, world view, values and standards of behavior that are the very things by which both measure improvement and growth (Hill, 1969). Regardless of whether these guiding beliefs are founded in a formal theory or in an informal perspective of life, it is toward these beliefs that the therapist explicitly or implicitly attempts to persuade a patient in the course of treatment. Either by design or circumstance, the effective therapist exerts a persuasive influence over a patient to acquire the system of beliefs and values that the therapist has found appropriate.

There have been numerous books, chapters, and papers in recent years devoted to assessing the forces of persuasion in psychotherapy (e.g., Bergin, 1980; Beutler, 1978, 1979b, 1981; Brehm, 1976; Brehm & Brehm, 1981; Frank, 1973; Frank, Hoehn-Saric, Imber, Liberman & Stone, 1978; Goldstein, 1971; Johnson & Matross, 1975). The focus of these various writings differs, but all come to certain basic and fundamental conclusions. Of most significance to the current discussion is the demonstration that an important ingredient in psychotherapy effectiveness is the patient's coming into confrontation with certain discrepant viewpoints and values which are held by his therapist. Since there is no uniformally agreed upon set of "therapeutic values," there is no uniform agreement about what comprises a "healthy" belief. Hence, the amount of benefit observed is often a function of the acquisition of the therapist's particular viewpoint about such diverse and personal topics as religion, discipline, sex and philosophy. These changes are no less important when they have not been directly discussed and may not even be considered relevant by one or another of the principals involved.

Additionally, there are variations among patients in the degree to which they are willing to adopt a point of view espoused implicitly or explicitly by another individual. This persuasability or "reactance potential" will dictate how strong a stand a therapist can take and still maintain the persuasion. In applying these concepts to psychotherapy, Brehm (Brehm, 1976; Brehm & Brehm, 1981) cautions that those who are high on this reactance dimension should be handled without challenging their sense of freedom. The therapist must avoid taking control in these instances since "reactance" describes an individual's propensity to respond oppositely in the face of an influence effort. At times this may mean waiting before initiating treatment (e.g., Frances & Clarkin, 1981b) or taking periodic therapy vacations (e.g., S. S. Brehm, 1976) in order to "allow" change. Hence, viewing psychotherapy as a process in which persuasibility and influence power varies may dictate a therapeutic strategy which is responsive to patient variations.

There is reason to believe that many of the salient forces in therapeutic persuasion can be determined before treatment begins and can be used to maximize the amount of therapeutic gain experienced through this process. To do so, however, means that both patients and therapists must be open to the fact that there are certain interpersonal matches that are more facilitative of growth than others. Many clients have been helped substantially by one individual while finding others totally ineffective. Certainly every therapist has experienced success when others have failed and failure where others later succeeded. This clinical knowledge, however, has not been used formally to assist the development of a patient-therapist match that is conducive to therapeutic progress.

The interpretation of psychotherapy as a persuasion process boldly underlines the need for prospective patients to know beforehand the values and attitudes that will govern the particular treatment they receive. At the outset it should be clear to both patient and therapist that, although the therapist's theoretical orientation is an indirect reflection of personal values and partially determines targets for treatment change, other personal attitudes, attributes, and beliefs of the therapist may be far more important to the treatment than can possibly be indicated by a knowledge of the therapist's theoretical conceptualizations alone (Beutler & McNabb, 1981; Frank, 1981; Schwartz, 1978; Strupp, 1978; Walton, 1978). A formal theory simply provides a backdrop for the construction of a set of assumptions and goals that are used in the service of interpersonal persuasion. While the procedures advocated by different theories overlap in application with those of others, they do have some differentiating qualities (e.g., Beutler & Mitchell, 1981; Brunink & Schroeder, 1979; Sloane et al., 1975). Nonetheless, formal theories and personal philosophies intertwine at the level at which the therapist decides to construct an intervention.

As with any persuasion process, the different methods employed and the timing of their use will have different effects on different individuals. The suitability of a given therapist and treatment operation can only be determined by an inspection of the personal beliefs and expectancies of the patient and his therapist and the manner in which changes in these belief systems impact improvement.

Concepts in Interpersonal Persuasion

Many variables that contribute to attitude persuasion and change have been extracted from empirical observations and integrated into descriptive theories of interpersonal influence. Typically, these relationships are empirically studied in social environments where an overt and explicit attempt is made on the part of one individual to change another's attitudes or beliefs. As a result of such studies, much knowledge has accumulated about the conditions under which an individual will be persuaded when confronted with information that is discrepant with his or her own values. Some of these principles will be described briefly, as they relate to psychotherapy.

The Structure of Values. Rokeach (1973) has suggested that belief and attitudinal systems are ordered in hierarchical fashion, reflecting the intensity of one's belief and investment—in other words, one's values. To clarify this issue further, think of "personality" as a collection of attitudes, values, and beliefs that dictate and determine behavior and feelings. Indeed, all three of these concepts (values, attitudes, and beliefs) are defined as predispositions to respond in certain ways to given situations or objects, all composed of cognitive, affective, and behavioral components. If the progress of personal development is assured to be the process of organizing belief systems along a dimension of importance, the relationship between beliefs, attitudes, and values becomes more apparent. "Value" reflects the place along the continuum of importance on which a given belief is based. By the same token, beliefs are the most nuclear of the three elements, with collections of beliefs comprising attitudes and collections of attitudes, arranged on a hierarchy of importance, comprising values. Indeed, when conceptualized in this manner, one can see the structure of personality as a series of concentric circles, each representing beliefs that are more or less central to the manner in which one is identified. The most central beliefs and collections of beliefs, therefore, are those that are used to identify *who* and *what kind* of person we are. The beliefs and attitudes that provide answers to these questions are values that are central to one's entire behavioral organization. This core of beliefs is considered by the person to be capable of verification by total consensus among observers. Beliefs about one's sex, age, name, etc., qualify for this core of identifying beliefs.

Progressing from this central core to more peripheral beliefs and attitudes (e.g., those in which there is less value investment attached), less than 100% agreement is anticipated by the subject. The more central the belief, the more disruption to the personal, cognitive, and behavioral organization of the individual if that belief system is changed. As belief systems progress more toward the periphery of cognitive organization, they become increasingly less important to the integral definition of the individual and, therefore, less susceptible to threat. While a significant change in one's very peripheral beliefs can occur without feeling life stress, intense protective resources and emotions are mobilized if the belief to be changed reflects directly upon the sense of self-identity.

The centrality of the belief system that is tapped relates to at least three things (e.g., Rokeach, 1973). First, the centrality of the belief system reflects the amount of ego (i.e., emotional) investment that one has in a given attitudinal position. Second, it determines the ease of changing that positon; the more central the belief system the more difficult the change. And it also reflects the amount of interattitude change that is likely to accompany an alteration in the target attitude. Central belief systems are more interactive, being the support of those belief systems that are more peripheral to them. The degree of emotional investment in these beliefs reflects the place along the dimension of importance accorded the belief and therefore, its place in the value hierarchy. Since innermost attitudes and beliefs receive nearly 100% consensus, it is easy to discount any variation. An individual is most vulnerable when he/she has learned to anticipate less than total agreement with a belief. In such cases, the individual must give credence to the possibility that the belief may be false. Value laden beliefs about the world, the governing rules of man, the source of personal control, and the conditions of one's worth all reside in these vulnerable belief systems. Yet to change these still important beliefs is to change the underlying structure of many assumptions that govern behavior and dictate perceptual field.

Cognitive Dissonance and Change. One of the most comprehensive systems of interpersonal persuasion and one which has been most consistently applied to psychotherapy was originally developed by Leon Festinger (1957). The basic tenant of *Cognitive Dissonance Theory* is that discrepancies among belief systems have motivational properties that prompt a person to reconstruct cognitive experience in a way that promotes the perception of consonance or harmony among separate beliefs. That is, when individuals are confronted with a discrepant communication they either: (1) assume an attitudinal stance that is like that of the persuader, (2) withdraw from the relationship in order to avoid being confronted with the discrepancy, or (3) assume an even more rigid stance against the propositions being presented while, at the same time, devaluing the antagonist (Brehm & Cohen, 1962; Zimbardo, 1969).

Three variables that determine which of the foregoing alternatives the individual will choose are: (1) the degree of dissonance or discrepancy between one's own belief systems and the position being advocated, (2) the recipient's investment in being free of external control and, (3) the perceived credibility, competence, and attractiveness of the individual whose argument is being considered. Hence, when one's beliefs are challenged by the discrepant opinions of a valued authority, cognitive dissonance may be restored either by devaluing the authority or changing one's beliefs. Ordinarily, the more powerful and attractive the persuader, the less one's investment in maintaining autonomy, and the greater the discrepancy between the listener's and the persuader's beliefs, the more likely the listener is to change opinions. Psychotherapy will be facilitated for most people when it is conducted by someone who is perceived as credible, competent, likeable, and whose opinions are respected. The less credible and likeable the therapist is perceived, the less discrepancy the client can tolerate between his own and the therapist's belief systems before rejecting the therapist, withdrawing from treatment, and/or devaluing the treatment process. For better or for worse, the very fact that one member of the dyad is labeled a "therapist" and is frequently called "doctor," lends an inordinate amount of credibility to the relationship even before any persuasion is initiated.

Therapeutic Growth. As the objective world is confronted, a person is placed in relationship to elements or information that are both at dissonance with previously established assumptions, attitudes, and values and demonstrate the lack of consensual support available for his/her opinions. The pressure to resolve dissonance between discrepant values or beliefs or among the various components of those values or beliefs is thought to motivate change (Zimbardo, 1969).

Psychotherapy is designed to confront an individual with sufficient awareness of dissonant elements in her belief and informational systems as to mobilize her to resolve these dissonances in a manner judged by the therapist to be helpful and useful. That is what Frank (1973) has referred to as the patient assuming the therapist's assumptive world. The choice among treatment alternatives must both reflect the particular value stance of the therapist and consider the forces likely to produce the most beneficial change for a particular patient.

As a process of interpersonal persuasion, psychotherapy is a set of values, philosphical assumptions, and methods designed to induce awareness of those personal beliefs which are inconsistent with others. This awareness ultimately requires a readjustment of the belief-value hierarchy in order to reestablish consonance. At times, unrecognized dissonance may arise between the behaviors and cognitions of a given attitudinal object as, for example, when one acts angry but denies the presence of anger. At other times, psychotherapeutic change may entail reordering the nature of a response to a given object so that it is consonant with one's response toward another. In either case, the therapist serves both as an attitudinal model and as a persuasive force and cannot usually persuade another individual to make any change in which the therapist does not appear to have some investment or belief. Hence, therapists are engaged in an effort to persuade patients to become more like they (the therapists) perceive themselves to be.

Examples of Dissonance Development. Before giving intensive consideration to the techniques that might accomplish a relatively stable consonance within an individual's belief and value systems, it may be useful to speculate on some of the problems and processes that may give rise to unrecognized dissonance. When left on their own, individuals are frequently unaware of contradictions in their value-belief structures (Beck et al., 1979). They erect protective padding around their belief systems in order to maintain a sense of constancy in their environment. However, an individual's efforts to seek consonance are complicated by certain features of the cultural language system. It has long been known that the absence of differential verbal labels hampers the development of discriminative responses (e.g., Beutler, 1970; Bruner, 1957; Goss, 1961). For a child, discriminating among cognitive and behavioral components of attitudes may be relatively simple because of the existence of an external reference to which such labels may be applied and feedback obtained. Since emotional states can only be inferred, the period in which a child is developing discriminative labels for internal states may be critical. Frequently during this period, a child may be taught to mislabel his/her internal responses. Such mislabeling occurs, for example, when a child is encouraged to express sorrow for an aggressive act about which either glee or anger is felt.

Likewise, culturally derived value and belief discrepancy may be perpetuated in contradictory and inconsistent parent-child communication patterns. For example, when a consequence occurs on one occasion following a given behavior and an unpredictable but different consequence occurs on another occasion following the same behavior, the two contradictory behaviors vie for dominance on the value hierarchy and anxiety results. This is akin to what Horney (1939) has called "basic anxiety" and is seen in writings on learned helplessness and depression. This latter literature indicates that there is a need for one to either *predict* or *control* the consequences of behavior in order to avoid subjective distress (Abramson et al., 1978).

Another communication pattern that engenders culturally supported dissonance is the double bind communication described by Bateson et al. (1956). A child raised by a parent who simultaneously communicates opposing values may become emotionally withdrawn in order to be protected from the unresolveable dilemma of conflicts between two different values.

Dissonance Induction and Psychotherapy. In psychotherapy, the defenses that have been constructed against awareness of discrepant values are undermined in a systematic fashion. Extrapolations from empirical findings suggest that therapeutic progress may occur as patients compare their own belief systems with those of a valued therapist. The power of the treatment relationship to facilitate such a comparison relies less upon *technique* than upon the therapist's interpersonal *style*. Persuasion is best accomplished by a credible and attractive persuader. If these therapist characteristics are not present, the logical power of the message is compromised for most patients.

In an interesting application of these attitude-dissonance concepts of personality organization, Rokeach (1964) systematically confronted three psychiatric patients with discrepancies in those belief systems that usually receive consensus. All three men shared two fundamental assumptive beliefs. Each believed that he was Jesus Christ, and each held the opinion that there could only be one such Christ. The rationalizations, avoidances, and struggles of these individuals as they attempted to reconcile their own sense of identity with the discordant and often adamant beliefs expressed by their colleagues is most revealing. To a lesser degree, each individual in psychotherapy is confronted with a similar dilemma—an authoritative and credible individual (a therapist) who presents a set of beliefs that is discrepant in one way or another from one's own and that is given credence because of his or her professional credentials and/or personal attributes.

An understanding of the interpresonal persuasion process leads to the prediction that increasing the discrepancy between the patient's and therapist's personal beliefs and philosophies will increase both the likelihood of change and the patient's sense of improvement. At the same time, it is reasonable to expect that clients will leave therapy rather than be treated by individuals whose personal belief systems are inordinantly discrepant from their own (Bergin, 1980), especially if this discrepancy is not offset by the therapist's perceived competence and likeability. However, to the degree that one is unimpressed by "professional credentials" or is reactively competitive with authorities, some dimensions of initial similarity between the therapist and patient will be important in order to help establish a sense of collaboration, respect, and attraction (Arizmendi, 1982).

The persuasion process is expected to be influenced by the amount of effort or involvement maintained by the patient. The amount of effort expended typically reinforces the meaning of newly acquired beliefs. Within some limits, the amount of effort that is invested by a patient in seeking therapy and maintaining himself in that process determines the amount of gain realized and perhaps, even the credibility attributed to the treatment source (Beutler et al, 1972; Goldstein, 1971). That is, if one invests energy, faces difficult situations, and confronts anxiety, the sense of relief and benefit will be substantially greater than that experienced by someone who sits relatively passively in the therapeutic environment or otherwise fails to expend energy. Therapists may be well advised to be therapeutically frustrating. Nonetheless, if the frustration exceeds the limits set by the attractiveness and perceived competence of the therapist, the therapeutic effort itself will ultimately be frustrated (Beutler et. al., 1975).

In contrast to the usual theory of psychopathology, persuasion theory confronts the unique relationship of each therapist with each patient. Regardless of the techniques, strategies, or manuevers implemented in order to facilitate growth, it is the personal qualities—the attraction between the patient and the therapist, the ability of the therapist to communicate that he is a credible source of help, and the willingness of that therapist to provide a reassuring and safe atmosphere—that will dictate the success of the treatment. Much of this volume will be devoted to how a therapist is able to communicate these important variables. The following chapters will consider ways in which therapists succeed and fail in providing help. Before approaching these nuclear issues, however, the reader will note that a major therapeutic burden for the success of persuasion efforts in psychotherapy is placed on concepts of credibility, trustworthiness, attraction, empathy, and caring—the so-called "nonspecific" influences in psychotherapy. It bears stressing that these variables are nonspecific only in the sense that they do not uniquely characterize a given theory. Descriptively, most of these characteristics are common to most therapeutic relationships, though not to all psychotherapists.

SUMMARY AND IMPLICATIONS

This chapter has: (1) distinguished between descriptive and inferential theories; (2) discriminated between theories of psychotherapy and theories of personality or psychopathology; (3) maintained that the former are only inconsistently related to the latter in application; (4) asserted that psychotherapy is fundamentally a persuasion process in which attitudes, assumptions, beliefs, and perceptions of life are systematically altered; and (5) observed that this therapeutic persuasion process appears to be influenced by the same variables that affect any persuasion process.

The use of the term "persuasion" does not imply that all therapists should or will design the specific and complete outcomes of the influence process. Nor does it suggest that the therapist should force a patient to accept a given set of "solutions" of the therapist's choosing. Indeed, much of psychotherapy, as has been stated, takes place without a formal design and on the basis of mutual compatibility between the principals involved.

The interplay between the patient's reactance potential (i.e., investment in his/her own sense of freedom and concomitant ability to accept alternative beliefs) may interact with the perception of the therapist as attractive, safe, credible, and trustworthy and thus influence change (Tennen et al., 1981). In all respects, it is a *perception* that the patient has of the therapist rather than the actual presence of those so-called therapeutic qualities which carries the most force in influencing therapeutic gains (Gurman, 1977). Hence, the therapeutic persuasion process is strongly mediated by the therapist's efforts to create a perception on the part of the patient which will then precipitate a behavioral and attitudinal shift. This latter point is illustrated in the experiences of the patient described in Chapter 12. When he talked of the two effective therapists in his life, there was a notable discrepancy between his own views of one of them and those of other clinicians. He described his male therapist as a "gentle," "patient," "considerate," "challenging," and "responsive" man. These are hardly the qualities that the therapist's mentors focused upon. To the training faculty, this particular therapist was a moderate rebel who had little patience, little investment in supervision, and was difficult to challenge. Yet to the patient, the most powerful element was the therapist's willingness to talk and provide direction.

The first task of persuasive psychotherapy is to match a patient and a therapist in such a manner that their assumptive worlds (Frank, 1973) are sufficiently compatible to facilitate a collaborative alliance and sense of safety (Strupp, 1981b). Thereafter, the persuasive process is one of moving a patient through an experience of evaluting his assumptive world using the therapist's as a contrasting standard.

A later chapter will discuss various dimensions of similarity and dissimilarity that are likely to make the therapist-patient match effective. However, such compatibility matching only sets the stage for the rest of the treatment process. Compatibility alone is neither psychotherapy nor persuasion. The next task must be for the therapist to perform the activities, both verbal and nonverbal, that encourage the growth of positive perceptions of the therapist. Both the matching process and the procedures for facilitating these attributed and "nonspecific" qualities are the foundation of effective psychotherapy. However, by systemically employing procedures which enhance positive person perception, these attributes will lose their *nonspecific* status and become powerful, *specific* contributors to all forms of treatment. Yet even this does not complete the therapy process.

Beyond both matching and positive attribute enhancement are sets of techniques and strategies that are more or less effective at bringing the patient into the therapist's assumptive world. The value of any collection of these techniques depends upon both the nature of the patient-therapist match and characteristics of both the therapist and the patient. Hence, the next step consists of selecting those techniques that will be most able to effect the assumptive world of *this* patient who holds *this* view of life and maintains *these* coping styles when applied by *this* therapist. Lastly, the task is to change and adjust those procedures as the patient's assumptive world, character style, and dynamics are affected by the persuasive process.

3
Characteristics of the Therapist

THERAPIST PERSONALITY

In his book, *The Art of Psychotherapy,* Storr (1980) details the dynamics which he assumes lead an individual to seek a career as a psychotherapist. Storr observes that the characteristics of the effective psychotherapist may be disparate in many ways with those necessary to function effectively in most social roles. Research has not supported Storr's view that psychotherapists have a common set of personality qualities, nor the contention that passivity is a quality to be valued among therapists. Nonetheless, there is ample reason to believe, as Storr suggests, that the therapist's mental health and ability to cope with his own psychological dilemmas may be critical in affecting positive outcome (Bergin & Lambert, 1978; Garfield, 1980; Luborsky et al., 1971). Bergin and Lambert have observed that therapists who are poorly adjusted emotionally can even produce deterioration among their patients. In a now classic review of the literature, Luborsky, Chandler, Auerbach, Cohen and Bachrach (1971) conclude that the therapist's psychological well-being is the most consistently important therapist ingredient contributing to positive outcome. Research has clearly indicated that patients of less pathogenic therapists develop more foresight and planning, show less cognitive disorganization, and are generally psychologically healthier themselves at the end of treatment (VandenBos & Karon, 1971). Indeed, hostile and competitive therapists tend to produce reciprocal client behavior, while supportive therapists engender support-seeking and low levels of hostility from their patients (Mueller & Dilling, 1968).

The reciprocity of patient and therapist qualities applies to a wide range of behaviors, including self-disclosure and self-confidence (e.g., Becker & Munz, 1975). This observation has led Strupp (1973) to observe that the therapist's attitude toward the patient should include respect, interest, understanding, tact, maturity, and a firm belief both in his own treatment effectiveness and in the psychotherapy process. An anxious therapist who is hesitant in confronting the client and yet is controlling of the treatment process is frequently not able to maintain the patient in treatment (Fiester, 1977).

While one might argue that the necessity of emotional stability augers in favor of all therapists being recipients of psychotherapy, the evidence for the desirability of personal therapy for the therapist is not well-established (Garfield & Bergin, 1971). We have all known therapists who appeared emotionally insecure and were still effective. This appears to be the exception that proves the rule. If the experience of Rosenhan (1973) is any example, patients may be more quick to perceive psychopathology than highly trained staff, since they are less dissuaded by the power of the demand characteristics of the environment. Therefore, it is logical to assume for the most part that the patient is usually able to perceive the stability of his or her therapist and will gain more from one who is stable and psychologically healthy than from one who is not.

Beyond the conclusion that the psychotherapist must be mentally healthy, little can be concluded in the literature regarding the value of certain personality variables. In a study of 95 renowned therapists, for example, Geller and Berzins (1976) found wide diversity in personalities and interests. The results also suggested relatively low correspondence between personality dimensions and adherence to particular treatment modes.

A recent review (Beutler & Anderson, 1979) of those personality, demographic, and sociocultural traits over which the therapist has little control revealed that these variables do not have a consistently strong relationship to treatment outcome. While there is some argument in favor of matching a patient and therapist on the basis of sex, race, and socioeconomic background, the evidence has been inconsistent in indicating the strength of such matches. Therapists representing a wide variety of personality styles, either sex, and a diversity of sociodemographic backgrounds can apparently be effective with an equally wide variety of patients. The importance of demographic, ethnic, and personality similarities between patient and therapist may be primarily in the initial stages of treatment. It is at this stage that a patient who is learning to trust may seek some common ground upon which such trust can be initiated (Luborsky et al., 1980). After this initial stage, during which the therapist's attractiveness and the establishment of a patient's desire to continue treatment are major factors, such variables lose much of their impact (Beutler & Anderson, 1979). During the initial stages of therapy the socio-ethnically different therapist must help the patient to find the common ground upon which trust can be established. Emphasizing commonalities rather than differences at this early point in treatment is most likely to help the patient through the initial struggle of commitment. Beyond this point, differences that exist between a patient and therapist may become more potent agents of change than the similarities (Beutler, 1981).

CHARACTERISTICS ATTRIBUTED TO THE THERAPIST

In his early work, Rogers (1957) speculated that certain characteristics of the therapist were both necessary and sufficient to produce positive treatment gains. These characteristics included being able to accurately understand and empathize with the patient, to accept the patient and his dilemma unconditionally, and to remain consistent with one's own feelings during the course of the therapeutic communication. Much research has now been devoted to a consideration of these issues but with some inconsistent findings. Typically, such variables have been assessed by means of outside raters who observe patient and therapist interactions and then rate the therapist's skill at communicating in a warm and empathetic manner. When assessed in this way, it appears that such offerings on the part of the therapist are neither sufficient nor necessary. Indeed, some research has even suggested that certain of these qualities are negatively correlated with treatment gains (Bergin & Lambert, 1978; Truax & Mitchell, 1971). At other times, research has suggested that the foregoing qualities are only important if one is practicing Roger's form of client centered therapy (Mitchell, Truax, Bozarth & Krauft, 1974). Indeed, the inconsistent results in regard to these qualities has been such that they would not have been included in the current presentation were it not for several recent findings.

More specifically, in a review of facilitative therapist attributes, Gurman (1977) has observed that when the patient makes judgements of the therapist's empathy, regard, acceptance, and genuineness, there is a consistent correlation between the level of these variables and treatment outcome. The fact that these characteristics represent the contribution of both the patient and the therapist (e.g., Frank, 1981; Strupp, 1981b) is therefore significant. While it is difficult to specify the manner in which empathetic understanding affects treatment gain, if the patient perceives such empathetic understanding (present or not) the likelihood of gain will ordinarily be facilitated. Moreover, research is increasingly shedding light on ways in which such perceptions can be facilitated. The effective therapist has the ability to communicate warmth, acceptance, and empathetic regard to patients. While methods of communicating these qualities may not be recognized when observed by experienced clinicians, the dimensions are nonetheless important to the treatment process. Indeed, many authors (e.g., Neuhaus & Astwood, 1980; Storr, 1980) suggest that acceptance, understanding, and empathy are the most important qualities of the treatment relationship.

In addition to the conditions originally detailed by Rogers, credibility, trustworthiness, and attractiveness all appear to have some importance in facilitating treatment gain (Beutler, 1978). Like beauty and empathy, attractiveness and trustworthiness are in the eyes of the beholder. Attractiveness may be facilitated by personal and demographic similarities and may exert its greatest impact during the early stages of therapy as a catalyst for establishing trust and commitment in the treatment process. On the other hand, credibility and "expertness" tend to have more long-term effects on the treatment process and are primarily a function of the therapist being perceived as a knowledgeable, educated, and helpful individual who has both the skill and training to bring to bear on the patient's dilemma. A patient's perception of these qualities can also be enhanced by certain structures of the treatment relationship itself or of the setting in which it occurs. For example, a relatively formal office decor complete with diplomas and certificates may facilitate the initial perception of credibility and expertness (Bergin, 1962). Likewise, therapist language expression (Schmidt & Strong, 1971), style of dress (Amira & Abramowitz, 1979), interpersonal distance (Hall, 1964; Sommer, 1969), and posture (Harper, Wiens & Matarazzo, 1978; Mehrabian, 1972; Mehrabian & Williams, 1969) are used as cues in the patient's development of a positive perception of the therapist.

It is probable that most accepting, credible, and interested therapists do in fact display these attributes very naturally through their posture, word, expression, and dress. But it is also possible that even these accepting and trustworthy therapists could further enhance their effectiveness by exaggerating those behaviors which promote the patient's sense of well being. Nonetheless, it is unlikely that the unaccepting and uncaring therapist can successfully portray a contradictory loving and accepting manner for long. Therapists who are incapable of relating warmly to most patients should be screened out in the course of training. On the other hand, those who are understanding and caring but who want to enhance and increase their effectiveness may find it valuable to exaggerate certain voice qualities, postures, and dress, and to utilize distance and touch in a manner that facilitates treatment process and outcome.

EDUCATION OF THE THERAPIST

The question of who can practice psychotherapy has long been an issue among the mental health professions as well as within the population at large. Neuhaus and Astwood (1980) have observed that the prevalance of pop psychology and the proliferation of various human development and growth potential movements have left the public with the illusion that all people share the major skills by which therapeutic change is initiated and maintained. Indeed, since psychotherapy is a noninvasive treatment procedure and takes place primarily through language and movement, the lay person has some difficulty distinguishing between the type of help that is provided across the back fence and that which may be provided within a psychotherapist's office. Since almost everyone has had the experience of providing counsel to someone who is appreciative, many people believe that they have a special gift for developing this type of relationship. Unfortunately, therapeutic skills are seldom transmitted by way of gift. While individuals may vary in their degree of helpfulness as well as in their ability to empathetically relate to another, this is *not* psychotherapy.

Psychotherapy is more than the act of providing help, counsel, or kindly attention. It is, in fact, a combination of art and science. An often unexpressed but nonetheless major aspect of psychotherapy is in the perception, anticipation, judgement, and other diagnostic-prognostic processes that may proceed concomitantly with the verbal exchange. An often unrecognized quality of the psychotherapist is the ability to judge his/her own limits of power and to make appropriate referral when additional or different treatment is needed. A large share of the knowledge that is gained in becoming a psychotherapist is in the acquisiton of a conceptual system that recognizes the significance of certain problems and patterns and judges whether or not the patient is amenable to this or some other form of treatment. A good psychotherapist is first an accurate observer, an astute conceptualizer, and an individual who is knowledgeable about alternatives to and indicators of psychotherapy.

The danger in the proliferation of untrained therapists is not so much in their doing damage to individuals who are appropriate candidates for this mode of treatment as in their failure to recognize those who are not. Sometimes the subtleties of psychopathology and personality are such that they cannot be perceived without familiarity with a language system that has been specifically developed to assist in this perception. What is being expressed is a variation of the hypothesis that one perceives what one has words for. The presence of a conducive language system facilitates logical thought and conceptualization. The independent practice of psychotherapy is probably best left, at least for the time being, for those who not only have intervention and relationship skills, but ample theoretical knowledge and formal training to recognize the subtleties of personality and psychopathology that dictate the need for alternative modes of treatment.

It should be observed that the foregoing suggestion is made in the absence of hard evidence. However, a recent Meta analysis of studies comparing formally trained therapists and paraprofessionals has presented surprisingly strong evidence in favor of formal training in treatment effectiveness (Stein, 1982). Definitive answers, however, still await definitive research.

Nonetheless, many of the helping skills of the psychotherapist are not obtained within a formal education setting. Indeed, Truax, Silber and Wargo (1966) have suggested that formal training programs may sometimes result in a decline of those skills and attitudes that often facilitate effective therapeutic transactions. Nor are formal credentials a guarantee that the therapist has these skills and interpersonal abilities. Formal credentials only guarantee that the therapist has had a specified amount and type of training as well as experiences believed to increase the probability of having the requisite diagnostic awareness, technical skills, attitudes and knowledge which would allow appropriate referral. Formal credentials only serve as a safeguard and should not solely dictate the selection of a therapist.

PROFESSIONAL DISCIPLINE OF THE THERAPIST

Formal discipline has little bearing upon treatment effectiveness. However, individuals from different disciplines apply different sets of theoretical constructs, beliefs, and technical procedures (Orlinsky & Howard, 1975). If the interpersonal skills which are largely independent of training are more important than either theory or technique (Lambert & DeJulio, 1978), one would expect little difference either in these skills or in treatment outcome as a function of professional discipline. Only in those cases where discipline-specific treatment strategies or values are uniquely appropriate can differences in outcome among disciplines be expected.

Different types of professional training seem to orient individuals toward the application of different theories. While most mental health professionals probably consider themselves to be eclectic, it is likely that the professional socialization process leads psychologists to place relatively high value on conditioning and learning theory and psychiatrists to place more value on psychoanalytic philosophy and biological dispositions. Obviously, psychologists are probably less likely to rely upon medications to assist in the treatment process than psychiatrists, whose medical background is oriented in this later direction. At this point in time, one can only wonder about the impact of this potential discrepancy.

While most research literature (Frances & Clarkin, 1981a; Luborsky et al., 1975) suggests that psychochemical agents facilitate the effects of psychotherapy among most patient groups, there is some evidence (Rush, Beck, Kovacs & Hollon, 1977; Rush, Hollon, Beck & Kovacs, 1978) to suggest that this additive effect may not occur with some types of psychotherapy and patients. In cognitive therapy, for example, the objective is to teach the patient that he has greater control over his life and functions than he has heretofore believed. This viewpoint may be incompatible with the simultaneous administration of psychoactive chemicals which implicitly communicate that the patient does not have control over his feelings and behavior. While there is no doubt that psychoactive medications have been a substantial boon to improved emotional health and outlook, research suggests that this benefit often derives more from how one perceives the chemical influence than from the influence itself (Beutler & Jobe, 1976; Davison, Tsujimoto & Glaros, 1973).

Current opinion and research is beginning to indicate that the recent proliferation of medications and medical knowledge on one hand and psychotherapy and psychotherapy knowledge on the other, may have resulted in a knowledge base that is too great for any one individual to encompass. The future may see psychiatry return to its medical heritage and psychotherapy left to those trained specifically in a broad range of psychological theories, techniques, and procedures (e.g., Beigel, 1979).

EXPERIENCE OF THE THERAPIST

The role of the therapist's experience is somewhat more clear cut than the issue of formal training. We have long assumed that experience both homogenizes therapists (Fiedler, 1950) and facilitates treatment gains. A recent research review (Auerbach & Johnson, 1977) tends to confirm this point of view but not as strongly as we have previously believed. Experience tends to smooth out the differences that exist among individuals adhering to different philosophies (Sloane et al., 1975), and experienced therapists behave considerably differently in therapeutic relationships than inexperienced ones (Beutler & Anderson, 1979; McCarron & Appel, 1971; Strupp & Hadley, 1979).

The enthusiasm and commitment of inexperienced therapists tend to offset their lack of technical proficiency. As therapists become more experienced, they become at once more facile in applying treatment and, unfortunately, more pessimistic about the benefits of it (Berenson, Mitchell & Moravec, 1968; Berenson, Mitchell & Laney, 1968). Enjoyment, enthusiasm, commitment, all seem to be important in facilitating those qualities which are therapeutic. Judging from the impact of therapeutic "enthusiasm," it may be that "If you are not enjoying therapy, you are doing it wrong."

THERAPIST BELIEFS, VALUES AND ATTITUDES

While we may all agree that it is "bad" for a psychotherapist to have severe emotional problems, it is a more unlikely judgment for us to suggest that his values are *per force* "inappropriate," facilitative, or interruptive of the treatment relationship. Nonetheless, research suggests that relatively ineffective therapists have different attitudes toward their patients and themselves than more effective ones. An examination of therapists selected because of their variability in judged competence (Beutler et al., 1980; Strupp, 1981b) has revealed that therapists judged to be highly skilled and effective tend also to be relatively consistent and realistic in their views of their own success rates. They are characterized by their sensitivity to patient's dysphoria and hold nondefensive attitudes that allow them to focus on the therapeutic relationship and directly approach areas of resistance and defense (Strupp, 1981b). In contrast, less effective therapists are more variable. Like successful therapists, some appear to be relatively realistic in their judgments of their own lack of treatment effectiveness, while others show significant, protective distortion in their views of therapy-induced change. This factor may account for the observation that therapists frequently provide incongruous judgments of treatment effects when these judgments are compared with those of the patient (Garfield, 1977).

Another attitude that characterizes relatively ineffective therapists is their tendency to view their patients through rose colored glasses, minimizing the degree of psychological distress, dysphoria, and resistance they encounter (Beutler et al., 1980). It is rather paradoxical that these therapists tend to see their patients as less in need of treatment than do more highly skilled therapists, perhaps suggesting their pessimism about the effectiveness of treatment.

Hence, the effective therapist is one who is both able to approach difficult issues presented by the patient, confront patients with their own resistance, provide support, and at the same time accurately perceive both his own failures and the patient's unhappiness. The corollary of this latter observation is seen in the conclusions of Hoyt (1980) that good sessions are viewed similarly by patients and therapists and are attributed to similar processes. The observation is also consistent with that of Orlinsky and Howard (1967), who emphasize the advantage of the mutually perceived collaborative psychotherapy relationship as an indicator of a helpful treatment session. Good sessions are characterized by greater correspondences between patients' and therapists' viewpoints than bad sessions. Perhaps less effective therapists defensively protect themselves from the patient's negative observations and bad feelings about therapy. Mutuality of influence is an important ingredient in treatment, and the therapist who will allow himself to be influenced by the patient as well as to influence the patient increases his impact.

Psychotherapy literature is also becoming increasingly attentive to issues of belief systems, moral values, and interrelationships between cultural and personal values. Bergin (1980) has strongly asserted that psychotherapists must be more cognizant and accepting of their patients' theistic belief systems. He has maintained that we must allow room in the therapeutic environment for a theistic determinism in which the therapist supports both the religious patient's reliance upon God and his commitment to sexual monogamy and impulse restraint. While few therapists would argue Bergin's point in the abstract and would maintain that they accept the patients right to theistic concepts, the intensity of reaction to Bergin's point suggests that a cord has been struck.

Our own research (Beutler, 1971, 1979; Beutler et al., 1974, 1975) has indicated that patients and therapists do not need to share a common theistic belief system in order to be compatible. Therapists are well-advised to be accepting of their patient's belief systems, nonetheless. If the therapist's latitude of acceptance in regard to theistic concepts does not include the patient's preferred beliefs about the subject, treatment gain may be impaired. While therapists are as variable in most of their belief systems as their patients (Beutler et. al., 1978), not all therapists seem able to accept divergent theistic views in their patients.

At the very least, therapists should be aware that their particular beliefs are not usually subject to validation. Moreover, beliefs must be understood not only as preferred opinions about an object or subject, but as including the unstated latitudes encompassing both acceptable and unacceptable alternatives (Sherif & Hovland, 1961). This is to say that any attitude can be represented not by a statement of preferred belief but by a series of statements ranging from one extreme to its opposite. While one's preferred belief is best represented by a single statement within this continuum, the latitudes of acceptance, rejection, and noncommital represent, respectively, those alternative positions which are considered acceptable, unacceptable, and inconclusive. While preferred beliefs may be divergent across therapists, it seems reasonable to suggest that their latitudes of acceptance should accommodate a wide variety of alternatives which may be presented by patients.

SUMMARY

Collectively, the effective therapist is emotionally healthy and integrated. He is able to maintain an accurate perception both of his own effectiveness and of qualities that facilitate the patient's experience and displays a willingness to approach difficult issues collaboratively. The therapist's emotional health is a significant contributor to positive treatment gain, but there is no evidence of a general personality style, theoretical orientation, or set of philosophical and personal attitudes that uniquely characterizes effective therapists. Moreover, there is no clear indication that ethnic, sexual, or sociodemographic similarity to the patient linearly enhances treatment effectiveness. However, some personal similarity in background and viewpoint may facilitate the initial attachment necessary for the development of the helping alliance (Luborsky et al., 1980). Once a helping relationship is established, however, the relationship can tolerate a great deal of diversity without negatively influencing treatment effects. What seems to be more critical than initial similarity is the therapist's realistic, positive attitude toward his own therapeutic ability, the patient, and the overall efficacy of psychotherapy.

The effective therapist is willing to both respect and collaborate with his patient as an equal. Respect for differences, willingness to abrogate moralistic judgments, and a commitment to maintaining a professional role, all foster the therapeutic alliance. Aside from being empathic and willing to listen without intrusion, the effective therapist is able to discuss difficult issues even as they arise within the relationship and maintains the therapeutic focus on the treatment goals. Focused and egalitarian communication conveys the therapist's professional confidence and attitudes toward the patient which are more important than theory in teaching the patient a helpful approach to life and conflict resolution.

4
Patient Characteristics and Dimensions of Change*

As suggested in Chapter 1, the most influential factors in determining either successful or unsuccessful treatment outcome are contributed by the patient (e.g., Lambert & DeJulio, 1978). Psychotherapy appears to be most effective when the patient is amply motivated to undergo intensive self-scrutiny and modify his/her own behavior. The unmotivated, noninsightful patient is also amenable to psychotherapy, however (e.g., Garfield, 1980; Goldstein, 1973; Karon & VandenBos, 1981). While it has been suggested that those who are least in need of treatment are the ones who are most likely to benefit from psychotherapy (Eysenck, 1952; Schofield, 1964), this conclusion may be unjustifiably harsh. As we are begining to find the limits for which psychotherapeutic strategies should be applied, we are also finding that a wide variety of patients can benefit from psychological interventions when the therapist is willing to alter the procedures in order to fit the patient, rather than assuming that the patient will acclimate to the procedure (Garfield, 1980; Goldstein, 1973).

Nonetheless, psychotherapists have usually failed to fully define their interventions in terms of their interactions with potentially limited patient variables. The patient uniformity myth (Kiesler, 1976) has pervaded research into clinical arenas. These concerns underline the necessity of considering psychological interventions within a much broader perspective than is possible from any one theoretical framework alone. Due consideration must be given to cognitive, emotional, and behavioral elements when assessing patient change. We must, therefore, be concerned with the clinical implications of how change is conceptualized before discussing patient factors which might precipitate it.

---

*The author wishes to acknowledge the contributions of Drs. D. Kolb and T. Arizmendi to ideas presented in portions of this chapter.

DEFINING PATIENT CHANGE

Any attention given to the patient characteristics which potentially influence psychotherapy outcome must address, in part, the criterion being assessed. The rather thorny issue of what constitutes psychotherapy improvement must be approached. Even to the most naive, the criteria issue in psychotherapy is an extremely difficult one. Moreover, it is not one that has been successfully addressed by any school or theory of psychotherapy to date. Each theory has its own definition of improvement based upon the concepts valued by that theory (Glad, 1959). Indeed, this is an area in which research methodology could bear directly upon clinical practice.

Multiple Perspectives of Changes

In the past decade psychotherapy researchers have made significant advances in the development of methods for assessing psychotherapy change that extend beyond theory-specific values. In so doing, they have expressed the need for addressing the issue of psychotherapy improvement from a variety of perspectives (e.g., Beutler & Crago, in press; Lambert et al., in press; Mintz, Auerbach, Luborsky & Johnson, 1973; Waskow & Parloff, 1975) which are often illusive to the clinical practitioner. In spite of advances in developing measurement devices, however, researchers have not totally addressed the constructs that are considered relevant to the practitioner. In part, this lack of sensitivity to the practitioner's needs is a carryover from both the strengths and weaknesses of the behavioral movement. The behavioral schools have added to the fields of clinical practice and research on understanding of the need for specificity in assessing outcome. However, a narrow band, symptom focus is also the shortcoming of many of these approaches.

Storr (1980) has pointedly addressed these concerns, observing that all clinicians have had instances where patients have symptomatically or behaviorally improved but are neither considered nor consider themselves "improved." More frequently, patients who have not changed symptomatically or behaviorally, consider their therapy successful. This complexity reflects the multiplicity of the outcome problem.

Strupp and Hadley (1977) have suggested a tripartite model for assessing therapy outcome. A similar model might be applied clinically to assess improvement from three partially independent perspectives: of the patient, the society at large, and the clinician. Change in all of these dimensions would, of course, be most desirable. Nevertheless, the importance of change on a single measure must not be underemphasized. For example, among most voluntary patients, the dimension of greatest practical relevance is the patient's subjective impressions of benefit.

Changing Goals over Time

As already observed, symptomatic change is often independent of patients' posttreatment ratings; subjective benefit may bear little relationship to symptom change by the end of treatment. Research literature has suggested that while symptomatic behavior may initiate a patient's involvement in treatment, the process of treatment itself tends to result in the patient's initial goals being supplanted by the goals and objectives of the therapist (Hill, 1969). Translated, this means that symptomatic behavior may bring patients into treatment, but both their remaining in treatment and their subsequent impressions of its benefit will often bear little resemblance to these initial behavioral goals. This observation underlines the necessity of constantly evaluating the changing goals of treatment with the patient.

Symptomatic versus Structural Change

Just as one must distinguish between symptomatic change and improvement, one must also distinguish between the patient's manifest, situation-specific behavior and his characterologic style or personality. Many strategies embody a *narrow band* focus. That is, they are pointedly aimed at symptomatic change and leave surrounding style or function relatively untapped. Hence, the spread of effect in most of these treatment approaches in unknown. Other types of treatment, however, may have an impact upon one's coping styles and/or generalized personality constructs by focusing upon the conflicts assumed to support these patterns. While such *broad band* treatments may impact many areas, they produce correspondingly less change in any specific symptom. While there is little evidence that psychotherapies produce major changes in character structure, they do produce a significant impact upon attitudes, self-concepts, and the prevalence of certain coping patterns. While the therapist's initial concern must be with disruptive symptomatic manifestations when they are present, most patients who seek psychotherapy do not have any clear, external manifestation of symptoms beyond that of generalized unhappiness (Szasz, 1960). Hence, a truly eclectic therapy will discriminate between treatments on the basis of breadth of focus and subjective versus objective manifestations of distress.

The relationship between symptoms and personality must also be considered from another perspective—the more severe a symptom complex is, the less closely those symptoms will reflect a particular personality organization (Millon, 1969). In other words, psychological disturbance exerts a homogenizing effect such that individuals who represent a wide variety of character structures may develop similar symptom patterns. This observation has direct relevance for the assertion that any therapeutic focus must concern itself both with the symptom patterns and the nature of the patient's personality. While hypotheses about the patient's underlying dynamics may assist the therapist in providing a working focus for the treatment, attention to such dynamic structures does not lend itself well to symptom removal. Ideally, psychotherapy focuses both upon changing the patient's symptoms and modifying those values and conflicts which frequently maintain these symptoms.

A PREVIEW

It is the objective of this chapter to clarify the patient and symptom characteristics that will allow the clinician to anticipate the course of treatment and select the strategies needed to provide the patient with a satisfying view of his/her own change. This systematic form of eclecticism requires that a variety of techniques and assumptions from many theories be available in the practitioner's repertoire. The therapist's guiding conceptual orientation must be sufficiently broad to allow the incorporation of what appear to be divergent viewpoints.

Characteristics of the patient that are often thought to be rather uniformly related to therapeutic change across a wide vareity of interventions will be addressed in the next section. In subsequent sections, an attempt will be made to distinguish what may be more relevant treatment determining conflicts, personality types, and symptom patterns. A multidimensional, conceptual model of psychological distress will be presented from which a treatment program can be constructed. On one level, this model will address issues having to do with objective symptom structure and manifest coping styles which predicate treatment strategies. A later chapter will provide some of the relevant data that supports the decisional/prognostic value of these dimensions.

Another level of this model is borrowed and adapted from Millon (1969) and is designed to assist the therapist in deriving a working hypothesis of the multisymptomatic patient's motivating, social-interpersonal conflicts. These thematic attitudinal patterns can provide the integrative force or dynamic focus for organizing and interfacing therapeutic strategies for some patients (e.g., Malan, 1976; Strupp, 1981b). Awareness of these two levels of analysis will provide the groundwork for later discussions of how the flow and pattern of treatment strategies are applied.

NONSPECIFIC PATIENT QUALITIES

Certain patient characteristics are very important in facilitating treatment outcome, relatively independently of the therapy mode. Luborsky et al. (1971) reviewed nearly 200 studies of treatment outcome and observed that the largest number of variables found to be significant in this process were factors intrinsic to the patient. Other research confirms the observation that relatively stable characteristics of the patient contribute both to the ability of the patient to become engaged in the relationship and to its effectiveness (e.g., Luborsky et al., 1980; Marziali et al., 1981; Staples et al., 1976).

Patient Perceptions

In an earlier chapter, we have considered attributed variables of the therapist and their importance in treatment outcome. However, in numerous studies the work of therapists has been studied across a variety of patients. The findings indicate that these attributed characteristics are often as much a function of the patient as the therapist. For example, while credibility, attraction, empathy, positive regard, and understanding are typically thought to be "therapist offered" (Rogers, 1957), a significant proportion of these characteristics have to do with the patient (Gurman, 1977).

Patients who do poorly or drop out of treatment seem to enter therapy with a negative disposition toward its effectiveness, are resistant to persuasion messages, and filter their view of the therapist through their own negativistic perspective, remaining relatively intransient to the therapist's efforts. Even as rated by outside observers, attributed therapist qualities vary from moment to moment and patient to patient (Beutler, Johnson, Neville & Workman, 1973; Beutler, 1976; Gurman, 1973), again suggesting a complex relationship between patient behavior, therapist response, and the perception of facilitative treatment qualities. Hence, a patient's predisposition to value psychotherapy combines with therapist attributes and therapy procedures to facilitate the patient's positive view of the therapist.

Background and Adjustment

In spite of the early indications (e.g., Schofield, 1964), patient sex, age, and socioeconomic status are probably only indirectly related to treatment outcome. While conventional forms of relationship and insight-oriented treatment are typically most appropriately applied to individuals from middle to upper socioeconomic classes, this may be coincidental with the presence of a characteristic demographic background, interpersonal style, intellectual capacity, and expectancy (Garfield, 1980; Goldstein, 1973).

Sex, Age, and Ethnicity. Patient sex and age may be irrelevant to treatment gain unless they are significant issues to the patient in defining treatment course. For example, if a patient desires to work on issues related to her role as a woman in this society, she may be advised to seek treatment from a person whose credibility will be greater than the middle class, traditional male. This is not to say that a nontraditional, androgenous male cannot treat such patients, but it does acknowledge the importance of the patient's sense of influence in helping to determine both the therapist and the initial direction treatment will take.

A similar concern holds true for other aspects of the patient's background. Contemporary research (Abramowitz & Murray, in press; Banks, 1972; Beutler & Anderson, 1979; Jones & Zoppel, 1982; Satler, 1977) does not indicate that matching patients on the basis of sex or ethnic background is particularly facilitative of treatment outcome, except in the initial stages of treatment when the patient has certain expectancies of those who vary on these dimensions. An empathic, caring, and understanding therapist of whatever race, sex, and age can apparently help a motivated patient of whatever sex, ethnic background, and age. In regard to sex, in fact, it is the androgeny of the therapist (her or his ability to adhere to multiple sexual roles) rather than biological gender that tends to carry the day (Berzins, 1975). It is expected that the same rule holds true for ethnic and age related issues; it is the tolerance of the therapist for conflicts that revolve around these dimensions rather than the fixed characteristics themselves that will determine the power of the treatment relationship.

SES and Education. Similarly, while a patient's social class may determine the importance of adjusting expectancies and treatment procedures toward or away from an insight or experience focus, it is unlikely that social class *per se* mitigates against successful treatment. It is the flexibility and creativity of the therapist in accepting the various perspectives, beliefs, and intellectual variations of their patients rather than the beliefs themselves that determine treatment outcome. Unfortunately, therapists are neither very flexible, creative, nor likely to alter their treatment approach as a function of the patient being treated (Strupp, 1981b; Strupp & Hadley, 1979). Hence, patient characteristics such as demography, sex, and ethnicity probably still carry more weight than they rightly should in determining treatment gain.

A related patient variable is educational level. Patients with the best prognosis are those who have a high education and, in a corollary fashion, high intelligence. Unfortunately, psychotherapists have typically not paid attention to the intellectually low functioning patient. Therapists frequently find such individuals unattractive and poor candidates for psychotherapy (Nash, Hoehn-Saric, Battle, Stone, Imber & Frank, 1965). However, evidence consistently emerging from the literature suggests that programs that prepare these clients for psychotherapy significantly enhance the probability of obtaining a positive outcome (Goldstein, 1973; Heitler, 1976; Jones, 1974).

Level of Adjustment. The patient variable most consistently related to treatment outcome is the initial level of psychological disturbance (Bergin & Lambert, 1978; Luborsky et al., 1971). The more severely disturbed the patient, the lower the probability for successful outcome. However, it is possible that this finding reflects the inability of clinicians to adjust their expectancies for low functioning patients. Sometimes the patient's initial disturbance may even increase motivational variables (Kolb, 1981). A recent book provides convincing evidence that even psychotically disturbed individuals may respond well to appropriately oriented and geared psychotherapy (Karon & VandenBos, 1981). With appropriate modification of treatment approach as well as appropriate sensitivity, it is unlikely that patients should be excluded from psychotherapy on the basis either of intellectual level, socioeconomic background, or even initial level of disturbance.

Patient Involvement/Motivation

A patient variable that is apparently more important than background is the patient's involvement in the treatment process. Several authors (e.g., Baer, et al., 1980; Gomes-Schwartz, 1978; Kolb, 1981), have determined that among a variety of process dimensions, patient involvement most consistently predicts therapy outcome. Moreover, levels of patient involvement do not seem to differ significantly as a function of the type of therapist seen or the type of treatment provided, suggesting that it is, in fact, a largely patient determined characteristic. Nonetheless, a patient's involvement can be facilitated by the therapist's involvement, and both participants seem to find treatment most effective when the therapist is highly invested in it (Orlinsky & Howard, 1967).

Expectancy. A major element in ensuring initial patient commitment and involvement is found in the therapist's ability to create an alignment between early interventions and the patient's initial expectancies. Unfortunately, psychotherapy as usually practiced gives little credence to the patient's initial expectancies and operates on the implicit assumption that the patient or client must change to fit the orientation provided. Goldstein (1973) suggests that this is an unrealistic expectation of the patient and may have hampered significant therapeutic gain. Hence, one would be well-advised to ascertain both what brings the patient into treatment and what he/she hopes to get out of it. While patient expectancies change, the patient will either not become invested in the treatment or will disengage from the process unless some initial expectancies are met (Goldstein, 1971). The high dropout rate (Butcher & Koss, 1978) observed for most therapy probably reflects such a failure.

PROPOSED TREATMENT DETERMINING VARIABLES

Various authors have attempted to extract patient dimensions that dictate the appropriateness of various kinds of treatment. Conceptual level, intellectual level, and symptom pattern have all been proposed and researched. In a recent review, the author (Beutler, 1979a) determined that three relatively orthogonal patient dimensions seem to have specific predictive power in determining the effectiveness of several types of treatment. This chapter will outline these symptom dimensions and their implications for determining some aspects of treatment. The empirical support for the value of these dimensions will be addressed more specifically in Chapter 9.

Symptom Complexity

Symptom complexity can be artificially dichotomized into monosymptomatic, situation-specific behavior patterns and/or "habits" at one extreme and multi-symptom, neurotiform behavior patterns on the other. While psychotiform symptom patterns are more intense than neurotiform ones, they are not necessarily more complex (Millon, 1969). For most of our discussion, psychotic patterns will not be specifically addressed since they are probably least appropriate to psychotherapy.

The symptoms observed at one end of the complexity dimension can be seen as habits, reinforced but relatively nongeneralized through discriminative learning. These habits or "simple" symptoms are characterized by an orderly development from readily apparent earlier experiences wherein the symptom might have been appropriate or protective. Symptoms are considered to be "simple" if there has been little symbolic transformation and generalization. The symptoms can be seen as simple avoidance responses, positively reinforced habits, or inappropriate behaviors which occur because there are not appropriate ones in the patient's repertoire. The resultant disturbance is usually monosymptomatic, although not necessarily so. For example, a patient in the author's experience had a severely disturbing case of agoraphobia. He was confined to a four block area around his house and seemed unable to transverse outside of that area. An exploration of the history, however, revealed that the patient's disturbance began with a specific event that was clearly related to the current symptom pattern. As a naval air pilot, he was landing on an aircraft carrier when the plane ahead of him crashed. The patient apparently had an anxiety attack and nearly crashed his own plane as well. He was promptly removed from the ship to a base hospital. He never returned to fly and subsequently experienced increasing generalizations of travel fears. This patient's withdrawal from travel can be seen as a very direct generalization from an aversive event involving travel and flight.

On the other end of the continuum, we find the more typical psychiatric patients who not only have multiple symptoms with widely diverse effects, but these symptoms bear only a symbolic relationship to the currently precipitating cues, both internal and external. Often these individuals' current symptom patterns are either manifest in environments that appear irrelevant to their early experience and/or seem never to have been congruent with their environment. Indeed, thee patterns are maintained because of unrealistic attitudes, beliefs, perceptions, and expectancies that prevent extinction. Early internal conflicts and fears become generalized according to rules based upon these idiosyncratic perceptions and symbols. They are then reflected in symptoms whose association to the early learning pattern is very unclear. The more typical agoraphobic, for example, experiences an anxiety attack that seems unprovoked, occurs seemingly without an identifiably dangerous external event, and is repeated on a random basis, making the entire environment aversive and fear provoking (see Chapter 11). The lack of an isomorphic historical relationship between the precipitating stimulus, the initial symptom, and the ultimate stimuli-symptom connection, as well as the multiplicity of areas in which the behavior affects one's adjustment, indicate the elaborate avoidant patterns characterizing the end of the continuum we call *disturbances of adjustment.*

To some degree, the complexity or generality of the symptoms presented may reflect the adequacy of the patient's coping strategies. Patients with high levels of coping ability or cognitive complexity (Wilkins, Epting, & VandeRiet, 1972) may be able to constrict the spread of symptoms and limit their permutations. On the other hand, a patient who lacks adequate coping skills may allow even simple conflicts to pervade a variety of behaviors and be represented in a multitude of symptoms. Hence, symptom complexity can be indexed by determining either the discontinuous historical development of the symptom, the amount of symbolic transformation represented, the number of ways that pathodeviant behavior emerges, or by assessing the number of social areas in which the patient's functioning is impaired.

Reactance Potential

Reactance is a concept originally described in social psychology literature (Brehm, 1966). The concept has been fruitfully applied to clinical phenomenon (Brehm, 1976; Brehm & Brehm, 1981), however, and seems conceptually similar to various aspects of "resistance" as described by Goldstein, Heller and Sechrest (1966).

Basically, reactance refers to an individual's investment in maintaining personal control and freedom and is described by one's unwillingness to comply with external constraints. As originally described by J. W. Brehm, reactance is a state that can be engendered in any individual the moment they sense that their choices are being limited. It is indexed by a movement in the direction *opposite* of that externally advocated. More than indifference or static resistance, it is counterphobic rebellion. However, the potential of interindividual reactance to any given environment may vary widely, thereby suggesting that reactance is a trait as well as a situational state of the organism (Beutler, 1978; Brehm & Brehm, 1981; Burger, 1981).

To some degree, reactance is dependent upon a person's attributional style and is descriptively related to the concept of *locus of control* developed by Rotter (1966). Those with a perceived internal locus of control over personal reinforcement have been found to exhibit high levels of reactance (Beutler, 1978, 1979a) and to be specifically resistant to external influence. In contrast, those with a generalized belief that they and others are governed by external events are more likely to succumb to environmental manipulation (Biondo & MacDonald, 1971; Doctor, 1971). Externally controlled individuals appear to be low in reactance potential and, therefore, are theoretically amendable to overt persuasion efforts. Of equal significance is the observation that those with low reactance tend to become more reactant during successful psychotherapy (Gillis & Jessor, 1970; Kilman & Howell, 1974; Widman, 1978).

While a person's generalized expectancy of internal or external control is associated with reactance, these perceptions may be exacerbated in pathological states. For example, Abramson et al. (1978) have suggested that while normal individuals are prone to self-attribute positive events and externally attribute negative events, the reverse is true as depression accrues (Miller & Norman, 1981).

As a trait, reactance potential can be measured and assessed before the patient's choices are limited and can, therefore, predict the patient's resistance when confronting stress (Houston, 1972) or threatened loss of personal choices in therapy (Abramowitz et. al., 1974; Baker, 1979; Beutler, 1979a; Messer & Meinster, 1980). Motivational bias (Burger, 1981), stress tolerance (Houston, 1972), and clinical prognosis (Miller & Norman, 1981) are all effected by reactance potential. Moreover, by knowing the latitude of acceptance with which one evaluates external persuasion efforts, one can estimate the strength of a patient's reactance trait, and hence their probable resistance to therapeutic persuasion (e.g., S. S. Brehm & J. W. Brehm, 1981; Kelman, 1961; Steiner, 1970). In turn, one consequence of psychotherapy is to increase both a persuasible individual's sense of personal choice and his/her resistance to external influence. The paradox present in this observation is obvious, given the assumption that psychotherapy is fundamentally a persuasion process. If psychotherapy is successfully persuasive, it convinces people to be less persuasible.

Style of Psychological Defense

While reactance describes a person's interpersonal sensitivity to external demands, the style of psychological defense describes the methods of coping with internal and external conflict. Not surprisingly, concepts of reactance and types of psychological defense are relatively independent (Beutler, 1979a). Regardless of a person's sensitivity to interpersonal pressure, one may choose from a variety of defensive behaviors, roughly differentiated as *internalized* or *externalized* patterns. Using an internal coping strategy, an individual approaches conflict resolution by becoming preoccupied with his own internal imaginations. This pattern either exaggerates threat (e.g., intropunitiveness and sensitization) or avoids it through distraction, compartmentalization, or rationalization. Using an external coping style, the subject divests himself of internal stress by projecting blame or displacing conflict outwardly (e.g., somatization and acting out). External methods of coping are more primitive, tending to occur spontaneously at earlier periods in the person's life. Internalized coping styles, in contrast, require higher cognitive resources, and hence, spontaneously occur at later periods in normal development (Valiant, 1971).

Different authors have described and researched the significance of defensive styles in various ways. The repression-sensitization (Byrne, 1961), internal versus external coping styles (Welsh, 1952), and the extroverted versus introverted dimensions (Eysenck & Eysenck, 1969) are all conceptually interrelated. The data (e.g., Roessler, 1973) suggest a common pattern to various constructs which have been labeled internalized and externalized defenses (Welsh, 1952). The reason for choosing this latter descriptive dimension in the current context is that it is easily translated into empirical terms and can be objectively assessed.

While a given patient may spontaneously vary to some degree in his use of internal and external coping styles, there is probably a good deal of stability in this pattern across time (Welsh, 1952). Nonetheless, at times psychotherapy may be designed to alter the patient's coping style and, therefore, the therapeutic approach must itself change as it exerts this influence.

PROPOSED TREATMENT ORGANIZING VARIABLES

Broad versus Narrow Band Focus

In developing treatment programs and in understanding the patient dimensions by which such derivations might be made, it is important to distinguish between symptom manifestations and the mechanisms by which they are maintained. In other words, a given symptom may represent a habit pattern disturbance in one patient and a disturbance of adjustment in another. By the same token, many types of individuals might develop schizophrenic behavior, depression, drug disorders, or phobias. Within a given symptomatic condition, therefore, allowance must be given in the treatment program to attend to the maintenance mechnisms as well as the symptoms.

Since the patient's initial concern is almost always with symptomatic change, the therapist's initial attention must also be to such changes, even while recognizing that the patient's perspectives and goals may also change. For patients with habit or monosymptomatic patterns, a symptomatic approach alone will be satisfying, but for complex patterns of adjustment, the treatment strategy must also address the patient's values and attitudinal belief systems that maintain emotional conflicts. It is assumed that early difficulties with significant others typically give rise to patterns of interpersonal contact which may have been initially designed for protective purposes but which are now disruptive, self-defeating, or even self-destructive. The role of these conflictual themes has been described by Davanloo (1978) and Malan (1976), among others.

The less specific a symptom pattern is, in terms of either historical etiology or interrelationships with other symptoms, the more the need to focus upon these underlying conflicts and their associated dynamic themes. In other words, where symptoms have a specific development and their manifestations are clearly obvious in terms of the historical significance of the behavior, such narrow band treatments may be sufficient to both produce patient satisfaction and symptom removal. However, when symptoms are not so isomorphically related to a historical etiology, are more generalized into numerous areas of functioning, and do not bear a clearly determining relationship with a precipitating event, patient satisfaction is often independent of symptom reduction (Schlamowitz, Beutler, Scott, Karacan & Ware, in press; Stampfl & Levis, 1967). These conditions cannot be expected to be satisfactorily treated with narrow band or symptomatic treatments alone.

As a patient's goals tend to become more broadly defined during the course of treatment, the therapist must be willing to adjust approach accordingly. In cases of complex adjustment patterns, these changes in strategy should be integrated by a common focus on changing the attitudes and values that underlie hypothesized dynamic conflicts. Indeed, while the emphasis in therapy frequently shifts among various symptoms and character styles, one does well to keep the inferred core conflict in mind and to use this awareness to guide the overall treatment program. Consistent and direct attention to this conflict as it is manifest within the therapy process itself may facilitate treatment gain (e.g., Strupp, 1981b).

Through complex symptoms, patients may exaggerate predisposing social and personality styles, even though the symptoms are not isomorphically and exclusively related to specific personality styles. One must be ready to address the multiplicity of levels which are suggested in the patient's complaints. Since acute symptoms or *states* often require immediate attention, treatment usually initially assumes a symptomatic focus rather than attempting to resolve the underlying *traits*. Later stages may then require a shift of focus. Attention to this trait-state distinction will be retained throughout the remainder of this volume.

Core Conflictual Themes

Once symptomatic complaints have been identified and it has been determined that the patient's problem represents a complex adjustment effort, the next step is for the therapist to define a working hypothesis about the conflicting social attitudes (i.e., core conflicts) being expressed and giving rise to the symptoms. In the procedure developed by Malan (1976), independent judges make speculations about the nature of the patient's dynamic conflict, based upon the patient's overt behaviors and expressed beliefs. Moreover, Armstrong, Yasuna, and Hartley (1979) have demonstrated that such conflict analysis is relevant both for behavior therapy and psychoanalytic therapy. Mintz (1981) has suggested that symptomatic as well as dynamic change is reflected in these conflicts, and Dewitt et al. (1980), and Kaltreider et al. (1980) have pointed to the feasibility of assessing core conflicts on common dimensions, rather than varying the concepts with each patient. The latter procedure logically increases the reliability of judgments and allows a more solid base on which treatment gain can be assessed.

Dynamic attitude and value conflicts which are reflected in interpersonal relationships can be usefully conceptualized without the initial time investment and detailed speculation usually given to this process by dynamic theories. Hypothesized interpersonal themes do not need to be so unique that they characterize only one individual or particularly elaborate in the beginning phases of therapy. Since they are inferential, proposed core conflicts or themes can only be working hypotheses, not realities. Therefore, if a common set of conflicts can be applied across patients, it makes for greater uniformity and consistency in applying treatments. A medium level of extrapolation may be much more suitable than either the symptomatic level usually applied by behavioral analysis or the intensive dynamic core analysis advocated by dynamic theorists.

Dynamic conflicts can be conceptualized as a set of social-interpersonal values toward attachment and separation which are acted out in consistent behavioral themes when the subject establishes relationships with others (e.g., Millon, 1969). In the following pages, the terms "attachment" and "separation" will be used to describe the patient's relative values, and the term "conflictual theme" will describe the dynamic interplay of these values with interpersonal events.

It is assumed that recurrent interpersonal patterns reflect social attitudes toward attachment and separation which manifest themselves in symptoms and distress, that all individuals value both separation and attachment, and that the relative balance between these drives and external resources characterizes the social conflicts that motivate or drive behavior. Persuasive forces in psychotherapy are often designed to change these attitudes and values.

Detached Patterns. On one extreme is the *detached* individual who characteristically engages in little social activity and experiences little in the way of overt arousal. Such persons may maintain few social relationships, avoid intimacy, and appear to have little social interest or sensitivity. To the detached individual, the life theme or struggle is to avoid both attachment and true separation. The avoidant-detached pattern, however, may belie the degree of internal struggle or discomfort. Moreover, the pattern generally becomes a conflict only when efforts to remain detached or to avoid interpersonal confrontation are frustrated. In this sense, the conflict is between the individual and the competing, perceived demands of the external world.

Prescriptively, the goal of therapy among individuals with detached patterns is to facilitate the development of internal values of attachment and separation. Hence, the procedures invoked in therapy are those that encourage the development of interpersonal relationships both with the therapist and others. The evocative verbalizations of the therapist emphasize the individual's avoidance of attachments and fear of social encounters, while the directed patterns encourage and facilitate such approaches. This focus is the integrating force of therapeutic interventions—the common and directed core.

Attachment Patterns. The attachment seeking individual orients his existence around the establishment of bonds with individuals whom he perceives as stronger than himself. He denies or avoids separation and seeks attention. The role pattern may vary from one of "pleaser" to "victim" depending on the patient's level of reactance. The implicit attitude or assumption is that he is weak, others are strong, and that he is incapable of surviving or escaping hurt alone. The attachment-oriented individual is fearful of making overt attempts at separating from even painful relationships because of the risk of irreparable emotional or physical abandonment. The attachment conflictual style is characteristic of an individual who avoids being alone and becomes frustrated, depressed, or angry when insufficient attention is obtained from others (e.g., inadequate and hysterical personality patterns). He/she gravitates toward others, often passing through sequential relationships designed both to bolster his/her needs for attention and to provide reassurance to salve his feared inadequacy. In other words, the attachment conflict is between excessive attachment needs and an external world that is believed to be unsupportive. The attachment striving is not usually gratified through any available or realistic amount of interpersonal contact, producing a sense of futility and a never ending search for external security.

Conflict occurs because the process of growth brings with it social expectations of autonomy and individuation which are discordant with one's level of attentional strivings. One may have learned to expect a degree of reassurance and support from significant others which, with age or situational change, is not possible in the existent world. But the struggle is not between competing drives within the individual as much as between the attachment drives of the individual and the expectations of autonomy perceived to be present in the environment.

The integrating force of therapy is designed to persuade attachment striving individuals to place increased value on autonomy and to experience a greater sense of personal identity and self-motivation. Both evocative behavior on the part of the therapist and directed patient activities are designed to reduce the fear of losing significant others and to gain a greater sense of individuality, independence, and self-control. The externalizing, attachment striving individual may be self-dramatizing and present conversion symptoms, while the internalizing one may be depressed and develop psychophysiological and/or hypochondriacal symptoms. Likewise, variation in reactance levels contribute to a correspondent continuum of responses ranging from hostile to passive-dependent.

Separation Patterns. A similar struggle between an internal drive and a perceived or actual external reality occurs in the case of the individual with a separation conflictual theme. Such individuals have strong needs to separate from dependency relationships. Conflict occurs when the external world refuses to accord this individual the status of power which is demanded. The push toward interpersonal distance, like that toward attachment, only becomes a conflict when the perceived interpersonal environment fails to support the expression of the interpersonal value. In the meantime, the patient's response to separation struggles ranges from aggressive indifference and static resistance (low reactance) to being narcissistically preoccupied with achieving gratification of needs by either victimizing others or rebelling against authority (high reactance). Concomitantly, the separation behavior ranges from actively to passively aggressive.

While the struggle of the attachment driven individual is to avoid emotional loss, the separation struggle is to avoid nurturance and commitment. While attachment conflicts arise from fear, separation conflicts produce anxiety in the face of perceived helplessness.

The therapeutic task among separation striving individuals is to persuade them to place greater value on attaching to others. The integration of the therapist's evocative and directed strategies is in the common goal of facilitating the patient's empathetic sensitivity and willingness to receive nurturance. Procedures that encourage listening, social responsivity, and compliance are integrated into the scenario of the therapeutic process.

Ambivalent Patterns. Those who maintain equally balanced drives toward attachment and separation are said to be ambivalent. Unlike either attachment or separation conflictual styles, ambivalence is purely an internal conflict. In this state, one is plagued by strivings to maintain both love and separateness.

While the primary conflict is between two sets of opposing interpersonal values, this is not to discount the importance and influence of external factors. While those with either dominant attachment and separation values are drawn into treatment because of their perception of a nonsupportive external world, the ambivalent person is in a perennial struggle with himself. Both the attachment and separation striving individual experience conflict only when their strivings are thought to be externally frustrated, but the ambivalent person's struggle cannot be resolved as long as he/she has to choose between values that appear to be incompatible.

The ambivalent individual may manifest a wide variety of disturbing symptoms while coping with this conflict. The ambivalence between nurturance and separateness frequently serves to immobilize individuals with low reactance into a state of stable discomfort and to produce recurrent, unstable crises in the relationships of those with high reactance. The low reactant, ambivalent patient may establish stable, unsatisfying relationships that allow neither commitment nor exit, while the high reactant may vacillate widely from being hostile-dependent to rebellious. Moreover, depending upon the dominant defensive style, very different patterns of behavior evolve. The externalized, ambivalent patient may develop either phobias or compulsions; the internalized one develops psychophysiological disorders or becomes ruminative, depressive, and obsessive.

Unlike the attachment patterns, the ambivalent person is oriented around achieving separation without sacrificing love, and the therapeutic focus becomes one of encouraging greater acceptance and more flexibility in approaching the duality of one's values toward attachment and separation. The therapeutic task with the ambivalent individual is to allow the individual to accept his/her bipolar nature and to introduce an "and" between the separation and the attachment strivings rather than the usual "or." In other words, the patient's usual effort to decide between one or another striving is self-defeating, but the acceptance of this ambivalence and the discriminative channeling of attachment and separation urges in noncompetitive ways serves as a focal point of treatment intervention. Strategies are developed, therefore, that encourage the individual to tolerate discrepancies and to find outlets for both attachment and separation strivings.

SUMMARY AND CONCLUSIONS

Both nonspecific and treatment specific patient dimensions may determine treatment outcome with a given therapist. While many nonspecific patient variables seem to be very important in determining psychotherapeutic success, this is primarily because of the unbending nature of most therapists' approaches to their patients and their lack of sensitivity to the various dimensions on which a discriminative treatment program can be developed. Patient variables exert their impact only through the ability of the therapist to sense the patient's expectancies and moods, adapt their interventions, and convey an image of helpfulness and interest. Ways in which these perceptions and facilitative qualities are developed and enhanced will be described in a subsequent chapter.

The dimensions of patient personality and symptom pattern potentially assist the therapist in selecting categories of psychotherapeutic procedures. Clearly, the relatively simple conceptual system developed in the preceding pages does not do justice to the intricacy of human functioning. For example, while the analysis of core conflicts along a single dimension may roughly parallel on a different level of abstraction more elaborate and theory specific concepts of "life theme," "instinct," and "object relations," the current structure lacks the intricacy of detail and fullness of explanation of more elaborate, inferential theories. One can fine tune the foregoing structure by adding theory specific concepts which, in turn, would lend greater intricacy and explanatory color to observed behavior.

The value of a relatively simple conceptual structure rests upon the eclectic necessity of establishing a theoretical framework on which a wide variety of approaches can find a suitable place. Detailed elaborations of personality have heuristic value, but their therapeutic advantage has not been demonstrated. In fact, detailed understanding is an exciting process of discovery for the therapist (and perhaps even for the patient) and indeed has value in the pursuit of science. Nonetheless, much improvement takes place without insight and many helpful attitudes, beliefs, and insights are achieved after rather than before symptomatic improvement (Bandura, Blanchard, & Ritter, 1969). In the interest of eclectic efficiency, therefore, a simple model of conflictual themes and a description of empirical dimensions associated with therapeutic effects in different modalities is likely to be of greater value to the practitioner than the heuristic understanding.

The conflictual themes described here are assumed to reflect variations in the value given to separation and attachment. As such, these themes are the attitudinal systems at the very core of persuasive psychotherapy. The patient's method of coping with these value conflicts results in unhappiness and psychological symptoms. Then the goal of psychotherapy may be to change these values or associated beliefs. By utilizing a model such as described here to both determine treatment focus and select therapeutic procedures, the therapist is free to subsequently invoke more specific explanatory concepts from those theories that best fit the therapeutic approach selected. Since the correspondence between theory and practice is so low, it makes as much sense to fill in the theoretical system following the development of practice as it does to utilize the more conventional approach of confining oneself to the procedures that follow from an *a priori* held theory.

5
Assessing Patient and Therapist Compatibility

The preceding chapters have established the premise that psychotherapy is a persuasion process. The current chapter is the first of three devoted to applying the principles of persuasion and influence heretofore described. This and Chapter 6 are devoted to the assessment process. The following pages approach this problem with an eye decidedly toward matching patient and therapist on various dimensions related to their assumptive belief systems, in so far as these are compatible with the process of therapeutic persuasion. In this sense, the type of assessment described in the current chapter is one that is largely unconventional in current psychotherapeutic practice.

Chapter 6, concentrating as it does upon characteristics of the patient, is more typical of the clinical orientation and perspective familiar to most practitioners. Nonetheless, before repeating the patient-focused mistakes of the past, and thereby undermining the potential power of the persuasive interaction, the reader's attention will be directed to the importance of a psychotherapeutic relationship where the patient and therapist have compatible views of life. After all, we have expressed the view that psychotherapy is a process wherein the therapist shares his/her philosophy of life with the aim of the patient acquiring that perspective of the world and achieving some level of comfort in his/her existence. If, as we have suggested, psychotherapy is characterized by a patient changing his assumptive world, and if that change is predicted upon the attitudes modeled by the therapist, then it behooves us to specify a means for evaluating the dimensions which are salient to this process.

We have already discussed psychotherapy as a process designed specifically to encourage the patient to adopt the therapist's assumptions and views of life (i.e., to undergo value convergence). Yet it is not logically possible for every patient to adopt each therapist's assumptive world with equal ease. It is also self-evident that the persuasion process need not attend equally to all of the specific values, attitudes, or beliefs that characterize the patient's lifestyle in order to be effective. Numerous studies of patient and therapist interface have been conducted to assess the nature of compatibility. However, such studies have failed to evolve a clear set of guidelines on which matching might take place. As a consequence, the current chapter must remain speculative, but will, nonetheless, serve to underline the theoretical and practical importance of compatibility matching. In this process, we will present some tentative guidelines for implementing compatible matching of the assumptive worlds of patient and therapist.

CONVERGENCE, SIMILARITY AND IMPROVEMENT

Convergence and Improvement

A recent review of research on the effects of psychotherapeutic persuasion (Beutler, 1981) has documented a consistent and relatively strong relationship between the degree to which a patient acquires the therapist's attitudes (convergence) and the amount of therapeutic improvement attained. In this review, both convergence and improvement were assessed on a wide variety of dimensions. Given this diversity, it is surprising that 70 percent of the 22 studies designed to evaluate the degree to which increasing patient-therapist belief/value convergence is associated with positive treatment outcome supported this relationship. This figure represents more than a fourteen-fold increase over the percentage of positive findings expected by chance alone. While even the casual reader of literature in this area will become aware that the dimensions on which convergence has been assessed are entirely too broad to make the concept directly applicable in any individual case, both the prevalence and magnitude of the convergence-improvement relationship is persuasive. Linear correlations approaching those occurring between IQ and school achievement have been consistently found (Arizmendi, 1982; Beutler, 1971; Beutler et al., 1974, 1975).

Dimensions assessed in studies of convergence have included broad ranging personality patterns, interest patterns, collections of various beliefs, and even specific value systems. For the most part, single indices derived from a variety of more specific dimensions have been employed as a means of assessing similarity at the beginning and end of treatment. The fact that the relationship between convergence and improvement remains consistently high in spite of the wide variety of dimensions assessed argues for the potency, prevalence, and breadth of this phenomenon. Whether assessing similarity in a concept as broad as "personality" or as specific as "belief in God," the general conclusion of such studies remains the same. The more that the patient's values and beliefs become similar to those of the therapist during the course of psychotherapy, the more the patient will express satisfaction with treatment and the more both the therapist and external observers will consider the treatment successful. Moreover, at least some of the studies employed measures of specific rather than general symptoms as indices of improvement, and still found results which are consistent with the overall trend.

Since none of the studies reviewed suggest that a negative relationship occurs between convergence and improvement, we can conclude that most patients who improve either become more similar to their therapist in belief and value systems or (to a lesser degree) retain their prior perceptions during the course of treatment. The effective therapist is apparently able to either motivate the patient to assimilate a new set of values and beliefs that are more in line with those of the therapist, or is able to explore important therapeutic issues without engendering the patient's reactance and resistance to the therapist's values. In at least one of the studies devoted to this topic, those patients who became less similar to their therapist, seeming to indicate a reactance against their therapist's point of view, became worse by the end of treatment (Rosenthal, 1955).

While improved patients are more likely to assimilate the therapist's assumptive world than they are to retain their own status quo, we don't know whether the preponderance of patients who both improve and converge with their therapists are better off than those few who improve but do not converge. Nonetheless, the conclusions that convergence is (1) a central process in most effective psychotherapy and (2) a probable consequence of most successful treatment appears justified. Certainly, few other variables associated with improvement have shown either the consistency or magnitude of relationship as has convergence (Luborsky et al., 1971).

Similarity and Convergence

While establishing the importance of convergence in effective psychotherapy, the nature of the patient-therapist relationship that facilitates such convergence is quite complex. Even though convergence is probably a reflection of collaborative interactions created within the psychotherapy hour, it is apparent from persuasion literature that certain indwelling similarities and dissimilarities between patient-observer and therapist-persuader are also important. Generally, persuasion literature is consistent with dissonance theory and suggests that, other things being equal, the greater the disparity between the beliefs conveyed by the persuader (therapist) and those of the listener (patient), the greater the likelihood of belief convergence and assimilation. This finding is most consistent, however, if the initial disparity between listener and persuader is not too great and/or if the credibility of the persuader is extremely high. When the persuader's credibility is low, the listener seems to find it easy to discount the communicator's discrepant opinion unless some other reason can be presented to enhance the persuader's likeability or credibility (Aronson, Turner & Carlsmith, 1963; Bergin, 1962; Strong & Schmidt, 1970).

In the previously cited review of psychotherapy research (Beutler, 1981), five of eight research studies suggested that the greater the initial disparity or difference between the patient's and therapist's assumptive worlds, the more influence the therapist was able to exert on the patient to engender convergence. This finding is five times greater than chance expectancy and is especially interesting in view of the belief held by most therapists that a patient and therapist must initially share a set of similar assumptions in order to facilitate a positive relationship. However, if the therapist presents a model for change and change is desired, some differences between patient and therapist are logically imperative. In fact, the data suggest that the credibility inherent in the title "therapist" is probably sufficient to support rather large differences between patient's and therapist's assumptive worlds to be facilitative of convergence.

Nonetheless, the data do suggest that patient-therapist simlarity in certain demographic, social, and religious background characteristics facilitate the initial development of a helping relationship or positive contact with most patients (Luborsky et al., 1971, 1980). The relationship between amount of patient-therapist similarity and convergence of beliefs and values appears to be much more complex than the one between convergence and improvement. While the convergence-improvement relationship in psychotherapy seems to occur across a very diverse variety of assumptions, belief systems and personality variables, the relationship between initial dissimilarity and convergence is probably more specific to the nature of the dimension on which similarity is being assessed. For example, patients apparently are initially more trusting of a therapist whose social background and expressed preferences are *similar* to their own than of one whose background is markedly different (e.g., Atkinson, Brady & Casas, 1981; Holzman, 1962). Thereafter, however, the patient apparently contrasts many of the therapist's assumed beliefs and attitudes with his own values and uses the therapist as a model for judging his own subsequent behavior, thoughts, and feelings. The greater the distance between a patient's and therapist's beliefs and values, the greater the dissonance apparently induced and the greater the patient's motivation for restructuring his/her assumptive world (Beutler, 1976, 1981).

While the foregoing states the general rule, it is also likely that patients are more forgiving of any lack of similarity in demographic background than we usually give them credit for. For example, while patients seem more willing to trust those who are ethnically similar to themselves during the initial stages of therapy, the very accepting therapist seems able to overcome these differences for most patients without impairing the effectiveness of treatment (Abramowitz & Murray, in press; Beutler & Anderson, 1979; Sattler, 1977). Moreover, once beyond the first few therapy sessions, one again observes that differences in cognitive systems, assumptive worlds, and values appear to be more important to treatment gain than demographic similarity (Beutler, 1981). Hence, while demographic similarities do facilitate the development of a helping alliance, their absence is not an insurmountable problem in most cases. This latter conclusion is aptly attested by Goldstein (1973), who maintains that therapists can adjust their treatment strategies to the patient's expectations and role demands in order to effectively work with clients who are different than themselves and who are typically thought to be poor risks for psychotherapy.

Similarity and Improvement

These latter points are brought into relief when one reviews research studies that have specifically addressed the relationship between initial similarity and improvement. The reader will note that this is a slightly different question than the one addressing the relationship between initial similarity and convergence.

While it has been suggested that a relatively consistent relationship exists between (1) patient and therapist convergence and subsequent improvement, and (2) patient and therapist initial belief system dissimilarity and subsequent attitude convergence, the relationship between initial belief system dissimilarity and subsequent improvement is less certain.

A review (Beutler, 1981) of 40 studies designed to assess the relationship between initial belief system similarity and subsequent improvement revealed the following distribution among four alternative findings: a positive relationship ($n=16$), a nonsignificant relationship ($n=8$), a curvilinear relationship ($n=6$) and a negative relationship ($n=10$). A slightly more favorable ratio is observed in support of a positive relationship between similarity and improvement than in support of a negative one. This balance shifts in favor of a negative relationship, however, when one discards subject analogue studies (all of which find a positive relationship) and looks only at those that utilized real clinical populations and actual therapists. Nonetheless, the presence of such a large number of contradictory findings underlines the necessity of looking more specifically at the values, beliefs, and personality variables being assessed. Indeed, when this tact is followed, two major findings emerge. One finding suggests that certain characteristics of the patient differentially affect his response to initial patient-therapist belief similarity. The second finding suggests that there are some specific belief systems on which patient-therapist similarity is associated with improvement and others on which dissimilarity appears to be beneficial.

More specifically, among some patients, initial dissimilarity precipitates both convergence and improvement, whereas among others similarity alone is therapeutically facilitative. In a recent study in the author's laboratory (Arizmendi, 1982), it was determined that individuals who presented paranoid character patterns of suspiciousness and distrust manifested a decidedly different response to a therapist whose beliefs were dissimilar to their own than less highly reactant and externalizing individuals. Among this group of highly reactant individuals who manifested externalizing (projective) defenses, high amounts of attitudinal convergence with the therapist resulted in high improvement only if the patient and therapist were initially quite *similar* on a variety of value and belief dimensions. If the patient and therapist were initially *dissimilar* on these dimensions, improvement occurred only if convergence did not. This pattern was found to be rather different than the more usual and expected one in which high dissimilarity resulted in both convergence and improvement and wherein high similarity tended to attenuate both convergence and improvement.*

A similar relationship was proposed nearly two decades ago by Goldstein, Heller, and Sechrest (1966). Collectively, it might be suggested that reactant and distrustful (separation seeking and externalizing) individuals are threatened by converging with a therapist who presents a divergent point of view. Therefore, they resist convergence in the interest of maintaining separation and, indeed, will only manifest improvement if convergence does not occur. Resistance appears to be less when the threat of losing interpersonal identity is lessened (Goldstein et al., 1966).

The second line of evidence suggests that patient-therapist dissimilarity on some beliefs or values is inconsequential to improvement, while dissimilarity in others is very directly related to such improvement. For still others, dissimilarity may even negatively affect improvement. Even though findings in this latter area must remain tentative, they do underscore the need to look more specifically and in greater detail at some hypothesized dimensions of belief system compatibility which might facilitate treatment effects.

Dimensions of Compatibility. There are numerous dimensions on which it seems to make little difference whether patient and therapist share the same or similar beliefs or values. For example, shared beliefs or disbeliefs in the existence of God (Beutler et al., 1978) seems to bear little relationship to positive treatment outcome as long as the patient and therapist are able to share (i.e., are similar with respect to) more practical, social-religious philosophies about the nature of life. Recent unpublished data gathered by the author on a wide variety of patients and therapists indicates that similarity in the emphasis placed both upon humanistic values of courage, forgiveness, and politeness bodes well for determining a positive treatment outcome. That is, a patient and therapist who value or devalue these humanistic and social values to a similar degree are seemingly better suited to work together than those whose values in this area are discrepant.

In contrast, there are other dimensions in which discrepancy among patient's and therapist's values plays a major role in motivating a patient to engage in

---

*In these results, convergence reflected a ratio of amount of change to amount of change possible in order to control for statistical artifact.

and benefit from psychotherapy. For example, Berzins (1977) found in a large-scale, crossvalidated study that discrepancies between patient and therapist dependency needs were strong contributors to facilitating therapeutic outcome. Beutler et al. (1974, 1975) have confirmed this observation and suggested that discrepancies in the patient's and therapist's beliefs about sexual and marital attachments and interpersonal security facilitate a therapeutic bond. In a current study using the Rokeach Value Survey and a wide variety of psychiatric outpatients and their therapists, consistently clear and strong indication is now being obtained to indicate that patient-therapist discrepancy in the value placed upon social attachments and close friendships precipitate therapeutic growth. When such discrepancies are combined with similar social-demographic and humanistic values, an even more substantial amount of the variation in treatment outcome is accounted for.

A common pattern emerges from these diverse findings. Those values, attitudes, and beliefs in which patient and therapist *differences* are predictive of therapeutic gain have themes of attachment and separation in common. Ideally, therapists and patients might be counterbalanced in those values that reflect the conflictual themes described earlier, with the attachment oriented therapist working most effectively with the separation-seeking patient and vice versa. The interpersonally insecure therapist might be better equipped to deal with those who inordinately exaggerate a sense of safety and vice versa (Beutler et al., 1978).

While one might assume that most therapists are autonomous and secure in their sense of attachment and most patients are support-seeking and perceive the world as unsafe, such a speculation is not uniformly true. There are insecure and attachment-seeking therapists just as there are secure and separation-seeking patients. Even though this does not bode well for these therapists' effectiveness (Garfield, 1980), they might do best being matched with patients whose beliefs and feelings stand at some contrast to their own. Since patients appear to construe the therapist's behavior as a model for their own change, contrasting values may call into question their own assumptive worlds and foster therapeutic changes.

In short, it seems that matching patients and therapists in terms of dissimilar conflictual themes will facilitate the patient's movement through treatment. Therapists whose separation strivings contrast with patients who have attachment strivings seem to provide a suitable alternative philosophy to provoke cognitive dissonance. Similarly, separation-striving patients who ignore and defend against their attachment struggles may find a more compatible role by observing therapists who are comfortable with intimate attachments and able to establish close relationships. In addition, it seems that the collaborative alliance and therapy outcome is further enhanced if the patient and therapist share common life philosophies. This pattern may provide the basis for the mutual trust needed to initiate and maintain the relationship.

ASSESSING SIMILARITY AND PERSUASIBILITY

Belief and Value Matching

The importance of the therapist's ability to accept the patient has been discussed in the abstract for many years. Extrapolations from social persuasion literature, however, suggest a means by which such acceptance can be assessed before the patient-therapist relationship is initiated. This strategy stands at some contrast to the usual clinical research paradigm which measures acceptance only at the end of treatment. Moreover, these social persuasion research methods provide a way in which the viability and flexibility of the therapist's assumptive world can be assessed, along with actual similarity in preferred beliefs. Assessment of patient and therapist "latitudes of acceptance" using such procedures has confirmed the clinical impression that patients whose beliefs and assumptions about the world fall within the therapist's latitude of acceptance are more likely to experience treatment as a positive influence in their lives than those whose beliefs fall outside of the therapist's acceptance latitude (Beutler et al., 1978). Moreover, patients have reported being more satisfied with their therapists, even if not improved themselves, when they have been treated by one whose preferred beliefs and assumptive world also falls within the patient's latitude of acceptance (Beutler et al., 1978).

If one can identify the core conflictual assumptions that both the patient and the therapist make about the world and can then measure the alternative assumptions to which both are willing to concede, a direct assessment of each one's latitudes of acceptance can be determined. Indeed, previous research has suggested this possibility and even provided a means for making such assessments (Beutler & McNabb, 1981). It is important to observe, however, that patients and therapists may hold very similar preferred beliefs or assumptions and yet not share latitudes of acceptance. This pattern occurs when latitudes of acceptance are very narrow, reflecting the disposition of the individual to hold beliefs tenaciously and rigidly. Fortunately, improvement in psychotherapy appears to be more a function of the therapist's latitudes of acceptance encompassing the beliefs of the patient than vice versa (Beutler et al., 1978). This is fortunate, since it might logically be expected that patients are more rigid in their latitudes of acceptance than therapists.

One of the implications of this is the suggestion that therapists should objectively assess both their underlying assumptions of the world and the flexibility with which these assumptions interact. Therapists should work to broaden their latitudes of acceptance and accept as patients those whose assumptive systems are within the therapist's latitudes of acceptance. This, it may be assumed, will allow the therapist to respond in an accepting and tolerant way to the patient's expressed beliefs and views of the world, even though these beliefs are divergent. While this suggestion seems sensible from a clinical perspective, making it operational becomes more complex. Typically, it has been possible to determine a therapist's ability to accept a given patient only after the treatment relationship has been initiated. For effective matching to take place, such evaluation must be initiated before treatment as part of the initial decision-making process regarding the patient's future care.

A tentative means for making direct assessments of latitudes of acceptance and rejection on the dimensions previously discussed has been partially reproduced in Table 5.1 (cf. Beutler & McNabb, 1981). This assessment method is based upon research on some variables that comprise the dynamic themes of attachment and separation.

Each scale reproduced in Table 5.1 represents a set of beliefs ranging from one extreme through a neutral position to the opposite extreme. One's basic assumption or dominant belief about each dimension is represented by his "preferred belief." However, other beliefs might also be tolerable and the range of beliefs encompassed by the furthermost *acceptable* belief statements represent one's latitude of acceptance. Ideally, a patient's *preferred belief* will fall within the therapist's latitude of acceptance on each of these dimensions. Such a pattern should facilitate the development of a compatible relationship, especially if preferred beliefs are also quite discrepant. Moreover, if the patient's latitude of acceptance encompasses the preferred beliefs of the therapist on each of these dimensions, it is likely that the patient will be more satisfied both with treatment and the quality of the therapeutic relationship, facilitating the perception of the therapist as a credible, empathetic human being (Beutler et al., 1978).

It should be understood that the specific attitudinal object of the scales presented in Table 5.1 are not considered exhaustive of attachment related themes. What is being illustrated is a method for assessing both latitudes of acceptance and preferred beliefs. The fact that a modest amount of research has accumulated to suggest that certain patterns of similarities and dissimilarities between patient's and therapist's belief systems on those specific dimensions partially represented in Table 5.1 should not be taken as license to prematurely employ these and only these assessment areas in deriving patient and therapist matching systems. The broad range of values, which are partially, but not completely represented by Rokeach (1973), along with speculations about hypothetical conflictual themes, form a basis for a broader perspective. The work of others, as well as the unpublished work reported here supports the value of such broad ranging attitudinal and value dimensions. This is not to lose sight, however, of the concomitant importance of assessing one's latitude of acceptance as well. Sharing acceptable, but different points of view about attachment needs and world threat while retaining similar and mutually acceptable views of other sociodemographic values and interests, seems to represent the most effective patient and therapist match at this stage of our knowledge.

Conveying Compatibility

In addition to assessing both similarity and mutual acceptability of patient's and therapist's belief systems, much can be accomplished toward facilitating the psychotherapeutic relationship through the therapist's systematic emphasis of either similar or dissimilar backgrounds and perspectives. Ideally, the therapist does well early in treatment to emphasize demographic and social agreement with the patient in as many respects as possible, especially in values regarding humanistic philosophies and social achievement. This suggestion contradicts the passive role of the therapist usually advocated. Indeed, psychotherapy literature to date fails to support the value of the passive therapist and generally argues on behalf of the therapist taking a relatively active, though not necessarily directive role in treatment (e.g., Beutler et al., 1980; Beutler & Mitchell, 1981; Goldstein et al., 1966). However, in doing so the therapist must not lose sight of the patient's reactance level.

Uniqueness theory (Snyder & Fromkin, 1980) maintains that individuals who are very similar to one another will, through the course of their interactions, become increasingly different in an apparent effort to establish autonomy and identity. Similarly, most individuals who are not highly reactant but who are initially quite dissimilar will tend to converge with their therapist over the course of time. Apparently, interpersonal relationships are characterized by a striving toward similarity but a resistance to excessively great similarity. Perhaps this observation comprises a parallel with J.W. Brehm's (1976) notion of reactance potential. If so, it follows that individuals with high reactance potential and strong investments in their own autonomy and self-assertiveness should be treated by a therapist who is willing to express human ignorance rather than by one who emphasizes authority and power. Generalizing both from recent research from the Arizona psychotherapy project (Arizmendi, 1982; Kolb, 1981) and particularly persuasion literature, one would expect that highly reactant individuals may be especially prone to withdraw from therapy if the therapist becomes too directive and authoritarian or emphasizes too strongly his/her differential status to the patient.

Tennen et al. (1981), for example, maintain that among patients who characteristically manifest high levels of reactance, an authoritative and high status therapist is contraindicated. They suggest that, "in fact, it may be generally advisable to down play one's status as an expert. There may even be pitfalls in the therapist being very well liked or respected by the client" [p. 16].

Other findings (Kolb, 1981) confirm this latter speculation among reactant patients who also utilize the externalizing defensive style of projection. Among these markedly suspicious and separation-striving patients, significant negative relationships were found between such therapist qualities as support, direction, empathy, and acceptance on one hand and therapy outcome on the other. These

Table 5.1. Value Compatibility Scaling

Instructions

1. Read the nine statements under each topic heading carefully.
2. As you read mark a plus (+) by those statements that you agree with.
3. Mark a minus (–) by those statements that you disagree with.
4. Reread those statements that you have marked with a plus, and put another plus by that *one* statement under *each* heading that best represents your real feeling about the topic.

1. WORLD THREAT

__I am constantly aware that this world is really an extremely threatening, frightening, and hostile place.

__I usually am aware that this world is really a very threatening, frightening, and hostile place.

__I often think that in many ways this world is threatening, frightening, and hostile.

__Once in a while I think that this world is rather threatening, frightening, and hostile.

__In general I feel rather indifferent about the world, it neither frightens me, concerns me, nor makes me happy.

__Once in a while I think that this world is rather beautiful, friendly, and loving.

__I often think how, in many ways, the world is beautiful, friendly, and loving.

__I am usually aware that the world is really extremely beautiful, friendly, and loving.

__I am constantly aware of how absolutely beautiful, friendly, and loving the world is.

2. PREMARITAL SEX

__Premarital sex is absolutely wrong under any conditions.

__It is vaguely possible that there may be very rare circumstances in which premarital sex should not be absolutely wrong.

__Although premarital sex is basically wrong, there are probably some occasions or circumstances when it might be all right.

__Although I do not approve of premarital sex under general conditions, I am certain that many conditions justify it.

__I am honestly not sure whether I basically approve or disapprove of permarital sexual relationships.

__Although I basically think that premarital sex is all right, I am certain that under many conditions it could be wrong.

__Although permarital sexual relationships are generally all right, in my opinion there are probably some circumstances under which they are somewhat wrong.

__Only under very rare circumstances can I possibly conceive of permarital sex as being wrong.

__It is absolutely absurd to think of premarital sexual relationships as wrong under any conditions. They are absolutely good, proper, and necessary.

3. CHRISTIAN PHILOSOPHY

__The Christian philosophy of life is absolutely the only sound one and I am all for it.

__Although the Christian philosophy of life is by far the best one available, occasionally other philosophers have better ideas about some things.

__Although the Christian philosophy of life is basically the best one available in my consideration, I sometimes find things of greater value in other philosophies.

__Although I think that the Christian philosophy of life is somewhat better than others in some ways, I think that other philosophies very often have better ideas about some things.
__The Christian philosophy is probably no better or worse than any other philosophy.
__Although the Christian philosophy of life has many valuable points, I don't think that it is the best one available, by and large.
__Although the Christian philosophy of life has some value, it is in most ways second rate as philosophies of life go.
__The Christian philosophy of life is of little real value as philosophies go, and says little or nothing that is not better said by others.
__The Christian philosophy of life is totally unsound, and cannot be applied to today's world with any significant benefit.

---

relationships were directly contrary to those found with other patient samples in our study population (even other samples of highly reactant patients). There are apparently instances where therapists may systematically desire to alter their image of attractiveness and credibility as a function of the patient's general distrust of external demands.

In contrast, patients who are not highly reactant are probably easily engaged in therapy by emphasizing the therapist's strengths and power. Since most patients do, in fact, tend to be low on the reactance dimension (Kolb, 1981; Lefcourt, 1976), either because highly reactant patients do not seek therapy or do not stay in therapy, this stance of competence is the one most frequently found to be helpful in psychotherapeutic contacts. Therefore, once the therapist has assessed the patient's reactance potential, the general stance that should be taken early in therapy to deal both with similarities and differences from the patient's own background and attitudes can be determined.

These suggestions do not mean that therapists should systematically and directly inform patients about their own background or share personal information with them. What it does mean is that the therapist should not be particularly shy in talking to patients or expressing agreement, especially in the initial stages of treatment. It is important for therapists to confirm patient expectancies and to help these expectations come into line with what therapy can offer. In the course of this, patients will typically ask therapists questions that are designed to elicit information about the therapist's attitudes, goals, beliefs, and even background. It is on these occasions that therapists might systematically alter their responses either to emphasize background similarities and status differences (in most cases) or to deemphasize differences in power and status, as in the case of the highly reactant and externally defended patient. It is also at these opportune times that the therapist can exaggerate or minimize his/her own passive or active stance in therapy in order to counterbalance the dependency-inactivity or extraverted character style of the patient.

Both by combining patient-therapist matches on the basis of relatively stable characteristics of each one's belief systems and assumptive worlds and by modifying one's approach in order to emphasize similarities or differences, it is expected that a suitable compatibility and alliance can be achieved early in therapy. Methods for furthering the helping alliance through verbal and non-verbal strategies will be addressed in more detail in the next chapters.

SUMMARY AND CONCLUSIONS

In an effort to make some of the concepts of persuasion and psychotherapy practical and applicable, the current chapter has attempted to operationalize the relationship between certain patient characteristics, on one hand, and the roles of convergence and patient-therapist similarity on the other, as applied to successful treatment outcome. It was observed, for example, that among most patients, a consistent relationship seems to exist between the degree that one acquires the viewpoints and beliefs of the therapist and the value of the therapy process. The relationship between initial dissimilarity of patient and therapist belief systems and subsequent convergence is less clear but still relatively consistent. This lack of clarity seems, in part, to be a reflection of the fact that different beliefs and values have a different impact on convergence. The picture becomes even more inconsistent, however, when one inspects the role of interpersonal dissimilarity in predisposing improvement or therapeutic gain. Here the personality style of the patient as well as the specific attitudinal dimensions being assessed determine the way in which patient and therapist belief similarity will affect treatment gain.

Collectively, this suggests that while most patients respond favorably to a therapist who represents a similar social background and a set of attachment-separation values and beliefs in contrast with their own, the highly reactant, separation-seeking, and externalizing patients resist convergence if their therapists' belief or value perspectives are too discrepant from their own. These patients only improve if convergence *does not* occur and, conversely, tend to converge with their therapist and show improvement only when they are initially quite similar in their values and viewpoints.

In a similar fashion, different values affect the relationships between convergence, improvement, and similarity differently. Discrepancies between patient's and therapist's valued beliefs relating to attachment needs appear to most directly mediate among these variables (Beutler et al., 1978, 1974). Accordingly, a tentative and suggestive means has been presented for assessing compatibility, similarity, and acceptability of patient and therapist attitudes on some specific aspects of these dimensions. Nonetheless, the role of patient factors in influencing the relationship between convergence, similarity, and improvement underlines the necessity of evaluating more than just the belief systems held by the patient and therapist. Hence, there is a legitimate place for more formal evaluation with a decidedly patient focus. It is to such evaluation that the reader's attention will now be directed, giving some special consideration to the preparation of the patient for therapy, once the relevant dimensions affecting the persuasive process are understood.

6
Evaluating the Patient and Setting the Stage for Therapy

TREATMENT VERSUS CONSULTATION ASSESSMENT

In a previous chapter some of the major characteristics and dimensions on which patients should be assessed were described, and the need for evaluating both interpersonal sensitivity, coping styles, and symptom intensity was expressed. The importance of distinguishing between coping styles, coping adequacy, and source of conflicts was also stressed. A later chapter will address how these dimensions might dictate the implementation of certain treatment strategies. However, before proceeding to this second phase, some guidelines for reliably assessing these dimensions must be provided.

Any assessment procedure must be attuned to the types of questions to be answered and the purpose of the evaluation before treatment is started. In this chapter it will be assumed that the patient is seeking to enter therapy as a result of some initial level of internal motivation and distress. In this context, issues having to do with determining whether the patient is appropriate for individual psychotherapy will be addressed, along with some guidelines for determining his/her appropriateness for other treatment modalities. However, since the primary concern here is with individual psychotherapy, the indicators for this type of treatment will be addressed most thoroughly. Excluded from this consideration of patient evaluation will be those instances where the primary question is diagnostic-consultive and there has not been an active effort to seek psychotherapy on the part of the patient. The procedures suggested here may be inadequate to answer a variety of specific diagnostic questions with the degree of thoroughness that is important when providing consultation to another professional. To understand this is to understand the nature of a therapy-oriented evaluation.

In the usual therapy-oriented evaluation, the evaluator is also to assume the role of primary therapist. Hence, a degree of flexibility is allowed to mix therapeutic and diagnostic (actually, prognostic) activities, a latitude that is not frequently given in the case where the evaluator is serving as a consultant to another therapist. It is doubtful, for example, that formal assessment can provide any information that a therapist cannot discover alone over the course of time (e.g., Meehl, 1960). When treatment relevant information is needed rapidly, however, formal assessment is warranted.

The primary effort when evaluating a patient for psychotherapy is to determine whether a restrictive alternative to the outpatient environment is immediately necessary, whether initial supplemental use of medication is indicated, and to obtain initial indications of the personality organization, structures, and functions of the patient in order to outline the initial treatment. At this point, unlike the case of providing consultation to another, we can confine our questions to the form and focus of psychotherapy to be developed at the initial stage. These initial conceptualizations can be modified as treatment unfolds.

Maintaining a distinction between the evaluative roles of consultant and primary therapist is important from several perspectives and is a function of several realities. First, while a consultant can usually afford to spend many hours with the patient in the process of developing a treatment recommendation, a patient who comes in specifically seeking individual psychotherapy has immediate therapeutic expectations which must be met if treatment is to be continued. Taking five or six sessions before therapy begins in order to formulate a diagnosis and develop a conceptual analysis as is traditional in many therapies (e.g., Davanloo, 1978; Malan, 1976; Neuhaus & Astwood, 1980) may contribute to premature drop out and is often unfeasible in the five sessions that characterize most clinic-based psychotherapy (Butcher & Koss, 1978) and the eight sessions typical of private practice settings (Koss, 1979).

Moreover, while even an extensive diagnostic and assessment process is often therapeutic, its aims are quite different than the longer term focus of psychotherapy itself, and the willing patient's expectations for treatment must be respected from the beginning. Therefore, diagnostic efficiency allows the diagnostic-prognostic process to intertwine with the therapy process, unfolding the finer nuances of the patient's personality structure and function during the treatment itself. It is wiser to assume that therapy will be brief and then to revisit this decision later, than to do the opposite and have treatment end before it's begun. It is not practical to emphasize the diagnostic function to the exclusion of the therapeutic one when the aim is primarily the latter.

ASSESSING EXPECTATIONS AND MOTIVATIONS

The dimensions of patient expectation that are relevant to psychotherapy include the length of time that treatment is expected to last, its expected success, and the assumed roles in the treatment process of both the therapist and patient. Within the first therapy session, some effort should be made to both provide some of the structure expected by the patient and to define roles that are realistic to the intervention being applied and compatible with those expected. Especially at these early stages, therapists should talk to their patients and should be willing to answer questions about treatment. The assessment process, thereby, allows the therapist to establish therapeutic contracts (either formally or informally) early on that define both the patient's and therapist's roles and the initial length of treatment trial. A trial period is defined in order to explore the therapeutic process and reevaluate treatment goals. This process will be described in greater detail later in this chapter.

In the course of the first interview, the patient's expectancies can be explored while addressing three cardinal questions: "*Why* are you here?" "Why are you *here*?" "Why are you here *now*?"

"Why?"

Emphasis on the "why" of the patient coming to treatment lends understanding to how he perceives his primary problem and the degree of anxiety or distress surrounding it. The patient who is in little distress is often attempting to initiate treatment in order to appease others. These patients are especially prevalent in institutional, inpatient settings, and the therapist must decide if the treatment available is appropriate or can be modified sufficiently to mobilize the patient's involvement. The variations of response around the issue of "why," therefore, become critical in understanding whether one is treating the patient or the dissatisfaction of significant others. Certain types of highly reactant patients seldom seek treatment of their own volition. In these instances, dramatically different interventions are needed.

"Here?"

An emphasis upon the "here" of seeking treatment clarifies some of the patient's expectancies about the particular setting or therapist from which service is sought, allowing one to contrast this image with that held toward other therapists or other settings. At times, patients seek treatment not from the most effective therapist or institution, but from the one whom they perceive to be least likely to upset their status quo. This pattern even occurs in very anxious patients who, in spite of their anxiety, have no desire to confront the issues that they intuitively sense will be required for successful treatment. If the patient needs to perceive the therapist as being relatively helpless in order to be reassured about the safety of the situation, some initial emphasis upon the patient's rather than the therapist's power is required. In contrast, if the patient appears to be seeking therapy on the basis of needing some immediately strong and powerful intervention, it does little good to undermine one's own potency by emphasizing the helplessness of the therapist's role. It is probable that therapists do themselves a significant disservice by emphasizing too strongly and quickly certain weaknesses which they find apparent in therapeutic strategies. Even the experienced therapist may feel frustrated by a lack of power and may prepare for failure by emphasizing that there is little to offer except support. To most patients, the expectancy that their therapist has power is a very important ingredient in the treatment process and augers for success, rather than failure. This is the concept of "hope" found to be a common ingredient in success by Frank (1973).

Even if a psychotherapist uses the same interventions, suggestions, and comments as one's "close friend," he/she may be more powerful because of this expectancy of power. It is not advantageous, therefore, for a therapist to undermine the patient's expectancy of help by depriving the patient of this singularly powerful conception and anticipation.

Despite the value of therapeutic optimism, the therapist's power must be frequently readdressed at later points in treatment so that unrealistic expectations of the patient do not result in undue disappointment. Neither the therapist nor the patient should expect more than is possible from the relationship. It is easy for the therapist to become trapped by the patient's high expectations of and enthusiasm for the treatment process. It is fun and exciting for a therapist to be highly valued after a patient starts noticing changes. Yet this pinnacle of success can also place undue pressures upon the therapist to maintain ever escalating heights of therapeutic impact. The therapist must be prepared for a fall from grace by anticipating its inevitability and addressing it the moment that the patient begins to show signs of disappointment. This shift of focus is the fine tuning of therapeutic strategy and has little to do with the technique or philosophy of treatment.

"Now?"

A third dimension of the patient's expectancies are assessed by the question of "why are you here *now*?" The emphasis upon "now" is designed to highlight the perceived changes that have occurred in the recent past and that have enhanced or produced the patient's motivation for treatment. This question determines the amount of stress that is needed before the patient will seek help. Some patients, by virtue of their unwillingness to seek help unless stress becomes severe, will only work well in crises. If this tends to represent the patient's pattern, either in seeking particular treatment at this time or in seeking other types of treatment or support from the environment, the goals of treatment must be modified.

Expectations About Treatment Roles

Direct questioning can often clarify matters relating to the type of treatment to be offered. There should be no objection to asking the patient what is expected and hoped for from treatment, both in terms of the process and the ultimate outcome. Clearly, the psychotherapist should make some determination of whether the patient's goals are compatible with his/her own and whether the therapist is willing to initially work toward these goals. Beyond this factor, however, obtaining an indication of the patient's expectations is often a demonstration to the patient of the therapist's interest and shows a degree of concern and involvement that sets the stage for establishing the collaborative atmosphere with which effective treatment is associated (Luborsky et al., 1980).

Ultimately, it makes little difference to the foregoing concerns whether the treatment offered is psychotherapy, hospitalization, or chemotherapy; all take place within a social network and interpersonal system. Therefore, an understanding of the patient's expectancies and a sense of collaboration with the treater is necessary in all. The quality of the patient-therapist relationship or match is a most important consideration (Frank, 1981; Strupp, 1981b). It is necessary, for example, to determine whether or not the patient feels able to relate to the therapist and wants the treatment which the therapist is able to supply. While it is not absolutely necessary that the therapist only recommend or supply those treatments the patient wants, it is important to both comply with some of the patient's wishes and to develop the sense of collaboration which allows for treatment to be successful.

On occasion, patients can benefit from hospitalization and medication even when they do not want them, but it is relatively rare that they benefit from psychotherapy if they do not have some understanding of and motivation for it. Frequently, an initial education about therapy and the roles required of the patient and the therapist enhances the development of facilitative attitudes and expectations (Hoehn-Saric et al., 1964; Strupp and Bloxum, 1973). Under some circumstances, it may be advantageous to withhold otherwise effective treatments until the patient's expectations are modified (e.g., Frances & Clarkin, 1981b). It is fruitless to implement a technically effective treatment in a context that produces a sense of defeat and failure. Instilling hope and providing information are the first tasks of the therapist (Frank, 1973).

Responding to a patient's expectations about psychotherapy also entails knowing what roles the patient wants the therapist to take: active or passive, teacher or student, saint or sinner, healer or collaborator. While many of these roles may be inappropriate or impossible, discussing them provides a framework for establishing a therapeutic contract, thereby increasing the chances of accruing the patient's commitment and benefit.

BACKGROUND INFORMATION OF SIGNIFICANCE TO THE EVALUATION

Subjective Complaints

An efficient and accurate psychological assessment necessitates obtaining certain background information. This background is important for determining whether psychotherapy is the treatment of choice and for assessing what forms and direction psychotherapy should initially take. A history of the problem also helps determine whether psychotherapy should be accompanied by medication or by added external structure. For example, recurrences of certain symptoms such as depression or the persistence of physical complaints often indicate the need for a physical examination in order to differentiate a disease-related process from many of the usual but general physical symptoms which accompany severe emotional states.

The patient's history, therefore, not only helps us define the problem in conceptually clear theoretical language, but clarifies the patient's subjective experiences with that problem. Patients should be asked to describe the kinds of thoughts that they have as the problem occurs, the feelings accompanying those thoughts, and any physical manifestations associated with them. Information about disturbances of sleep or sexual functioning, changes in appetite, motor activity, coordination, or sensory functions should be sought. Likewise, indications should be obtained of any perceptual distortions, hallucinatory activity, and changes in "personality" that the patient thinks have accompanied the described difficulty. From this information one obtains an indication of how severe the problem may be and the degree to which medical consultation is needed.

A patient with regressive physical manifestations of depression needs to be considered for antidepressant medications (Beck et al., 1979; Byrne & Stern, 1981), at least during the initial phases of psychotherapy. Likewise, the patient with hallucinations, recurrent suicidal ideation, or homicidal thoughts may need to be considered for hospitalization or environmental restraint. Patients with recurrent episodes of depression or excitement (or some combination of the two) that seem to occur either independently of or as exaggerated reactions to identifiable external events should be further assessed in order to determine if a bipolar affective disorder is present. In these conditions of severe disturbance, the treatments of initial choice provide for protection of the patient and structuring of the patient's environment. In these treatment activities, psychotherapy initially becomes an adjunctive rather than a primary treatment. Although some evidence exists that psychosocial intervention or psychotherapy is the treatment of choice for many chronic and debilitating conditions (Karon & VandenBos, 1981; Paul & Lentz, 1977), at present this is not a consensually supported hypothesis (Frances & Clarkin, 1981a).

The foregoing underlines, once again, the important diagnostic-prognostic function of the psychotherapist. Such a function requires a relatively high level of expertise and training. The therapist must know when more intensive evaluation or consultation is needed and be able to adjust his/her own time investment during the evaluation phase of treatment. While it is preferable to interweave evaluation and therapy, keeping formal evaluation relatively short, this is neither always possible nor desirable. Much depends on the therapist's diagnostic efficiency (i.e., speed and accuracy) and the confidence given to the psychological expertise of the referral source.

Family History

The presenting problem must also be clarified by reviewing the patient's family history. Indications of whether similar problems have been present in the family is important. Likewise, it must be determined whether family members have engaged in behaviors or manifest symptoms that are often precursors to the patient's particular symptoms. For example, a family or personal history of alcoholism is often found in those who are ultimately treated for bipolar affective disorders. Frequently individuals with a history of excited affect, disturbed thought, or severe depression attempt to medicate themselves, often resulting in a history of substance abuse. The family may be more sensitive to and aware of these patterns of abuse than they are to the depressive or excited affects themselves. Hence, a hypothesis of manic-depressive disorder must seek both cyclothymic disturbances in the patient's history and confirmatory indications of similar cyclothymic patterns of adjustment and/or substance abuse in other family members.

In addition to finding out the family's psychological history, other aspects of family history must also be addressed. These include a reasonably complete family medical history to determine whether chronic diseases that often affect the nervous system are present in the family. A history of loss through death, abandonment, or divorce also becomes apparent during history taking and can be obtained concomitantly with other information, shedding light on the situations to which the subject reacts. Individuals with a history of suicidal behavior, severe depression, and sleep disturbance are often found to have had a significantly greater number of personal losses among their immediate family than their less pathological peers (Feldman & Hersen, 1967; Hersen, 1971).

Another important aspect of the patient's history is information on how he or she relates to significant members of the family. Questions about how the patient perceived each of his parents as a child, whom among parents and siblings he believes he is the most like, and who would be the most disapproving of his life experiences will assist in determining the degree to which family members continue to be influential. Obtaining this information also brings to the fore data that is pertinent to understanding the patient's stability within his social and interpersonal network. Divorces, movement of the patient among relatives, and geographic mobility are signs of a poor prognosis in long-term, traditional therapies. It is through such divorces, interfamily rivalries, and shifts from household to household that one frequently learns to avoid the type of emotional commitment required in these treatments.

Living Environment

Once the family members with whom the patient most closely identifies and the most dominant problems of those family members have been determined, one has a hint as to the kinds of struggles the patient is having around his/her presenting problems and symptoms. To put this information into perspective, information about the patient's current living situation must be sought. Patterns and problems in the patient's marriage, sexual relationships, and continuing relationships with significant family members must all be determined. Information about how often the patient has separated from a spouse, discussed divorce, or experienced sexual dysfunction are all important for a determination of the patient's coping style and core, conflictual themes. The patient should be asked how he/she typically copes with both anxiety and external demands or rules. In this manner, some initial hypotheses about the degree of internalizing versus externalizing coping strategies and reactance level can be developed. In many instances it may be desirable or even necessary to have contact with significant others in the patient's life in order to obtain a clear picture of the patient's functioning, interpersonal style, defensive style, and conflictual theme. This must be done with the patient's knowledge and consent, however, and it is preferable to have the patient present in order to avoid the development of undue distrust.

Interview Behavior

In addition to the patient's verbal responses to questions about his history and family relationships, observations of patient behavior within the interview are also important. One can often observe signs of anxiety by the patient's expressions and movements and might well make note of the areas being discussed at these times. Such discomfort may indicate areas of significant conflict and serve to highlight discrepancies between the patient's overt behavior and inner states. The manner in which words are used, the quality of these words, and the educational background all provide information about the patient's intellectual efficiency. A patient's history of psychological disturbance sometimes reveals changes in his level of functioning with stress events. Modulation of voice, tremors, and clonic movements may also suggest qualities of affect that highlight behaviors in need of attention.

While it is desirable for this information to be obtained as rapidly as possible, the most pressing initial concern must be to determine if external protection and structure is needed, if it is advisable to obtain psychoactive medications, and if the patient poses a suicidal or homicidal threat. Once these issues are resolved, the therapist can afford to spend time integrating more therapeutic and evaluative functions. The additional information needed can be sought in the initial stages of therapy. Gathering this additional information may in fact be therapeutic as well as setting the therapist's treatment focus and directing the selection of initial treatment procedures. In the meantime, the therapist should concentrate on establishing an accepting, understanding, and peaceful atmosphere, relying on reflections, restatements, and questions rather than structure making and interpretation. While the degree to which one establishes structure for a patient will depend in part upon characteristics of the patient (e.g., reactance levels), the foregoing statement emphasizes the value of allowing the relationship to unfold, letting the patient experience the sense of freedom that often comes from being listened to. The degree to which the symptom is constricted or generalized, the degree of reliance on internal and external coping strategies, and the extent of reactance to external rules usually becomes apparent in this process.

Previous Treatment

In pursuit of clarifying these latter issues, a personal and family history is often supplemented by information about previous psychological and medical treatment experiences. In part, this information is obtained by asking the patient about his/her symptoms. Often, the patient will spontaneously report if previous treatment for these symptoms has been received. However, the therapist must not wait for this information to develop spontaneously. The therapist must ask directly whether the patient has had previous treatment for these or any *other* symptoms and of what that treatment consisted. A clear picture can only evolve when one has an idea of the nature of the therapy, the patient's initial expectations, and his/her current impressions of its success. If the patient had a positive response to previous treatment, it is generally a good sign that a similar treatment will be useful again. However, if the patient had a negative psychological reaction to the treatment, whether or not it removed the particular symptom of concern, it is useful to encourage the patient to clarify how the current treatment should differ from previous attempts. Within the first two sessions it is important to meet some of these expectations and even to address the inability to gratify others.

Strengths and Pleasures

One should also obtain information about the patient's strengths and weaknesses. Unfortunately, a good share of psychotherapeutic activity, especially in the assessment process, focuses upon weaknesses rather than strengths. Both from the standpoint of good therapy and good diagnosis and prognostication, some specific effort must be made to determine the patient's strengths (Neuhaus & Astwood, 1980). This information provides the foundation on which the therapy relationship can be developed, and it also provides important data about the patient's social functioning. If leisure time and pleasurable activities occur alone rather than in a social context, it may point to a separation-seeking or detached theme of life activity and the necessity of developing greater social contact in the course of therapy. If, on the other hand, the preponderance of pleasurable activities occurs in a social context, an important source of support for maintaining the patient's progress and growth is revealed.

Encouraging pleasurable activities is clearly a way of helping the patient defeat depressive tendencies and find alternatives for self-defeating behaviors (Lewinsohn & Libet, 1972). It should be clear, however, that one must distinguish between pleasurable activities in which the patient continues to engage but now without pleasure and activities which would still be pleasurable but in which the patient no longer engages. The key determination in making this distinction is an indication of the patient's perception of and persistence in seeking pleasure. Lewinsohn and Libet (1972) have aptly illustrated that depressed individuals construe the world in a way that prevents them from experiencing pleasure, even though they may continue to engage in "pleasurable" activities. At other times, however, psychological disturbance leads an individual to reduce the amount and duration of pleasurable activities, even though pleasure is still obtained from them. The experience of *anhedonia* is a poor prognostic sign and may suggest the necessity of a more vigorous medical and situational treatment regimen than would the failure to engage in activities which are still pleasurable.

ASSESSING THE PATIENT'S CONFLICT THEMES AND STYLE OF FUNCTIONING

Like any assessment device, historical information only provides hypotheses about the areas that seem significant for making treatment decisions. These hypotheses must be crossvalidated before a reliable set of treatment concepts can be developed. One method of crossvalidation consists of obtaining a formal measurement of the patient's current functioning. Formal assessment procedures range from a mental status examination to standardized psychological tests, varying in complexity, reliability, and generalizability.

It should be kept in mind that any psychological test, whether based upon externally standardized norms and objective responses or subjectively validated interpretations, is able only to represent one sample of the patient's behavior. Each assessment device has its own set of demand characteristics and is administered in a different social-interpersonal context. By being aware of the degree of structure provided by each task, the amount of stress imposed by the various interpersonal milieus, and by keeping the method of applying each instrument reasonably constant, one is able to obtain a broad sampling of behavior. Thereby, we can comfortably generalize our findings to a variety of defensive response styles which might occur outside of the assessment confines. In observing performance patterns and differences, apparent contradictions can be resolved between instruments or observations in terms either of the reliabilities of the different instruments used or the demand characteristics of and amount of structure imposed by the various presentations.

In the interest of obtaining a full sampling of circumstances under which different defensive functions are performed and symptoms are manifest, multiple measurement procedures are advantageous. For example, one type of information can be obtained about the patient's cognitive functioning, degree of psychological disturbance, and coping style from history and questions directed at the patient's current behavior. Behavior observed through self-report inventories provides yet a different view of the patient, since these instruments do not entail direct face-to-face contact and allow us to expose the patient to a different set of demands. Variation in these methods of assessment often reveal significant differences in the patient's responses to social and nonsocial environments.

Cognitive Evaluation

A face-to-face administration of questions designed to assess intellectual functioning as is present in the mental status examination or clinical interview is often important but may well be supplanted by a standardized, short, self-report inventory designed to tap these same cognitive functions with greater validity. The extent of multiple and formal measurement procedures should be dictated by the therapist's confidence, prior observations, time, and the patient's complaints.

For most purposes, the amount of information obtained from a long, intensive mental status interview or individually administered intelligence and projective test does not justify the time investment. While unable to tap the wide range of abilities often sought in the mental status examination or individual intelligence test, paper and pencil questionnaires are useful screening devices to be supplemented later if a question is raised about specific cognitive impairments. With most English speaking individuals who are literate beyond the sixth grade, an instrument like the Shipley Institute of Living Scale (Paulson & Lin, 1970; Shipley, 1940) may effectively reduce the amount of time investment required by the therapist in the diagnostic process during the beginning stages of therapy.

The therapist must be satisfied that an accurate indication of the patient's level of cognitive functioning, degree of investment in cognitive tasks, and efficiency of problem solving activities has been obtained. Some indication of how organized a patient's problem-solving efforts are, the amount he/she decompensates under stress, and various areas of decompensation in conceptual abstract reasoning is necessary in order to determine if the patient is a suitable candidate for psychotherapy. Ideally, the patient should have at least an average level of intellectual ability, even though it may be somewhat diminished as a result of his/her emotional state. The cognitive processing strategies used by the patient should be relatively conventional, without severe distortions or personalizations of the material.

While one might wish to delve deeply into the patient's cognitive and emotional organization (e.g., Neuhaus & Astwood, 1980), most individuals who seek psychological and psychiatric treatment either do not have major emotional disorders (Szasz, 1960) or they are readily manifest. Hence, expending intensive effort looking for serious disorders is simply inefficient. Once issues of immediate protection and dangerousness are reasonably resolved, one is well-advised to base decisions upon the logical probability that severe manifestations of disturbance will either be readily apparent or will become apparent early in treatment. It is only where the history and a current status assessment are discrepant that more serious and intensive evaluation may be required before a defined treatment approach is begun.

Personality/Coping/Symptom Variables

As with cognitive level and efficiency, paper and pencil evaluations of the patient's personality can frequently be helpful in inferring the symptom complexity and the defensive styles of the patient. Assessment of reactance potential can frequently be determined by understanding the patient's perceived locus of control (Beutler, 1979a; Brehm & Brehm, 1981). The Rotter (1966) Locus of Control Index is a reasonably suitable instrument for this latter assessment although not specifically designed for that purpose. Other indications of these dynamics can also be obtained by observing and reflecting on the patient's history of response to stressful situations.

Determination of the patient's coping style and degree of symptom complexity can be obtained by such instruments as the MMPI (Dahlstrom, Welsh & Dahlstrom, 1972), the Eysenck Personality Inventory (Eysenck & Eysenck, 1969), and the SCL-9OR (Derogatis et al., 1976). These are paper and pencil instruments that require a minimum amount of therapist time and yet yield reliable, empirical data by contrasting each patient's responses to those of homogeneous subsets of the patient population.

The MMPI, for example, provides reliable information of external and internal coping styles (Welsh, 1952) which can be crossvalidated by historical information. Likewise, the Eysenck Personality Inventory yields estimates of type of psychological defense (internal versus external) and degree or adequacy of psychological control. The second dimension probably closely reflects the degree of symptom generality and is similar, in this respect, to the manifestations of symptom generalization derived from the SCL-9OR. However, the SCL-9OR (Derogatis et al., 1976) assesses symptom intensity in two ways. One method reflects the average intensity of expressed symptoms across a multitude of areas (Global Severity), and the other is computed as the average intensity of symptoms derived from coding only those on which the subject admits some symptomatic behavior (Positive Symptom Intensity). If an individual has a very specific and focal symptom, the positive symptom intensity will be very high as compared to the global severity scale. In generalized disturbances, both indices will be high.

Core Themes and Conflicts

Direct indications of the patient's core, conflictual themes are often difficult to obtain from paper and pencil assessment devices. However, the dynamic pattern may be observed in the history of the patient's relationships with significant others, and many of the values that underlie these themes can be assessed in the manner suggested in Chapter 5. As Millon (1969) has suggested, individuals whose early history is one of inconsistent overprotection and/or abandonment frequently develop an attachment conflictual theme (see Chapters 13 and 15). This pattern is repeated in numerous relationships where there is a consistent expression of having been ungratified by others and of wanting more attention and closeness. In many instances, the patient has become a "pleaser," trying to buy the nurturance and attachment which is required through sacrifice, but being frustrated when it is not forthcoming and unavailable in his/her environment. In some cases, he becomes a "victim," giving in a martyr-like way but not obtaining love. While those with other conflictual styles may also be victimized, the significance of the attachment style is in its prostitution—the act of buying love.

The separation theme is typically enacted in a life-long struggle seemingly designed to prove that one does not need others. This pattern reflects a denial of attachment needs and may be enacted specifically to convince oneself and others of this individuality. Interpersonal relationships and life themes are enacted among such patients, in order to separate oneself from nurturance and parenting (see Chapter 14). As indicated earlier, some individuals (particularly those who have low levels of reactance) manifest this separation need through apparent ignorance or active disregard of others' desires to attach, coupled with unconventional behavior. However, other individuals (i.e., those with higher levels of reactance) make assertive moves in a direction opposite to that requested by those who desire to establish attachments with them. Consistent but passive (internalized) or active (externalized) rebellion is an indication of a reactant, separation struggle.

Detachment is characterized by an apparent lack of energy or investment in other people. While both attached and separation-oriented patients interact and involve themselves with others through asocial and unconventional behavior, the detached individual simply does not. Certain schizoid qualities, lack of energy, or fatigue represent their chronic approach to relationships. In one sense, the detached person appears to have simply given up efforts to understand the expectations and desires of those outside himself. Although gratification is sought through isolated, nonsocial activities, some of these patients have high levels of social anxiety. Such anxiety signals an internalization of conflict and belies the overt lack of social interest.

Finally, ambivalent individuals are characterized by a life theme of either stable interpersonal distances or erratic, crisis generation in personal relationships. In the first case, the individual establishes a certain amount of closeness but is unable to move into true commitment. By the same token, he/she seldom closes doors and ends relationships. Stable ambivalence is most often observed in low reactant individuals or what Millon has described as "passive ambivalent" patterns. The example of Lynne in Chapter 11 is a case in point. In other instances, however, the attachment and separation strivings are acted out sequentially, with swings between over-involvement followed by exaggerated separations. This latter pattern typically characterizes the high reactant ambivalent—one who generates crises in relationships but never establishes either true intimacy or true separation. The case of Bill described in Chapter 12 is an approximation of this latter extreme.

While themes may be clarified as treatment proceeds, two points should now be clear: (1) the values and attitudes reflected in these dynamic life themes are the final targets of change among patients with disorders of adjustment, and (2) patient and therapists who are matched for contrasting (i.e., dissimilar) values and attitudes toward attachment and separation may be most effective and compatible. Such dissimilarity may maximize the process of dissonance induction which appears to be central to therapeutic movement.

Diagnosis

Once the foregoing information is obtained, a formal DSM-III or ICD diagnosis should be recorded for the purpose of future correspondence. Like a theoretical system, diagnostic nomenclature allows communication among individuals within the helping professions. Establishment of the DSM-III decision tree and multi-axial labels approach (American Psychiatric Association, 1980), therefore, furthers the aim of facilitating communication. While these diagnostic schemes do not clearly differentiate specific approaches to psychotherapy, they do lend some credence to decisions having to do with the patient's suitability for nonspecific and general treatments. At least some diagnoses may provide relatively specific indication for forms of psychoactive medications but are not yet clear in differentiating the types of hospitalization and/or psychotherapy that are recommended.

Formulating Treatment Hypotheses

The final stage of the assessment process is to collate a picture of the patient from the various hypotheses, extracted, in turn, from the diverse methods of evaluation, and then to formulate an initial treatment focus and prioritize a set of procedures. The therapist should not lose sight of the fact that this plan dictates only the initial stage of treatment and makes postulations about ways in which the patient is expected to change to be crossvalidated later. It also suggests probable ways in which treatment will be altered in order to accommodate these patient changes.

The specifics of an initial treatment plan will be described in greater detail in Chapters 9 and 10. At this point, it is sufficient to understand that the methods of deriving evaluation data should be varied in order to accommodate a wide variety of patient experiences and responses to environmental demands and then should be attuned to answer the specific questions of patient level, degree, and type of functioning, both in terms of symptoms, character styles, and interpersonal sensitivity. Information gathered at this stage is designed both to allow the therapist to develop an overall treatment plan and to explore and modify the patient's expectations in light of realistic goals.

TREATMENT CONTRACTING

Treatment Length

The treatment contract involves several specific steps and usually occurs at the end of the first or second interview. The formal assessment procedures are most efficiently given during and after the initial interview and when their purpose has been explained. Many times, however, paper and pencil tests can be administered before the patient's first appointment. When established as part of a formal office practice and presented to the patient when the appointment is made, this procedure is usually willingly accepted as an effort of the therapist to understand the patient's problems and to come to the initial therapy session informed.

By the end of the initial session, the experienced therapist who has adequate preliminary data is usually able to construct a picture of the patient and, thereby, an initial treatment plan. Even though this plan may not be in a written form at this stage, with experience it is usually sufficiently organized to begin developing a treatment contract with the patient. It is at this point that the therapist shares expectations for treatment and both compares and contrasts them with those of the patient. This is followed by an invitation to negotiate and collaborate, wherein divergencies are explored and suitable alternatives are derived.

It is initially important to negotiate a period of time during which psychotherapy will be conducted before its effectiveness is reevaluated. An effort is made to give the process as well as the patient time to go through the normal vacillations of improvement and discomfort so that a pattern of change can be observed over time.

In discussing goals, it is often helpful to point out that the therapist's goals for treatment cannot always be to make the patient feel immediately better but to help the patient explore very painful issues and conflicts that might initially cause even more discomfort. This approach must be modified both in those instances where an overt symptom (e.g., chronic pain or anxiety) is sufficiently problematic that immediate control over it must be established and when symptom removal and behavioral change is all that is needed.

In negotiating an initial time commitment for psychotherapy, sufficient time must be allowed for attitudes about the therapist as well as symptom changes to be observed. Luborsky and his colleagues (1980) have found that a number of interpersonal therapeutic qualities, if present by the third session, can predict the probable value of treatment. Such findings suggest that these early sessions are very critical. Even though research literature suggests that fewer sessions are sufficient for attitudes toward therapy to be established, the author prefers to be conservative and set an initial commitment of ten sessions. Many patients may not choose to go beyond this ten session commitment during which symptoms usually attenuate or dissipate, but the establishment of this structure allows most crises to pass and usually helps patients see their way through the moments of distress and symptom exacerbation which often follow painful revelations in early sessions.

Typically, the major changes induced by therapy take place within the first twelve to fifteen sessions, with decreasing rates of return noted thereafter (Smith, Glass, & Miller, 1980). It is possible that there is a transition point around ten to twenty sessions in which narrow band or symptomatic problems are resolved, and both patient and therapist are accessible to renegotiating broad band goals of treatment. Failure to resolve this transition might explain the occasionally observed tendency of patients who terminate therapy in the period of fifteen to twenty sessions to have lower treatment gains than those who terminate either before or after that time (Cartwright, 1955; Smith, Glass & Miller, 1980; Taylor, 1956).

Treatment Roles

While establishing the treatment contract, the therapist must negotiate a role as helper/collaborator. The limits of control should be well established in the patient's hands but at the same time, the therapist should not back away from asserting confidence in his/her own skill and in the power of the therapeutic process. The patient ordinarily wants to find a therapist who is competent, and it is important to reinforce this view in order to initiate effective treatment. Nonetheless, the limits of power must be negotiated so that the patient will be responsible for behavior outside of the session, for deciding whether or not to keep contracts or commitments made within the session, and for determining the problems addressed.

The therapist, on the other hand, must establish a role as one who can be counted upon to be there when needed, to assist the patient in the exploration process, and to help find and negotiate a reasonable settlement to dilemmas. Frequently, this process of settlement will involve the use of homework or self-help training assignments. This aspect of the treatment should be explained at this point.

Treatment Process

Two final points must be made during the negotiation of the treatment contract. First, the therapist must get feedback as to whether the patient believes that he/she can work in this particular relationship and have confidence in the therapist. Allowing or encouraging the patient's participation in the process of exploring options will probably potentiate his being commited to the therapy process. This is true even of the patient with relatively low reactance but is especially true of those with high reactance (Brehm, 1976).

Finally, the therapist must stress the point that at some time in treatment the patient will have to take some risk in order to accomplish his/her goal. Gain seldom comes without cost; a patient must give up much predictability in order to let go of even destructive symptoms. The patient is usually invested in the status quo. The author finds the "magic shop" technique frequently helpful in illustrating this point as exemplified below.

The patient is asked to imagine that he is in a magic shop in which all kinds of goods are available, including happiness, satisfaction with life, a good job, and whatever the patient has described as his goals. The therapist then indicates that the patient may purchase, in this magic shop, whatever he wishes but that there is a price for which money cannot be substituted. Initially the price is set at a level which the patient will be unwilling to pay, such as "ten years of your life." This is used to illustrate that there may be a price that is too high and for which the patient may decide to keep his own unhappiness. It may then be observed that the price of having what he wants will probably not be "ten years of your life" but will in fact be the "willingness to take a risk and do the things which you have been avoiding."

Following is a discussion of fear and fear avoidance in which it is often helpful to illustrate that anxiety and other forms of psychological symptoms are functional behaviors which have become inappropriate as the individual has matured. I often use the example of Herman, a pet rat subjected to a Miller Box. The rat is placed in a box separated by a partition, the two chambers being accessed by a door which can only be opened by pulling a chain. On one side of the box is an electric grid on the floor and an electric light. The patient is told how Herman can learn very rapidly to pull the chain and to escape from the electric shock simply by trial and error. Moreover, it is suggested that Herman is smart enough that when the electric light is presented a few times, just prior to the shock, he arranges to never be shocked again. However, at some point in the experiment, after Herman learns his task well, the electric grid is disconnected so that he can no longer be shocked. At that moment, Herman's persistent avoidance of the light becomes "neurotic," in that it no longer serves a useful purpose.

At this point, it is helpful to observe that the patient's symptom is like Herman's escape, and that his electric light may be environmental events, images, or thoughts. Ultimately, patient and therapist come to the conclusion that the most efficient way to get rid of Herman's fear is to lock the door. At that point, the patient is questioned about how Herman might behave when he finds the door locked and the light comes on. The excitement, self-punitiveness, and anxiety that Herman experiences in this process are described. The therapist may then observe that no one is in the position of locking the patient's door and preventing him from avoiding his fears. Only the patient has that ability, and it must be clear that the therapy process will require that he be willing to shut the door, take the risk that the electric shock might be forthcoming, and both face and "check out" his fears. In the event that the patient complains that this would be easy if the therapist could guarantee that there would be no electric shock, one can observe that if this guarantee were made, there would be no risk. The price of the happiness a patient seeks is *risk taking*—being willing to approach fears, cut off escapes, and face what has been avoided.

The use of analogy and metaphor in the process of developing a contract and explaining psychotherapy prepares the patient for the exchange to come. These procedures can be supplemented by more formal and systematic "role induction" through interviews, tapes, and film (see Chapter 7). Once the boundaries of the contract are set, however, its very structure may help a patient find his way through the anxiety to follow. The patient and therapist can frequently revisit the explanation of Herman and the magic shop as the patient's anxieties and fears are confronted. Hence, establishing the contract even in this verbal and metaphorical form can do much to prepare the patient for therapy and see him/her through it.

SUMMARY AND CONCLUSIONS

This chapter has undertaken to describe the role of treatment oriented assessment for a patient who is motivated to seek psychotherapy. This assessment may be quite different than that undertaken when one assumes the role of consultant to another regarding diagnostic or treatment decisions. Nonetheless, even the therapy-oriented evaluation must address issues of the patient's safety as well as the viability of psychotherapy as a primary treatment option. With the prospective therapist serving the role of evaluator, however, the processes of evaluation and treatment can be intertwined.

Nonetheless, a period of evaluation is warranted, both to resolve the therapist's concerns about the appropriateness of psychotherapy and ancillary treatments, as well as to determine the form or structure that the treatment program will take. In this latter regard, evaluations of the patient's background, current cognitive level and efficiency, coping style and adequacy, degree of psychological disturbance, and basic conflictual themes are all relevant. Exploring the development of the patient's problem, relevant family experiences, current living environments, and previous treatment experiences will assist in the formulation of initial hypotheses and of an appropriate treatment plan.

In all of this, it cannot be stressed too strongly that the patient's expectancies for psychotherapy must be both understood, addressed, and modified if they are inconsistent with what can be logically expected. The development of a treatment contract is important, therefore, not simply because of the terms at which one arrives, but because of the process of persuasion and modification of expectation that occurs during contract negotiations. It is during this time that the patient's expectations are reformulated and he/she is prepared for the type of treatment the therapist is to provide. Since it is a contract, however, the patient also plays an active role, and the stage is set during this process of negotiations for the patient to be an advocate in his/her own behalf. Since the educative process is begun during this initial, evaluative contract, so is psychotherapy. It is relevant that we turn now to a consideration of how the process of psychotherapy can be facilitated.

7

Facilitating the Therapeutic Alliance

Contemporary social influence literature suggests that the persuasive qualities of a therapist/communicator are reliably communicated through voice quality, posture, activity, and message content (Franco & Kulberg, 1975). For example, the therapist's activity level (Beier, Rossi & Garfield, 1961; Overall & Gorham, 1962), amount of social interaction (Farina et al., 1977; Goldstein, 1973; Jennings & Davis, 1977), interpersonal proximity (Byrne, Baskett & Hodges, 1971; Horowitz, 1968), eye contact (Byrne et al., 1971; Grant, 1969), facial expressions (Kelly et al., 1971) and other nonverbal cues may facilitate the attribution of likeability and attractiveness. Nonetheless, not all patients are likely to be equally persuaded by a given voice quality, communication style, or by the personality attributes ordinarily assumed to be reflected in these dimensions. By systematically employing alterations of voice, facial expression, and posture to fit the individual patient's needs, a therapist might systematically alter the patient's perception, facilitate his persuasive potency (Verplanck, 1955), and encourage the patient's involvement.

Evidence suggests that the degree to which the therapist is successful in getting the patient involved and active in the treatment relationship is predictive of the effectiveness of that treatment (e.g., Beutler et al., 1980; Gomes-Schwartz, 1978; Kolb, 1981; Strupp, 1981b). While such involvement seems relatively independent of the type of psychotherapy employed, it is related to the type and quality of the therapeutic contact, which in turn is precipitated by the therapist's activity, self-disclosure, voice quality, and physical presence. While verbal and nonverbal dimensions assist in this process of establishing a collaborative exchange, these cannot be applied without regard for any counterbalancing characteristics of the patient which might be present. In this chapter, the reader's attention will be directed to ways in which verbal and nonverbal persuasive strategies may be implemented to increase facilitative collaboration as a function of various patient characteristics described in previous chapters. While a preponderance of these patient characteristics have relevance to the selection of therapeutic techniques or strategies, certain of them also play a direct role in assisting the therapist in deciding on the stylistic methods of communicating.

PREPARING THE PATIENT FOR THERAPY*

Some of the methods of preparing the patient for therapy during the course of the initial evaluation have been previously discussed. These methods have included structuring the therapeutic contract and defining patient and therapist roles. The necessity of deriving objectives for therapy towards which both the patient and therapist can work has been emphasized. Often, however, more systematic induction and preparation is required. Indeed, it's probable that a patient's participation in treatment is closely associated with preconceived notions of what happens in psychotherapy. Frank (1973) contends that it is the patient's faith that therapy can be helpful that is the prime determinant of therapy outcome. Success in psychotherapy, therefore, depends largely upon the therapist's ability to make the patient's expectations congruent with what actually occurs in treatment.

When the initial evaluation suggests a gross discrepancy between the patient's expectations and what is available, either in terms of roles, objectives, therapy duration, or therapy process, greater consonance can be achieved either by a structured learning program (Goldstein, 1973), a preliminary role induction interview (Hoehn-Saric, Frank, Imber, Nash, Stone, & Battle, 1964), or a preparatory film (Strupp & Bloxum, 1973). These procedures endeavor to teach patients appropriate in-therapy behavior and appropriate expectations for therapeutic process and outcome. The effectiveness of such procedures have been demonstrated. Those subjected to such experiences seem to change their roles in therapy, increase their participation, are less likely to drop out, and are more likely to experience positive outcomes than those who do not undergo such pretreatment experiences (Jennings & Davis, 1977; Warren & Rice, 1972).

Role induction procedures provide information about psychotherapy and its anticipated effects and, in many cases, demonstrate a typical psychotherapeutic session. An effort is made through the provision of descriptive and factual information to: (1) dispel misconceptions about therapy, (2) indicate the probable length of treatment, (3) underline the necessity of allowing treatment to be employed in a reasonable time frame, and (4) outline the patient's role both in and outside of the therapy hour. The information is usually presented optimistically, in such a way as to open the door to the potential for change. A realistic perspective regarding the course of emotional problems, their resolution, and their probable recurrence is also typically provided. Reassuring patients that conflicts, depression, anxiety, and anger are normal consequences of everyday problems and that therapy may provide a way for their continuing solution seems to provide reassurance and hope.

---

*Special thanks to Drs. D. Kolb and T. Arizmendi for their assistance in preparing this section.

Finally, emphasizing that the patient must be willing to take an active, risk taking role in mastering problems both within and outside of the therapy session, is often a means for counterbalancing the tendency for patients to remain dependent and passive (Strupp & Bloxum, 1973).

Goldstein (1973) observes that such role induction procedures are particularly valuable for the psychologically naive. In addition, those whose socioeconomic background precludes their being familiar with psychotherapy, and whose expectations are for a brief, therapist-directed treatment may also benefit from such pretherapy training.

Clinical experience suggests that those who develop externalized coping strategies (acting out, projection, and somatization) as well as those in greatest need of maintaining interpersonal control (high reactors) are likely to benefit from such role induction procedures. Role induction procedures assist the externalizing patient to begin a process of internalization. Thereafter, the patient may become increasingly introspective as their role is defined in therapy and as the limitations of psychotherapy are encountered. For those who have high reactance against the threat of loss of personal control, structuring the therapeutic relationship beforehand by means of readings, films, and tapes minimizes the potentially negative impact of an authoritative therapist. For example, it has recently been observed (Kolb, 1981) that patients who are highly reactant are prone to terminate from psychotherapy prematurely. Such early termination or drop out may signal that patient expectations are not being met and the role of "patient" is too threatening. The need for pretherapy role structuring may be indicated in these findings.

VOICE AND LANGUAGE CONTENT

Voice quality

Several authors (Schmidt & Strong, 1971; Mehrabian & Williams, 1969) have observed that the persuasive potency of a therapist is increased if he/she is willing to initially take a verbally active stance in therapy and to emit friendly comments. Such qualities increase the patient's attribution of warmth and empathetic interest to the therapist (Schmidt & Strong, 1971). Indeed, qualities of the persuader's voice have been found to imply reliable personality and emotional states (Kramer, 1963; Phillis, 1970; Scherer, 1971) among most people. While it is not certain that these attributed personality characteristics are accurate, there is clear social significance in various voice qualities. From a therapist's voice qualities, a patient is likely to infer the degree to which the therapist is accepting and positively disposed toward her (Welkowitz & Kuc, 1973). Indeed, evidence exists to suggest that by altering certain characteristics of delivery, a therapist can produce changes in the interpersonal qualities attributed to him/her (Bettinghaus, 1961).

While much research is still needed in this area, the current literature is sufficient to suggest that: (1) voice quality has a significant impact upon the process of attitude communication and change, (2) there are consistent attributions of personality and emotional states that are communicated through defined speech patterns, and (3) many of the personal characteristics attributed to a person on the basis of voice quality have been independently demonstrated to be facilitative of psychotherapeutic change.

The greatest implications for voice quality in psychotherapy may be found in the differential response of patients who vary in terms of reactance potential, core conflicts, and defensive styles. Patients exhibiting high reactance potential must be presented with a nonthreatening therapist. Lowering voice tempo and loudness may assist in the communication of such a nonthreatening attitude. Those who both externalize psychological conflicts, strive toward separation, and are highly reactive in their defensive styles, are negatively influenced by a therapist who is perceived as empathetic and warm (Kolb, 1981). This finding suggests that highly reactant and externalizing patients should be approached softly but relatively formally, utilizing one's voice to reduce threat but without portraying premature liking for the patient. A therapist should move slowly into the expressions of liking and even empathy with such patients.

Among patients who are highly reactant but less prone to externalize psychological conflict, empathy retains its power in influencing therapeutic gain. Patients who are relatively low in reactance seem to be able to tolerate more confrontation and verbal expressions which convey liking and regard than highly reactant patients. Likewise, verbal directiveness probably has more power to influence the low reactant patient than the more highly reactant one (Goldstein et al., 1966).

In many cases, the patient's reactance potential varies as a function of the topic addressed and the stage of therapy. As the patient's reactance potential increases around sensitive topics, a gradual lowering of voice can be used to maintain the intensity of the therapeutic exchange or encounter without unduly threatening the patient. As the patient becomes more relaxed, increasing the tempo and intensity of speech sometimes serves the function of re-engendering needed arousal. This is not to suggest that all therapy sessions must be intense and directed toward increasing patient arousal. It does suggest, however, that as patients tend to defensively move away from therapeutic material, either raising or lowering one's voice may facilitate redirection. The tempo and intensity of the therapist's voice change will ideally vary with the patient's inherent reactance potential as well as his dominant coping style and the amount of investment given to the particular topic.

Verbal Content

A second aspect of verbal presentation has to do with speech content. Categories of verbal response, their relative frequency, and the arousal they induce in a patient are all related to the persuasive power of a communication. For example, questions instead of factual statements seem to produce maximal persuasion (Zillman, 1972). Such an observation lends credence to Beck et al.'s (1979) reliance upon questions in attempting to persuade people to give up negative cognitions.

Similarly, research suggests that repetition and interpretation increase the persuasive potency of a message (Claiborn, Ward & Strong, 1981; Hovland & Mandell, 1952; Wilson & Miller, 1968). Indeed, the relative persuasive impact of verbal messages is apparently related to the amount of affect arousal potentiated by them. Although the exact effect of arousal on persuasion is not entirely clear, optimal levels appear to be present (Goldstein et al., 1966; Goldstein & Simmonson, 1971). Apparently, moderate arousal levels increase the power of the communication as compared either to very high or very low levels. Frank et al. (1978) has suggested that cognitive patterns in psychotherapy are most susceptible to change immediately following but not during intense arousal. Hence, verbal responses should be selected which maximize patient arousal during the first part of the session and allow opportunity for integration and conceptualization during the latter part of the session when arousal has become less intense. While this may be a general pattern for effective persuasion, it must be tempered by the qualities exhibited by the patient. Among those who are inordinately anxious or fearful of arousal, arousing communications may simply increase defensiveness (Janis, 1967). In therapy, one should probably avoid intense emotional arousal among these types of patients during the initial treatment stages, although such arousal may be a goal of treatment later.

As a therapeutic relationship becomes better established and the patient is more able to tolerate threatening emotions without withdrawing, increasing levels of arousal should be initiated as a primary therapeutic effort. Even then it seems likely that there is an optimal level of arousal for most persuasion and going beyond this level may actually impair the patient's ability to accommodate new concepts, self-attitudes, or assumptions about the world. A procedure that serves to decrease defensive tendencies while maintaining arousal is likely to produce maximal amounts of persuasion (Janis & Feschbach, 1954). With these considerations in mind, thought should be given to the various types of verbal responses that characterize psychotherapy and their effect on inducing arousal and persuasion.

It has been determined that therapists who are maximally effective are also those who are both interpretative and confrontative in their relationships with low reactant patients and are likely to be perceived as empathic and warm by those patients (Claiborn et al., 1981; Berenson, Mitchell, & Laney, 1968; Berenson, Mitchell & Moravic, 1968; Strupp, 1981b). They tend to confront discrepancies between their own and their patient's perceptions of the relationship, talk about issues of transference and countertransference, and focus their interpretations upon personal strengths as well as weaknesses. Ineffective confrontations concentrate largely upon patient weaknesses and fail to address discrepancies between patient and the therapist views of the patient or relationship.

Physiologically, there appear to be clear differences in the amount of arousal precipitated by interpretations, questions, and reflections (Lacey, 1959). Confrontations and interpretations, when provided by an experienced therapist, tend to produce less intense and more productive arousal levels than when provided by novice therapists (McCarron & Appel, 1971). It appears, therefore, that experienced and effective therapists can safely use more confrontation and interpretation in achieving optimal arousal than their less experienced and/or less effective counterparts.

However, S.S. Brehm (1976) suggests that it may be advisable, when confronting highly reactant patients, to downplay one's status as expert, minimize interpretations, and even to deemphasize one's likeability. She also suggests that strongly persuasive communications delivered by a liked and credible individual may be less potent among reactant patients, than those delivered by someone who is perceived as weak. Among such highly reactant patients, attempting to increase the attribution of credibility, attractiveness, and likeability may produce threat and increase resistance. Therefore, in working with these patients, the therapist may be advised to retreat from confrontations and interpretations and emphasize selective ignorance, questions, and reflections. In contrast to the usual relationships, patients who are highy reactant and/or who are invested in establishing their own autonomy (core conflicts around issues of separation) might benefit most rapidly from a therapist who deemphasizes areas of similarity and remains relatively detached until well into the treatment relationship (Arizmendi, 1982).

NONVERBAL COMMUNICATION

Posture

A growing body of research testifies that nonverbal communication styles are powerful forces in the psychotherapeutic persuasion process. A communicator discloses personal beliefs and feelings as much through nonverbal communication patterns as verbal ones. The observation that postural, gestural, and facial expressions belie a person's basic values and opinions has received notoriety in the popular press (e.g., Nierenberg & Calero, 1971). Studies evaluating the persuasive potency of postural and gestural styles implicate body cues in the process of conveying acceptance, approval, and other significant attitudes of importance to psychotherapy. For example, body and facial cues convey the impression that the communicator is secure and comfortable (LeCompte &

Rosenfield, 1971; Tankard, 1970), that he likes the subject (Mehrabian, 1972), and that he is credible and reliable (Mehrabian & Williams, 1969). Additionally, body language both increases the persuader's attractiveness (Kleinke, Staneski, & Berger, 1975) and increases the power of both negative and positive statements (Ellsworth & Carlsmith, 1968). Whether or not the information thus conveyed is accurate, the listener or patient clearly believes that such information is a valid reflection of the therapist and responds to it accordingly (Ekman & Friesen, 1969; Ekman, 1964; Howell & Jorgenson, 1970). In view of the consensus of meaning attributed to facial and gestural cues (Kozel, 1969; Kozel & Gitter, 1968; Spiegel & Machotka, 1974), it seems logical to assume that such communication will have a potent influence regardless of its accuracy.

The potential impact of postural and gestural variables has such intuitive appeal, that numerous authors (Brammer & Shostrom, 1960; Harper et al., 1978; Polster & Polster, 1973) have described their therapeutic use. The tentative data available suggests that different therapists have characteristic postural-gestural styles that assist in conveying the therapist's interest to the patient (Smith, 1972). In marital relationships, improving a spouse's accuracy in reading body cues may even increase the likelihood of making a successful marital adjustment (Kahn, 1970). Similarly, within the therapeutic dyad, interpreting the patient's body language, using it to feedback communication discrepancies and, thereby, to introduce conflicts in feelings and attitudes might be therapeutic (Greenwald, 1972; Perls et al., 1951).

Proxemics

The study of interpersonal distance (proxemics) also has implications for communication of therapeutic persuasion. Like other patterns of communication, interpersonal distance may be used to vary the patient's arousal level. Sommer (1969), for example, maintains that implicit norms exist for the appropriateness of varying interpersonal distances, and that one's anxiety increases if these norms are violated. Other things being equal, arousal can be increased as a communicator moves closer to the listener. However, the inverse relationship between distance and arousal is in part a function of other variables as well. More specifically, when the relationship is an intimate one, a closer physical arrangement can be tolerated without threat than when the relationship is nonintimate. Indeed, the more intimate the relationship becomes, the more comforting a close physical arrangement. Conversely, the closer a therapist moves to the patient when discussing intimate topics, the greater the warmth, interest, self-confidence, and friendliness that will be attributed to him by the patient (Evans & Howard, 1973; Felipe & Sommer, 1966). For example, close distances may suggest to the patient that the therapist is being intimate and warm, whereas greater distances might suggest less involvement and more disinterest (Hall, 1964; Quinlan & Janis, 1975). Excessive physical distance tends to convey rejection, dislike (Kleinke, Staneski & Berger, 1975), and feelings of isolation (Spinetta, Rigler & Karon, 1974) in the patient. The therapist must be cautious, however, to maintain consistency between the degree of intimacy present, discussed, and expected in the relationship and to insure that all are in accord with the physical closeness established.

The foregoing suggests that positive postural and gestural cues by utilized when working with patients who tend to be toward the low end of the reactance scale. Even physical touch may assist in conveying support and comfort to such patients (Hubble, Noble & Robinson, 1981; Montagu, 1971). In contrast, however, the highly reactant patient and those whose core conflictual struggle is with establishing separation of identity might find such activities aversive. With these patients, the therapist may be advised to remain more passive and nonexpressive. Avoidance of touch in these relationships may be of particular significance.

It should be stressed that physical touch is an unresolved issue in psychotherapy. While there is much to be said for the value of touch in conveying warmth and support in usual social situations, its value in psychotherapy is still largely unassessed (Harper et al., 1978). Touch should be used gently and with patients who are relatively low on the reactance dimension, needy of support, and at a stage in therapy where dependency attachments are being fostered. Even then, touch should be confined to those varieties that do not have strongly dominant or sexual implications. By remaining at an eye level equal to or below that of the patient and touching only the patient's arm or shoulder, one probably reduces the potential for negative communication. While more active touch may be appropriate in group therapies where sexual and dominance implications are more readily observed and monitored (and hence controlled) by others, they are probably not appropriate for most individual therapies. More will be addressed about this general issue in later chapters relevant to certain therapeutic techniques.

Several authors have counseled against placing physical obstructions between the therapist and patient (Brammer & Shostrom, 1960; Storr, 1980) and have suggested the value of allowing a patient and therapist to confront each other at an angle, perhaps across the corner of a desk. A patient should not be trapped in the corner of a room and should be allowed some sense of freedom in the spaces provided around him. The therapist should be sensitive to any indications of the patient becoming unduly anxious and should vary interpersonal space accordingly. By altering one's position from a forward balanced, attentive posture to a relaxed, setback posture, one may vary the intensity of the therapeutic session and convey the messages of liking and acceptance which are appropriate to the therapeutic exchange (Strong & Dixon, 1971). Close distances and forward balanced postures, however, are not indicated in the cases of individuals who have both high reactance potential, externalized defenses, and dominant conflicts around the establishment of independence.

Such individuals may have much invested in the avoidance of intimacy and may find such confrontation and friendliness intrusive. They may counter by increasing their defenses against penetration, insight, or exploration.

Temporal-Environmental Factors

There are other characteristics of the physical environment that convey therapeutic qualities and to which the therapist should be sensitive, as well. Consistency in appointment times, length of appointment, and even the internal structuring of the session are all important, for example. It cannot be emphasized too strongly that negative qualities accrue as therapists are late for appointments or fail to provide a consistent message about the importance of the treatment relationship through the absence of overt indications of commitment. Internal structuring of the session, moreover, must leave ample room for the patient to develop and carry the responsibility for the topics addressed, even if not totally for the methods of working through them.

Research on the topic (Frank et al., 1978; Pope, 1979) tends to suggest that the effective therapy hour is characterized by high levels of activity on the part of both the patient and of the therapist. In effective sessions, however, the patient tends to be more verbally active in the beginning of the hour and the therapist more so in the latter portion of the hour.

"Internal structuring" refers to the therapist's willingness to follow a consistent pattern in working with the patient's problems. This pattern includes allowing the review of material that the patient considers important, setting an agenda with the patient for working on a given problem within the session, constructing an appropriate intervention, and then obtaining feedback from the patient about the adequacy of the intervention before moving on to other tasks. The internal structure should also be such that when there are issues that the therapist feels the need to address, they should be reserved until after the patient has had a chance to deal with his/her own agenda.

By insuring that active interventions are preceded by a commitment from the patient to cooperate, the therapist places the responsibility for resolution of the conflict with him/her. Likewise, ending each intervention or session with feedback about the effectiveness of that intervention allows a smooth transition from session to session or topic to topic. Such feedback also provides the opportunity to address any tendency the patient has to shift topics as a means of avoiding anxiety. Internal structuring of such a nature, with emphasis on feedback, is likely to increase the patient's sense of collaboration (Beck et al., 1979; Luborsky et al., 1981).

CONCLUDING COMMENTS

While it is recognized that the foregoing emphasizes an active therapist approach as opposed to the more traditional, inactive, and distant orientation, research literature has sufficiently supported the value of such activity to now consider it an ingredient of most effective psychotherapies. This is not to say, however, that activity of this nature implies directiveness. Indeed, it does not. Directiveness is a dimension that can vary widely within the confines of any given structure, even that implied here. Directiveness entails the selection of topic and the designation of how it will be handled both within and outside of the session. Internal structuring of the therapy session does not place constraint on either the topic or the method of resolution.

In his early work, Rogers placed the responsibility upon the therapist to provide warmth, empathy, and genuineness as a means of facilitating patient change. Clinicians are aware, however, that they cannot equally accept or regard all patients, and that there are tremendous variations in the therapy process which eventuates from diverse patient variables. The degree to which the patient participates and engages in the therapy process is one such variable. While therapists can do much to facilitate patient involvement and activity, they must be sensitive to patient variations in critical personality and symptom dimensions if they are to effectively do so.

A patient's willingness to become self-disclosing and introspective in psychotherapy also appears to be a function of the therapist's verbal and nonverbal styles of communication. For most patients, self-disclosure may be precipitated by the therapist's own disclosure of information which is relevant to the therapy process and pertinent to the conflicts discussed (e.g., Chittick & Himelstein, 1967; Jourard, 1969; McAllister & Kiesler, 1975). While it is not usually advisable for the therapist to disclose the nature of personal struggles or weaknesses, it is sometimes pertinent for the therapist to observe such similarities with the patient. Such disclosure may facilitate both a sense of positive attachment on the part of the patient and precipitate the patient's own self-disclosure. Perhaps the observation that amount of therapist and patient verbalization varies together is a corollary of the foregoing observation (Pope, 1979).

Too much personal empathizing must be guarded against, but it does not seem inappropriate to suggest that a caring therapist has shared some of the same struggles as a patient and that the patient's recognition of such similarities might be helpful. The type of disclosure utilized, however, might best be altered as a function of the patient's reactance potential and coping style. Patients who maintain a high reactance potential might prefer to see certain weaknesses in their therapist. Self-disclosures to these patients might take the form of planned therapeutic ignorance (e.g., Bruch, 1978). By manifesting some degree of uncertainty, the therapist may be disclosing the human frailities that will allow the reactant patient to lower his/her guard, without providing a major foothold to use later in efforts to avoid therapy or to manipulate the therapist. To the less reactant patient, the therapist might usefully be more willing to express empathy through more personal confessions, such as "we all have those kinds of struggles" or "I have experienced similar feelings."

By whatever method, facilitating the patient's personal involvement has beneficial effects on treatment outcome. In the Vanderbilt Psychotherapy study (Gomes-Schwartz, 1978; Strupp, 1981b; Strupp & Hadley, 1979), for example, neither the type of therapist nor therapy dictated treatment gain to the degree that patient involvement did. Research in the author's laboratory confirms this finding (Baer et al., 1980; Kolb, 1981). Therapeutic outcome is primarily the result of common effective ingredients that exist across therapies and that facilitate the active investment of patients in the process and their communication with the therapist (Frank, 1981). To most patients, a smile, friendly comments, and an expression of pleasure in seeing the patient are welcomed in the initial stages of therapy and seem to produce therapeutic benefit (Strong & Dixon, 1971). Such facial and gestural displays along with the establishment of relatively close interpersonal distances in the therapeutic relationship are likely to convey personal attitudes and attributes of the therapist that are more attractive and therapeutic than those conveyed by greater distances and more passive facial expressions. Even at this, however, the therapist might be well advised to allow the patient to assume responsibility for enlarging interpersonal distances through such activities as breaking eye contact or to altering physical distance. Nonverbal encouragement, when applied thoughtfully might do much to enhance the power of therapeutic procedures.

8

Varieties of Psychotherapy Procedures

Most psychotherapy theories pose a philosophy of human misbehavior and also specify a set of procedures considered to be effective either in altering human behavior or diminishing human suffering. Moreover, most theoretical approaches assume a correspondence between the procedures advocated and the philosophy of behavior upon which the theory is based. Certain human growth theories, for example, maintain that a permissive orientation on the part of the therapist facilitates removal of environmental demands which have impaired the natural process of growth. Other theories do not assume that man's repertoire innately contains the ingredients for emotional growth and thus, advocate an educative stance in order to facilitate what they propose is essentially a "learning process."

As yet, psychotherapy literature has failed to clarify how close the relationship between philosophy and strategy is. It does not seem unreasonable, however, to suppose that therapy techniques can be applied independently of the theoretical orientations or theories from which they spawn. Such an argument is supported, in part, by the observation that most descriptions of therapy technique are more apparent than real (Beutler & Thornby, 1982). Moreover, similarly experienced therapists from different "schools" seem to act in ways that are more similar to one another, than they do to less experienced therapists within their own school (e.g., Fiedler, 1950). It seems relatively apparent in observing psychotherapy as performed by various practitioners who, in turn, represent different theoretical orientations, that the differences among labeling systems belie the degree to which there is similarity in approach and orientation. The language systems by which theories are described capitalize upon jargon and artificial distinctions, and it is often difficult to tell what one actually does from how it is described.

This latter criticism is probably least justified when applied to behavioral interventions, which by virtue of their overt behavioral emphasis are more clearly and objectively described than the psychotherapies. A written distinction between implosive theory and behavioral contracting, for example, probably bears a much closer resemblance to actual differences in application than a written distinction between Sullivanian and client-centered therapy. Among the psychotherapies, writers tend to emphasize the patient's inner experiences, which are assumed to have nonspecific external, behavioral referents and to ignore the behavioral aspects of their own interventions (Hobbs, 1962; Sloane et al., 1975).

In the current chapter, it is our intent to inspect various theoretical schools in terms of observed differences in therapist behavior. Since there are hundreds of schools, and only a handful of studies that have investigated distinguishing therapy processes, some collapsing across theoretical boundaries will be necessary. We will restrict our review, therefore, to those therapeutic schools that have been either sufficiently investigated to allow them to be empirically distinguished from other theoretical approaches or are sufficiently well-developed in practice to be rationally distinguished.

Comparative psychotherapy process literature is beset by a number of methodological shortcomings which make it difficult to derive a catalogue of the techniques that uniquely characterize various schools. For example, few comparative psychotherapy process studies have utilized clearly defined criterion groups of therapists representing pure "types" of psychotherapy, and therapist reports rather than direct observations often form the basis of conclusions. There is also a great deal of inconsistency in the categories used to define and classify therapist behaviors (cf. Russell & Stiles, 1979). Nonetheless, comparative psychotherapy process research makes it possible to distinguish among essentially five models of psychological intervention: (1) psychoanalytic approaches, (2) interpersonal approaches, (3) phenomenological/experiential approaches, (4) cognitive approaches, and (5) behavioral approaches. The latter category can be further rationally subclassified into overt and covert behavioral models.

Most comparisons of the treatment process represented by these different theories concentrate upon aspects of the therapist's evocative, verbal behavior. However, many therapies also direct the patient to perform certain activities. Hence, a distinction between therapist evocative and therapist directed behavior (Frank, 1973; London, 1964) will be maintained for clarity throughout the following presentation.

THEORETICAL AND EMPIRICAL DESCRIPTIONS OF THE PSYCHOTHERAPIES

Psychoanalytic Therapy

Theoretical descriptions. It is impossible in a brief space to do justice to a theory as intricate and complex as that upon which psychoanalytic therapy is based. Psychoanalytic therapy is an evocative therapeutic procedure (Frank,

1973) which operates on the assumption that current psychological difficulties represent unsuccessful resolutions of past, instinctual conflicts (Fenichel, 1945; Freud, 1933, 1939). Significant life events, occurring either in actuality or in fantasy, produce sufficient pain or threat of reprisal that a person becomes "fixated" prior to conflict resolution. Hence, the individual continues to reenact in subsequent relationships the nuclear conflicts characteristic of earlier psychosexual stages. Such repetition is considered to be the inevitable result of repressing conflict, and the fact that a person is unaware of conflictual, primitive events does not prevent these events from contaminating current relationships. The battle between personality structures of ego, superego, and id, determines the manner in which gratification is achieved. Personality or ego patterns are the behaviors through which socially unacceptable but instinctual (id) impulses are expressed without unduly violating the person's moral constraints (superego). The ego both synthesizes the demands of the id and superego and administers the manner in which both receive partial but realistic gratification.

Theoretically, psychopathology can be reflective of six relatively distinct processes (Danieli, Loew, & Grayson, 1975): (1) psychosexual fixation at a stage of infantile conflict, (2) an intense struggle between the instinctual/biological impulses and counterbalancing social demands, (3) restriction of appropriate expression because of debilitating repression, (4) inability of the ego to maintain defensive structures against unacceptable drives for sex or aggression, (5) inability of the ego either to satisfy id-based impulses or socially-based superego restrictions, and (6) the inability of the ego to adopt a realistic perspective of either instinctual or social sanctions.

In the course of controlling undesirable impulses, defense mechanisms accrue, the most salient of which are repression and denial. These primary mechanisms allow the person to avoid recognition of situations in which there is threat to the internalized social norm (object of identification). Additionally, secondary defenses are utilized in order to channel available energy to other activities. For example, one may displace aggressive impulses through the mechanism of projection or channel sexual energy into creative endeavors through the mechanism of sublimation.

The primary role of psychological defenses is to keep instinctual drives and their ensuing conflicts out of awareness. Hence, the *unconscious* occupies a central role in psychoanalytic therapy and theory. The unconscious represents the house of the id, which in turn is the source of all energy from which both ego and superego evolve. Yet it is in this dark abyss that one hides his basic procreative and destruction urges. Hence, the unconscious is assumed to be an irrational, emotional, motivational system by which a person is seen in relation to his history.

Given this, it is clear that the basic goal of psychoanalytic therapy is to bring past and forgotten conflicts, fantasies, interpretations, and thoughts to current cognitive awareness. Psychotherapy consists of ways and methods of either freeing the patient from the excessive restraints and inhibitions of a repressive society and superego or increasing internal restraints against unmodulated impulses. The principal means used to instigate change are free association and interpretation. The therapist tries to promote the patient's understanding of the manner in which his symptoms have evolved and the functions they serve. In constructing treatment, the psychoanalytic therapist relies upon the assumption of psychic determinism, interpreting the functional significance of nearly everything the patient says or does. Hence, accidents and slips are analyzed as if they were designed, and dreams as well as fantasies are explored in order to determine the primitive, infantile, and symbolically represented conflicts that motivate them. In his role as interpreter, the therapist attempts to maintain a relatively neutral stance, usually aloof and rather distant, in order to facilitate a *transference neurosis*. This latter term means that the inevitable tendency of the patient to reenact genetic, family conflicts during his/her relationship with the therapist. Interpretation of the significance of the transference is an attempt to promote insight into the infantile origins of a patient's problems. Progressively, through transference interpretations, analysis of the symbolic content of dreams, free association, and confrontation of resistances, the patient is allowed to relive early conflicts and move through the sequential stages of development.

Dreams are considered in psychoanalytic thought to be a vehicle for transcending one's ordinarily strong impulses to monitor, control, and constrict awareness (Freud, 1900). The manifest content—the awakened state description of the dream—is considered to be a symbolic representation of a deeper, latent content. By analyzing dream symbols, it is hoped that some insight will be achieved into the early primitive conflicts between ego and superego which engendered the repression of certain thoughts and the binding of anxiety. Symbols are interpreted both in terms of the patient's free associations and from relatively consistent theoretical principles of symbol development.

Empirical descriptions

Research on psychotherapeutic processes in psychoanalytic therapy have generally found that the therapist's behavior is consistent with that expected on the basis of the foregoing principles. In terms of the theoretical systems to be discussed in this chapter, psychoanalytic therapy has most often been contrasted with various of the experiential therapies. However, data has also accumulated on types of therapist activities that discriminate psychoanalytic therapy from cognitive therapies, interpersonal therapies, and behavior therapies.

Table 8.1 summarizes comparisons between psychoanalytic therapy and other treatment orientations. Analytically-oriented therapists tend to focus

Type of Activity	*COMPARED TO PSYCHOANALYTIC THERAPY*			
	Interpersonal is:	*Experiential is:*	*Cognitive is:*	*Behavioral is:*
Expressive-evocative Behavior	Less interpretive; more active; similar in other verbal behavior; more emphasis on conceptual knowledge.	Less questioning and interpretation; more spontaneous; more active; less exploration; more self-disclosing; less teaching of conceptual knowledge.	More focused on knowledge; more verbal.	Similarly reassuring and analytical. More active; more empathic and reflictive; more information giving.
Directed Activity and Focus	Similar levels of planning and structure.	More directed activity. Less focus on childhood experiences. Less emphasis on unconscious processes. Less structuring of sessions and goals. Less dream interpretation and free association. More imagery and fantasy.	More directed activity (establishing contingencies). Similar amounts of emotional focus.	More directive activity; less dream interpretation and free association; less focus on childhood experiences; more goal directed and structured; less affective focus.
Relationship Style	More emphasis on the therapist's personality; more authoritarian, parental and status oriented; less understanding; less personal.	More personal and warm; more optimistic and positive; more humanistic; similar in emotional involvement; less formal; more consistent.	Similarly impersonal; more humanistic; similar involvement; less formal.	More personal and similar in levels of involvement; less formal; more supportive; more self-disclosing.
References	Sundland & Barker, 1962; Wallach & Strupp, 1964; Fiedler, 1950; Fey, 1958.	Sundland, 1977; Gomes-Schwartz, 1978; Strupp, 1958; Gomes-Schwartz & Schwartz, 1978; Lohmann, 1979; Fey, 1958.	Sundland, 1977; Larson, 1980.	Sloane et al., 1975; Lohmann, 1979; Brunink & Schroeder, 1979.

more upon childhood relationships and to assume a more passive and impersonal stance than many other therapies. Transference interpretations, as would be expected, have usually been a distinguishing element of the psychoanalytic therapist's behavior, and the treatment is clearly an evocative one in the sense that exploration on the part of the patient is strongly encouraged (Brunink & Schroeder, 1979). While the therapist frequently is inactive and unobtrusive, this is not necessarily a lack of emotional involvement, as witnessed by the fact that the therapist is also frequently directive in both developing treatment goals and structuring an approach to topics (Strupp, 1958). However, the psychoanalytic therapist tends to be somewhat more cognitive in his focus than behavior therapists and less affectively oriented than the experiential, behavioral or cognitive therapist (e.g., Larson, 1980). The same holds true in the dimension of directiveness. While the analytic therapist appears to be more directive than the experiential, client-centered therapist (Gomes-Schwartz, 1978), he is less so than the behavior therapist (e.g., Sloane et al., 1975).

Psychoanalytic therapists seem to be relatively similar to behavior therapists in the degree to which they offer interpretations, seek information, and employ approval and reassurance (e.g., Sloane et al., 1975). Psychoanalytic therapists tend to describe themselves as using support, providing encouragement, and as employing the directed techniques of free association and analysis of dreams, consistent with their overall theoretical structure. There is also a pronounced emphasis upon early life experiences (Strupp, 1955), and upon long-term and frequent contacts (Wallach & Strupp, 1964). At the same time, psychoanalytic therapists tend to be somewhat more understanding and perhaps more emotionally close than interpersonal therapists (Fiedler, 1950) but somewhat less alike than experiential therapists (Fey, 1958).

Interpersonal Psychotherapy

Theoretical descriptions. One of the early criticisms offered of psychoanalytic therapy was its lack of interpersonal awareness. Among the most noted critics were Sullivan (1953), Adler (1927), and various early authors contributing to the ego psychology and object relations movements. These movements have led many analytic therapists to emphasize interpersonal issues and the participant-involvement role of the therapist (e.g., Davanloo, 1978; Sifneos, 1979). For the purposes of our current discussion, the various interpersonal therapies have been grouped together, since none have received sufficient research attention in comparison to other theories to allow empirical differentiation among them.

Like psychodynamic therapy, interpersonal therapy is an evocative treatment, relying primarily upon verbally evoked discussion and therapist interpretation. Rather than focusing upon the intrapsychic meaning of various symbolic events, however, the interpersonal therapist is urged to focus upon the interpersonal meanings of power, prestige, and influence. To Sullivan, for example, psychopathology is not within the person but is an expression of interpersonal conflict. Accordingly, individual psychological patterns are designed for their interpersonal influence. Sullivan differentiates between the part of a person that is allowed to be accessed by others and the part that is private. It was Sullivan who conceptualized the self-system. He hypothesized that the "self" grows with experience and serves to protect one from anxiety.

True to the general scope of his interpersonal focus, Sullivan considers the self-system to develop from interpersonal interactions, but unlike other personality constructs, the self system arises out of the organism's anxiety. The self-system, therefore, is assumed to be composed of attitudes, habits, and behavior patterns (dynamisms) that serve to minimize threat. As the overseer of one's security, however, the self-system frequently excludes information or experience that is incongruent. The degree of this exclusion provides a general index of the degree of psychological disturbance. Typically, the self-system grows and develops by confronting anxiety and expanding to incorporate new information. Since its primary investment is in maintaining freedom from tension, however, and since new information is tension producing, there is a natural movement toward exclusion of information. While partly hereditary and natural, this tendency to exclude information from awareness is thought to result in the individual being insensitive to information that may otherwise be relevant and important.

Like Freud, Sullivan postulated that normal growth proceeds through steps or stages. Unlike Freud, he did not postulate that these stages derive from instinctual drives. Instead, they are assumed to reflect the normal maturation of an organism in a social world. The stages, therefore, are culturally dependent. Theoretically, the product of these stages is inevitably the development of some attitude or habit which characterizes the infant's relationship to his/her environment. In infancy, for example, interpersonal attitudes about gratification are developed while nursing. These attitudes are generalized through subsequent development to produce stereotypes of the nurturant object. The degree of this generalization, as well as its change from infancy to adulthood, is facilitated by the ability to organize experience using discriminative cognitive processes. It is through this cognitive development that the organism comes to differentiate experience, to separate from the environment, and to learn complex social patterns that facilitate a sense of well-being.

Psychotherapy from a Sullivanian perspective is primarily concerned with the quality of interpersonal communication. The reciprocity between the therapist and patient was considered to be of particular concern and led Sullivan to emphasize the importance of the therapist's personality and interpersonal skill in the process of treatment. Indeed, it is this emphasis on therapist expertise in the area of interpersonal relationships rather than in knowledge of personal psychopathology that characterizes Sullivanian theory.

The therapist, as a *participant observer*, is assigned the task of evaluating the patient's response as a reflection of the therapist's personal impact rather than of the patient's disturbance.

By way of contrast, to Adler the dominant theme of life is one of power and influence. The child is thought to be engaged in a basic struggle of competing with a world that has more power and influence than one's self. Feelings of inadequacy are thought to develop early in life and to result in relationships designed to compensate for this inadequacy. Hence, life themes evolve and describe patterns in which these interpersonal conflicts and independency struggles are enacted. As this description would suggest, man is a social animal in Adlerian theory. Like Sullivan, Adler's and later Dreikurs' Individual Psychology (Dreikurs, 1964) minimizes the role of sexual instinct, conceptualizing it as subordinant to a dominant life style or theme. These themes are controlled by the largely fictitious beliefs through which an individual perceives the world and the probable consequences of his/her behavior.

The process of Adlerian therapy frees the individual from the influence of personal fictions. Only with such freedom can experience be dealt with independently of the attitudes or beliefs originally taught by family, friends, and society as ways of maintaining social positions and behaviors. In the process of achieving these ends, psychotherapy designs to understand and evaluate recurrent styles or patterns of life. While life styles are individual and idiosyncratic, they are governed by similar strivings for social-interpersonal superiority and ascendance. Aside from the obvious influences of family and social systems on attitudes about living and value, each lifestyle also accrues by virtue of having a unique place within the social and family system.

Empirical description. Table 8.2 summarizes the various empirical studies that have contrasted the processes of interpersonal psychotherapy with other treatment approaches. Essentially, the data suggest that Sullivanians, particularly, tend to be more personal in their orientation than psychoanalytically-oriented therapists and place relatively little emphasis upon childhood experience. By the same token, they are less spontaneous and less personal than experiential therapists (Sundland & Barker, 1962), while being more verbal and less structured in their orientation than analytic therapists (Wallach & Strupp, 1964).

Adlerian therapists are similar to Sullivanians in being directive, even more so than analytic or experiential therapists (Fiedler, 1950). However, Adlerian therapists are also judged to be more punishing and authoritarian than analytic therapists, with a tendency to develop a critical and emotionally rejecting attitudes toward patients (Fiedler, 1950). These latter characteristics may not be shared by Sullivanian therapists. Nonetheless, the general emphasis upon interpersonal relationships, moderate levels of verbal activity, structuring and

Table 8.2. Comparison of Other Therapies to Interpersonal Therapy

Type of Activity	*COMPARED TO INTERPERSONAL THERAPY*			
	Psychoanalytic is:	*Experiential is:*	*Cognitive is:*	*Behavioral is:*
Expressive-evocative Behavior	Similar in most verbal behavior; more interpretive and less active; less emphasis on conceptual knowledge.	More spontaneous and flexible; more verbally active.	More information seeking and use of questions; more clarification and interpretation; less verbal; more directive.	(No information available.)
Directed Activity and Focus	Similar amounts of planning and structuring of sessions; less directive in setting goals and structuring treatment.	Less focused on the past; less directive in setting goals and structuring treatment.	More directive activity and structuring.	(No information available.)
Relationship Style	Less personal and authoritarian; less parental and status oriented; less punishing and critical.	Similarly focused on therapist personality.	(No information available.)	(No information available.)
References	Sundland & Barker, 1962; Wallach & Strupp, 1964; Fiedler, 1950; Fey, 1958.	Sundland & Barker, 1962; Wallach & Strupp, 1964; Fiedler, 1950.	Luborsky et al., 1982.	None

personal involvement on the part of therapists all seem to characterize the interpersonal schools. Luborsky et al. (1982), for example, in a study of a broadly based interpersonal therapy found that interpersonal therapists spend more time speaking than patients and yet are relatively nondirective. The distinction between structuring and directiveness might be seen in this contrasting observation.

Experiential/Phenomenological Therapy

Theoretical descriptions. Client centered and Gestalt therapies represent various permutations of the experiential therapy movement. Sufficient research has accumulated on both of these approaches to describe some of their distinguishing elements. These distinctions will be important in the later descriptions of treatment objectives.

In many ways, Carl Rogers (1951) can be said to have initiated the "third movement" in psychotherapy. With its focus on overcoming awareness inhibiting forces, client centered therapy is founded on a humanistic, phenomenological, and in many ways existential philosophy of people and their change. While not the first phenomenologically based treatment proposed, Rogers and his colleagues have certainly been the most active in attempting to evaluate the significance of their therapeutic efforts and to determine the relative value of this approach.

The principal conceptual ingredients of Roger's theory of change are the organism, the phenomenological field, and the self-system. The individual is assumed to react as an organized whole within his phenomenological field. His efforts are aimed at satisfying biological and psychological needs for growth. The latter "self-actualizing" drive is the motivating force of personality organization once biological needs are satisfied. Through the self-actualizing drive, a person is willing to both delay gratification and inhibit power strivings in favor of cooperation. Nonetheless, there are circumstances when a person fails to symbolize (e.g., label) his experiences and thereby inhibits both awareness and self-actualization.

The self-system is a differentiated portion of the phenomenological field which is assumed to consist of conscious perceptions and values regarding an individual's "I" or "me" experience. The self-system develops out of a person's interactions with the environment. Through contacts with others, a person introjects positive and negative self-perceptions. The actualizing drive is devoted to achieving consistency between an individual's experience and self-structure. When an experience is not consistent with a self-system, it is perceived as threatening and the self-system is assumed to make an effort either to accommodate the new experience, prevent symbolization of the experience, or distort the person's perception of the experience. The latter two alternatives represent the essence of psychopathology.

In freeing a person to experience his world, a therapist divorces himself from objective reality and attempts to understand the patient's subjective reality. In accomplishing this, the quality of the therapy relationship established is most important. Rogers (1957), for example, outlines certain "necessary and sufficient" conditions, which if continued over a period of time are assumed to allow the patient total freedom to experience constructive change without distorting experience. It is assumed that if the therapist is able to establish a sense of unconditional acceptance and regard for the client's experience and to communicate an empathetic stance with the patient's perceptual world, the patient's innate drive towards self-actualization will be freed of the constraints and demands of a controlling and unaccepting environment.

The basic techniques emphasized by client centered theory consist of verbal and postural communication of warmth and understanding to the patient. The therapist designs himself as a unique person in the patient's experience, taking an active and encouraging role. Verbally, the primary strategy advocated is *reflection* rather than either transference interpretation or confrontation. By permissively reflecting the emotional or affective components of a patient's verbalizations, the therapist attempts to help the patient label or symbolize emotional experience.

Gestalt therapy (Perls, 1970) finds a common conceptual bond with client centered therapy, both in its emphasis upon experiencing the present to the fullest possible degree and in the value placed on the holistic integrity of the individual. Gestalt philosophy revolves around several key concepts: the intensity and beauty of present experience, a person's responsibility for his own feelings and behavior, and the inherent motivation of any organism to gain closure or completeness (a somewhat different interpretation of self-actualization than that given by Rogers). It is assumed that the individual is most capable of achieving his desires when he is able to intensely experience both the internal demands and external restraints of any moment. When one lives in fantasy of either past or future events rather than in the present, he is diminishing his contact with the present. The degree to which contact with the moment is minimized parallels the degree of psychological disturbance experienced by the organism.

Another factor that prevents a person from experiencing himself and his environment is the tendency to disown or deny his own acts and feelings. Gestalt philosophy, therefore, places maximal emphasis upon the individual taking responsibility for all of his experiences, emphasizing his role in creating feelings, acting upon his environment, and in other ways designing his world. It is the struggle of the organism both to own and to disown his experience which occupies much of the focus of Gestalt therapy.

Gestalt therapy assumes that in the ideal world, one moves sequentially from one experience to another, isolating each from its background of external influences. This "figure-ground" relationship is retained while one integrates the experience fully with previous ones and moves on, drawing another experience into focus while the prior figure now becomes part of the ground (Polster & Polster, 1973). Difficulties arise, however, because of the organism's inability to let go of an experience until it is assimilated with previous experiences. Hence, as each new experience occurs, the necessity arises for previous perceptual sets to be broken in order to accommodate the new experience. If one attempts to disengage from a figure before having achieved closure with past experiences, the figure intrudes upon new experiences and prevents them from being set apart as undiminished figures.

It is a goal of Gestalt therapy to finish past experiences, allowing the discrepant elements in each of them to be assimilated within the individual's total experiential field. Accordingly, it is the objective of the therapist to force patients to break existing gestalts that have prevented the incorporation of experience and thereby to achieve closure. In Gestalt therapy, "experiencing" occurs at the boundary between the organism and his environment, as mediated through sensory and motor systems. It is at these boundaries that dangers are rejected, obstacles are overcome, and the person selects, assimilates, and appropriates the external world. The interaction of the organism and his environment at these boundary points provides a basis for the contact functions.

Contact functions serve to place an organism in intimate contact with his world, thus allowing growth, development, and life to continue. Gestalt therapy operates upon the same simple faith that is inherent in client centered therapy—that a person has the capacity for his/her own maturation and positive growth if allowed to experience his world as it exists. Boundaries between self and the external world, inner and outer experience, and fantasy and reality are all confronted through directed experience or experiments (Perls, 1970). Gestalt therapy is distinguished from client centered therapy by its emphasis upon "action" mechanisms or directed patient activities.

The purpose of experiments is to move patients through emotional barriers and to increase their arousal. Arousal and anxiety are, in fact, seen as the therapist's guidepost, since such arousal indexes the presence of unfinished experience. The varieties of experiments are many (Greenwald, 1972; Lefitsky & Perls, 1969; Polster & Polster, 1973), including enactment, dream work, the use of two chair or empty chair dialogues, doubling, and varieties of cognitive rehearsal and role playing. One may also be asked to play the opposite of one's cognitive and emotional experience or to exaggerate a sound or gesture. Movement, including gesture, distance, and posture is utilized, as is both free and directed fantasy.

Empirical descriptions. Collectively, Table 8.3 summarizes the comparisons of experiential therapies with other treatment approaches. Table 8.3 suggests that experiential therapies tend to emphasize body awareness and to utilize

Type of Activity	*COMPARED TO EXPERIENTIAL THERAPY*			
	Psychoanalytic is:	*Interpersonal is:*	*Cognitive is:*	*Behavioral is:*
Expressive-evocative Behavior	More questioning and interpretative; less spontaneous and active; more analytic-exploratory and less self-disclosing; less reflective and disclosing.	Less spontaneous and flexible; less verbally active.	More emphasis on teaching conceptual knowledge; more analytical and questioning; more verbal; less focused on the present.	Less analytical and flexible; more reliant on giving suggestions and questions; more directive than client centered but less than Gestalt; more facilitative than Gestalt.
Directed activity and focus	More focused on past; less use of imagery and fantasy; more emphasis on the unconscious; more goal directed; less reliant on physical activity and release.	More focused on the past; more directive in setting goals and structuring treatment.	Establishes contingencies more often; more use of homework; less emphasis on physical contact and release activity; less emphasis on body awareness and fantasy; more goal directed and prestructured; similar emotional focus and role playing technique.	More goal directed; less focused on emotional release; less reliant on use of imagery, physical release, and role playing.
Relationship Style	Less personal and warm; more pessimistic and less humanistic; more formal but less consistent.	Similar emphasis on therapist personality; similarly humanistic.	More impersonal and formal; less disclosing; more authoritarian.	Less personal; more formal and supportive.
References	Sundland, 1977; Gomes-Schwartz, 1978; Strupp, 1958; Gomes-Schwartz & Schwartz, 1979; Lohmann, 1979; Strupp, 1955; Wallach & Strupp, 1964; Fey, 1958; Larsen, 1980; Brunink & Schroeder, 1979.	Sundland & Barker, 1962; Wallach & Strupp, 1964; Fiedler, 1950.	Sundland, 1977; Zimmer & Pepyne, 1971; Meara, Pepinsky, Shannon & Merray, 1981.	Larson, 1980; Brunink & Schroeder, 1979; Lohmann, 1979.

directed fantasy and physical contact to a higher degree than either psychoanalytic, cognitive, or behavior therapies (e.g., Sunland, 1977). As contrasted with virtually all other therapies, the therapist is more likely to make verbal comments suggesting friendliness and warmth and to be maximally spontaneous in both verbal and nonverbal behavior patterns (Gomes-Schwartz, 1978; Strupp, 1958; Sundland & Barker, 1962). Experiential therapists, moreover, are more informal, self-disclosing, and prone to emphasize immediate states and the quality of interpersonal contact (Gomes-Schwartz & Schwartz, 1978; Larson, 1980; Meara et al., 1981) than most others. They tend to be more verbal than psychoanalytic therapists but less than cognitive therapists and, as expected, to rely more heavily upon reflection and restatement than transference interpretation and confrontation (Fey, 1958; Meara et al., 1981; Strupp, 1955; Wallach & Strupp, 1964; Zimmer & Pepyne, 1971). Experiential therapists also tend to be more understanding and accepting, truer to their theoretical convictions, and more pleasant and warm than either interpersonal therapists or psychoanalytic therapists (e.g., Fiedler, 1950; Larson, 1980).

Gestalt and client centered therapies can be distinguished by the therapist's directiveness, verbal activity, and the frequency of employing directed therapeutic strategies. As would be expected, Gestalt therapists tend to be more directive, more confronting, more verbal, and more prone to increase conflict between the patient and therapist, even at the expense of understanding and empathy (Brunink & Schroeder, 1979; Meara et al., 1981; Zimmer & Pepyne, 1971).

Cognitive Therapies

Theoretical descriptions. Broadly speaking, all psychotherapies are cognitive therapies. Anderson (1980), for example, has lucidly observed the cognitive elements in numerous psychotherapies ranging from psychoanalytic to behavioral traditions. Nonetheless, it is convenient to extract from the range of psychotherapies those whose primary emphasis is upon initiating a change in cognitions. These therapies can be conceptually differentiated from the covert or imagery based behavior therapies by their emphasis upon cognitive change as a mediator for affective rather than purely behavioral change. Likewise, they can be distinguished from the more traditional psychotherapies by their encouragement of restructuring awareness rather than acquiring it.

While there are numerous cognitive therapies, a number of well-defined cognitive systems can be extracted from available writings. In many ways, Albert Ellis (1962) was the pioneer of cognitive therapy, defining psychotherapy as a process of emotional re-education and counterpropaganda aimed at altering ineffective and destructive personal beliefs and values. Ellis defined the ABC's which underwrite the cognitive revolution. To Ellis, the situation (A) does not cause one's emotional reaction or destructive behavior (C). Instead, behavior and feelings are internally caused. It is one's irrational beliefs (B) which produce excessive emotional reaction. Ellis condenses problematic beliefs into eleven basic irrational ideas which he maintains occur as a result of living in an irrational family and society (Ellis & Harper, 1961). At the heart of these ideas is a confusion of what one wants and what one needs. By believing that one "needs" something or "should do" something that is not a necessity, one comes to act in an exaggerated, irrational and overdetermined way. The eleven irrational ideas include the assumed need for approval and love from others, the internal demand to be competent and adequate at all times, the idea of being dependent on others, and the notion that one should have excessively strong feelings about the problems or disturbances of others, one's own past life, or even real and present dangers.

Both Self-Instruction Therapy (Meichenbaum, Gilmore & Fedoravicius, 1971; Meichenbaum, 1977) and Cognitive Behavior Therapy (Beck et al., 1980) concur with Ellis' description of the ABC's. However, the therapeutic techniques utilized in these three procedures are quite diverse. While Ellis advocates that the therapist take a counterpropagandistic approach to the patient, both Beck and Meichenbaum advocate a more persuasive orientation, taking greater account of the patient's viewpoint of phenomenological field than that proposed by Ellis. Beck and Meichenbaum, moreover, disregard the utility of defining human problems in terms of a finite number of societal misconceptions. Instead, they opt for determining those unique characteristics of an individual's cognitive pattern that allows him/her to feel or act in a particular way.

In turn, the distinctions between Cognitive Behavior Therapy (CBT) and Self-Instruction Therapy (SIT) are also important. Self-Instruction Therapy designs to teach patients a method of solving problems. Both schizophrenic (Meichenbaum & Cameron, 1973) and impulsive adults and children (Meichenbaum & Goodman, 1971) have been successfully taught to modify their internal dialogues by paying attention to the current behavior inducing situation, their own physical cues, and the demands of the problem environment itself. Through self-instruction, problem solving processes are slowed down and irrelevant problem solving strategies are disregarded as they occur.

While CBT also attempts to teach a problem solving strategy, the emphasis is not upon self-instruction but self-evaluation and perceptual change. Patients are taught to monitor those thought processes that predispose them to disturbing feelings or behaviors and then to adopt a personal, scientific attitude, similar to that advocated by George Kelley (1955) in order to evaluate the truth of their beliefs. The depressed individual is taught to look for certain predetermined and recognizable patterns of cognitive distortion. Thereafter, testing and invalidating these perceptions is a fundamental tenet of the therapy process. Weighing evidence from past and current experience, constructing experiments to test the belief, and both constructing and practicing alternative beliefs which might represent more accurate realities are primary treatment strategies. The CBT therapist also utilizes a variety of behavioral tools, however. For instance, behavioral strategies aimed at increasing the patient's activity level are often seen as precursors to employing cognitive change and rehearsal strategies.

Cognitive therapies are often highly structured within and across therapy sessions. CBT, for example, occurs within a sixteen to twenty session time limit, and each session includes a review of homework assignments, an evaluation of cognitive patterns, the construction of experiments to assess identified beliefs, frequent feedback and the translation of experiments into homework activities. The primary verbal activities advocated are clarifications and questions. Transference interpretations are avoided. Beck et al. (1979) maintain that the therapist has the greatest impact if the patient is allowed to direct her own awarenesses. Hence, the therapist seeks to become a collaborator with the patient in understanding a disturbing belief, evaluating it, constructing an alternative, and practicing or rehearsing a new and more realistic belief system.

The concept of experiment to the cognitive therapist is conceptually similar to that described in Gestalt therapy. While the Gestalt therapist utilizes experiment to enhance emotional level, the cognitive therapist utilizes experiment to either promote awareness of a patient's destructive belief system or to systematically alter those beliefs. While experiments may take a nonverbal, imaginal, or physical form, most often they are a controlled, quasi-scientific endeavor. Once a feeling comes into focus, the patient is asked to specify the belief, thought, or image that forms prior to or during the feeling itself. This impression then becomes the focus for both validity assessment and the construction of further experiments designed to alter it.

Empirical descriptions. In empirical comparisons (Table 8.4) cognitive therapists have been found to focus more upon contingency learning and the development of a knowledge base than upon emotional experience, past or current, as a healing process (Sundland, 1977). Cognitive therapists tend to be more impersonal and verbal than experiential therapists and more humanistic than psychoanalytic or behavior therapists (Larson, 1980). Their orientation is typically toward problem solving, and their stance with the patient is one of educator. They are also highly directed toward specific goals. The structure of the session and the entire treatment program is relatively high, as compared to both analytic and experiential therapies. In many ways, cognitive therapists tend to be like behavior therapists in their goal directedness, but more humanistically oriented and flexible than either behavior or analytic therapists (Larson, 1980).

Table 8.4. Comparison of Other Therapies to Cognitive Therapy

Type of Activity	*COMPARED TO COGNITIVE THERAPY*			
	Psychoanalytic is:	*Interpersonal is:*	*Experiential is:*	*Behavioral is:*
Expressive-evocative Behavior	Less emphasis on conceptual knowledge; less verbal.	Less likely to seek information; fewer questions; less seeking clarification; less interpretive; less directive; more verbal.	Less emphasis on teaching conceptual knowledge; less analytic and questioning; less verbal and more focused on current state.	Less analytic, questioning.
Directed activity and Focus	Less directive; similar levels of emotional focus.	Less structuring in sessions; less directive.	Less contingency management; less use of homework; more physical; more likely to use imagery and fantasy; less goal directed and prestructured. Similar role playing and emotional focus.	More goal directed. Similar emotional involvement but less prone to release affect; less use of imagery.
Relationship style	Similarly impersonal; less humanistic; similar involvement: more formal.	(No information available.)	More personal and self disclosing; less formal and authoritarian.	More formal and less personal or self disclosing.
References	Sundland, 1977; Larson, 1980.	Luborsky et al., 1982.	Sundland, 1977; Zimmer & Pepyne, 1971; Meara et al., 1981.	Larson, 1980.

Behavior Therapies

Theoretical descriptions—Overt. Most efforts to modify overt behavior rest upon the principles of operant conditioning. Changes in human behavior are assumed to reflect changes in the relationship between an organism's behavior and the environmental consequences (Ayllon & Azrin, 1968). Two fundamental assumptions are relevant to understanding this class of treatment techniques. First, the operant therapist assumes that internal states of the organism are relatively unimportant, except as they are manifested in overt behavior. Hence, concepts such as anxiety, fear, love, interest, or anger can only be understood in terms of their behavioral consequences.

A corollary principle asserts that no organism behaves without a reason. The "reason," rather than being found in infantile instincts, as psychoanalytic theorists would have us believe, however, is to be found in the organism's history with situations similar to the present one. To the operant theorist, all forms of behavior derive in some manner from variations in reinforcement. A reinforcer is any environmental stimulus that increases the frequency or likelihood of the immediately preceding event. If the reinforcer is one that reduces some deprivation, it is referred to as a positive reinforcement (Ullman & Krasner, 1965). In contrast, a negative reinforcer is any consequence that has the power to increase the rate of a given behavior by its removal (Watson & Tharp, 1972). Contrary to popular conception, a negative reinforcer and a punishment are not equivalent. It is *escape* from a painful environment that is negatively reinforcing rather than the negative environment itself. Punishment serves as a third method of altering behavior and is an aversive event presented contingently upon the performance of an undesired behavior.

Reinforcers may be subclassified into two types. Certain stimuli tend to increase the probability of a response naturally, without previous learning. Food and water serve as such *primary reinforcers*. Other stimuli acquire reinforcing power because they have been consistently associated with primary reinforcers. A conditioned or *secondary reinforcer* serves as a substitute for a primary reinforcer. Money and praise, for example, are not inherently reinforcing but acquire their reinforcing power because of their association with primary reinforcers.

Behavior is not only determined by current, contemporary events, but also by the organism's previous experience with similar environmental circumstances. The concept of *stimulus generalization* maintains that an organism will behave in the present circumstance in a manner that is similar to that reinforced in other circumstances. The degree to which two situations will produce similar responses is a function of the degree to which the two circumstances resemble one another. Conversely, the extent to which one responds differently to similar environmental events describes the amount of *discriminative learning* achieved.

With an understanding of the foregoing principles, one can observe the ingredients of several contingency management procedures. In applying a token economy, for example, pathological behavior is first broken down into smaller units of response which are then targeted for change. These responses must be both observable and quantifiable, and measurement of their pretreatment frequency is used as a baseline for assessing subsequent change. By observing the antecedents and consequences of these target behaviors, the therapist determines the reinforcers that maintain them. A medium of exchange is then established in which a token is designated as a secondary or substitute reinforcer. Tokens then become reinforcers in their own right, and may be objects that have previously acquired a reinforcing value or a neutral object whose value is acquired in the course of the behavioral manipulation. Using the same principles, aversive consequences have been applied to a variety of behavior patterns, invoking principles of negative reinforcement.

Contingency contracting is another variation of the token economy, in which emphasis is given to allowing the patient to establish and control the reinforcers (Stuart, 1971; Weathers & Liberman, 1975). The principles of contingency management remain essentially the same but require greater patient participation. By the same token, such involvement attempts to establish the patient as a collaborator in this treatment rather than being a passive recipient.

Still another variation of these principles is applied in social learning theory (Bandura, 1969; Rotter, 1954). Here reinforcers are often symbolic rather than physical, and learning often occurs through imitation or modeling. The fundamental, theoretical differences between token or aversion-based programs and modeling programs rest in the manner by which an organism is reinforced. Modeling is a process of acquiring a cognitive and behavioral association between a model, the model's behavior, and the perceived consequences of that behavior. After observing the consequences of another's behavior, the observer is able to rehearse the same behavior in anticipation of a similar consequence. Thus, the behavior receives vicarious reinforcement.

Bandura (1969) suggests that four basic processes contribute to the efficacy and speed of learning by modeling. First, the therapist must endeavor to maintain the patient's attention both by helping the patient distinguish between target behaviors and their surroundings and by engendering the patient's sensory arousal. Therefore, verbal cues are often used to focus the patient's attention and to discriminate relevant behavior patterns. Second, the patient-observer must have the ability to symbolize the observed events, either through verbal or imaginal processes. The therapist helps the observer develop retrievable images of the behavioral contingencies by providing descriptions, verbal cues, and directions for covert rehearsal. Third, the patient must be capable of making the responses necessary to imitate the model. Complex behaviors may require some additional practice by the observer, bolstered by concrete reinforcers. Lastly, the therapist must develop a motivational system that translates imaginal or verbal material into behavioral events. Overt rewards may be utilized in this connection, but often feedback and self-observation may serve just as well. Once a target behavior has been modeled, a consequence or outcome similar to that obtained by the model helps to strengthen the behavior.

Modeling finds application in psychodrama and other "action" therapies. In psychodrama (Moreno, 1946) the person playing the protagonist's *alter ego* serves as a model for expression of congruent affect or underlying feeling. Similarly, other role-playing procedures utilize many of the concepts of modeling in allowing a person to observe, either in fantasy or in actuality, his/her own behavior or that of another. The common feature of these approaches is the patient's observation, at a risk-free distance, of a person engaging in defined behaviors with defined but valued consequences.

From the perspective of interpersonal persuasion, modeling places comparatively less emphasis upon the external control of the therapist than does token economy. It places high emphasis upon overt behavioral roles taken by both patient and therapist, with coercive forces serving only to underline associations, discriminate among relevant events, and clarify the relationships between social roles and their consequences. Clarification, instruction, and confrontation are the most used verbal techniques. While the appropriate interpersonal activity level and distance to be maintained is under some degree of controversy (Ullman & Krasner, 1969), interpersonal closeness is not considered to be a requirement.

Theoretical descriptions—Covert. The conceptual distinction between covert behavior therapies and the overt behavior therapies described in the foregoing section is not based as much upon their methodology as on their point of focus. Overt therapies are used in the current context to describe the object of change—overt behavior. Covert behavior therapies, in contrast, are primarily designed to modify covert or subjective experiences, such as anxiety, which mediate between experience and behavior (e.g., Wolpe & Lazarus, 1966). In this latter process, the methods most often employed rely on classical conditioning and extinction procedures. Systematic Desensitization (Wolpe, 1973), Implosive Therapy (Stampfl & Levis, 1967), and covert modeling (Cautela, 1973) are all examples of such behavioral approaches. In Systematic Desensitization, for example (Wolpe, 1973), neurotic behavior is assumed to represent a persistent learning of maladaptive behaviors to cope with debilitating anxiety. Anxiety, while rooted in the person's past experience, is assumed to be a subcortical, sympathetic representation of traumatic experience. Hence, amelioration of anxiety is best accomplished by a classical extinction process that involves the autonomic nervous system rather than voluntary, cerebrally controlled systems.

Borrowing from laboratory studies on classical extinction, Wolpe has applied a counterconditioning model to anxiety reduction. By this technique, an anxiety response is thought to be inhibited by an incompatible, more dominant response that is conditioned to similar cues. By introducing a powerful stimulus whose effect is antagonistic to anxiety, the organism acquires a conditioned inhibition of anxiety in the presence of anxiety cues. Anxiety gradually becomes less dominant in the patient's hierarchy of response and finally is assumed to dissipate. Originally, the counterconditioning response was relaxation and the anxiety eliciting cues were presented in imagery. In more recent applications, however, desensitization has been undertaken in vivo, teaching relaxation as an active coping strategy applied in the provoking environment itself (e.g., Goldfried & Davison, 1976).

In employing systematic desensitization, Wolpe emphasizes the importance of the therapist's understanding, warmth, and acceptance. These conditions, however, are not thought to be primary healing agents but simply serve as a means to encourage the patient's cooperation with the therapist.

The next task of the therapist is to derive a list of anxiety-provoking situations. These stimuli are then arranged in a hierarchy from highest to lowest arousal. A number of hierarchies, each reflecting a different class of stimuli, may be developed, and these hierarchies may in turn be placed on a scale reflecting the relative intensity of arousal associated with them. The therapist then proceeds to instruct the patient in an incompatible response. Among the responses that are considered antagonistic to anxiety behaviors are self-assertion, relaxation, and sexual activity. Assertiveness training, for example, typically applies both overt role playing and relaxation to lower anxiety levels attendant upon assertive responses. A state of hypnosis may even be achieved in these relaxation exercises, and the extinction process may be facilitated by suggestions given while the patient is in this state. The patient is then asked to practice this procedure on his own in his normal environment. As the patient acquires an antagonistic relaxation response, the therapist begins to instruct the patient in the procedures of visual imagery. Once both relaxation and clear imagery are obtained, the therapist begins to present visual images of fear-provoking stimuli drawn from the fear hierarchy. In later applications, this procedure may be supplemented by in vivo confrontations with anxiety-producing situations. Typically, desensitization is started at the lowest end of the fear hierarchy and proceeds to that producing maximal anxiety.

Numerous variations, including covert modeling (Bandura, 1969) in which the patient is asked to imagine a valued, significant other perform a task requiring either coping or mastery in the face of anxiety is also utilized in desensitization. Covert rehearsal (Kazdin, 1975) entails another variation in which the patient is asked to systematically imagine going through the act of either coping with or mastering the anxiety-producing task. Generally, a coping rather than mastery model is considered to be most efficacious (Anderson, 1980). That is, the patient imagines herself or a significant other engaging in a usually avoided act, gaining control of and coping with anxiety in the process.

Throughout the presentation of any such fantasy material, the patient is asked to remain as relaxed as possible. Traditionally, when anxiety is encountered, the therapist may terminate the anxiety-provoking stimulus and introduce a neutral or relaxing image, gradually reintroducing the anxiety producing stimulus until anxiety is no longer produced. It is unclear how necessary this latter procedure is, however. In covert modeling, for example, no systematic effort is ordinarily made to back off from anxiety when it begins to accrue. In fact, automated desensitization procedures are becoming widely used (Kahn & Baker, 1968; Marks, 1978; Rosen, Glasgow & Barrera, 1976), and such procedures frequently do not allow this degree of precision.

Numerous other covert strategies have been developed. For example, Implosive Therapy (Stampfl & Levis, 1967) combines two factor learning theory and traditional renditions of psychoanalytic theory. Stampfl and Levis (1967) hypothesize that the root of much pathology exists in the infantile experiences described by psychoanalytic theory. Memories of these events, however, are forgotten or pushed out of awareness in order to avoid the pain associated with them. If effective, this repression prevents a patient from contacting the original conditioning situations. The infrequent exposure one receives to such stimuli prevents their extinction. While systematic desensitization may eliminate anxiety associated with specific symptom contingent stimuli, Stampfl argues that it does little to extinguish the anxiety associated with the original learning situation. Since it is from this primitive nucleus that anxiety generalizes, Stampfl maintains that it is more efficient to flood the patient with imaginal representations of the original stimulus. This stimulus material is derived from hypothesized, infantile learning experiences associated with Oedipal struggles, dependency attachments, and disapproval of parental figures.

Likewise, covert sensitization (Cautela, 1977) has been successfully used to curtail certain habits, such as drinking and smoking. In this behavioral strategy, an effort is made to increase the anxiety associated with previously reinforced and reinforcing behaviors. By inducing a state of conditioned noxiousness, the therapist attempts to inhibit the targeted behavior. Covert sensitization parallels aversive conditioning, where the therapist applies negative reinforcement to instigate a decrease in the frequency of a given behavior.

Finally, renewed interest in hypnosis and advances in biofeedback strategies have added these tools to the armamentarium of the behavior therapist. Even though the procedures are conceptually distinct and hypnosis is not usually seen as a behavioral strategy, biofeedback and hypnosis have many characteristics in common. Directing the patient to focus upon particular subjective experiences, the provision of suggestion, and the aura of the "magical" all serve to induce these procedures with a powerful effect of suggestion. Moreover, they are both frequently applied to physiological experience, particularly in the control of pain, and both have been broadly applied to a wide range of medical

Table 8.5. Comparison of Other Therapies to Behavior Therapies

Type of Activity	*COMPARED TO BEHAVIOR THERAPY*			
	Psychoanalytic is:	*Interpersonal is:*	*Experiential is:*	*Cognitive is:*
Expressive-evocative Behavior	Similarly reassuring and analytical or questioning; less verbal; less reflective; less likely to give information.	(No information available.)	More analytical, questioning and flexible; less opinion and advice giving; less directive (Gestalt is not); Gestalt is less facilitative-supportive.	More analytic and questioning.
Directed Activity and Focus	Less directive; more reliant on dream interpretation; free association and focused on unconscious and childhood experience; less goal directed and structured. More emphasis on affective release.	(No information available.)	Less goal directed; more emotional release exercises, imagery, physical release, role playing.	Less goal-specific; more focus on release of affect through imagery; similar levels of involvement.
Relationship Style	Less personal and disclosing; more formal; less supportive and friendly but similar amounts of involvement.	(No information available.)	More personal and less formal; Gestalt therapy provides less emotional support.	More personal and less formal; less self-disclosing.
References	Sloane et al., 1975; Lohmann, 1979; Brunink & Schroeder, 1979.	None	Larson, 1980; Brunink & Schroeder, 1979; Lohmann, 1979.	Larson, 1980.

and somatic conditions (e.g., Fromm & Shor, 1979; Yates, 1980). Biofeedback operates on the demonstration that one can alter various aspects of biological functioning if the patient can efficiently and rapidly monitor minor changes in that function. In contrast, hypnosis capitalizes upon the patient's willingness to focus upon changes in experience and to accept therapeutic suggestions.

Empirical Summary of Behavioral Procedures. Table 8.5 summarizes the empirical differences observed between the activities of behavioral and nonbehavioral therapists. Essentially, behavior therapists tend to emphasize teaching the knowledge base of their procedures as a means for overcoming various forms of psychopathology. They seek more clarification than other approaches, are more directive in their statements and strongly goal directed, and do not place much emphasis either upon affective awareness or the obtaining of traditional insights (Larson, 1980; Sloane et al., 1975). Behavior therapists are, nonetheless, prone to respond in supportive and empathic ways, at least as contrasted to traditional psychoanalytic therapists (Sloane et al., 1975) and utilize a wide mixture of overt and covert conditioning techniques rather eclectically. They employ such directed procedures as relaxation training, systematic desensitization, aversive conditioning, role playing, and advice giving. They also are prone to give opinions and suggestions and to seek opinions and suggestions from their patients (Brunnick & Schroeder, 1979; Lohmann, 1979).

SUMMARY

One can observe from the foregoing, that many therapeutic interventions exist along a continuum of usage. Because of methodological differences, it is difficult to determine the degree to which the various therapy descriptors are independent. While factorial and clustering procedures have been used in several studies, the clinical descriptions of the factors obtained vary greatly from study to study as an undetermined function of the method used to code observations, the source of ratings, and the directness of the observations. Nonetheless, utilizing terms that seem conceptually/clinically reliable and relevant, it is possible to differentiate among the various theoretical approaches in terms of the type and degree of the verbal activity, amount of reliance on various directed activities, the breadth of therapeutic focus, and the amount of warmth, closeness, and informality encouraged. Table 8.6 summarizes the variations among theories by describing their relative rank order in reference to one another along various dimensions described in the foregoing pages.

While the hope, persuasiveness, and faith engendered in psychotherapy are important, Marks (1978), among others, suggests that we may have entered the

Table 8.6. Summary Rankings of Various Therapies on Therapist Behavior

*Type of Activity**	*Psychoanalytic*	*Interpersonal*	*Experiential*	*Cognitive*	*Behavior*
A. Expressive-evocative Behavior					
1. Verbal activity level	5	4	3 (Gestalt Only)	1.5	1.5
2. Reframing/reflection	3	4.5	1	4.5	2
3. Clarification/questioning	1	4	5	2	3
4. Interpreting/analyzing/advising	1	4	5	3	2
5. Teaching/informing	4	2.5	5	1	2.5
B. Directed Activity					
1. Use of directed activity	5	4	1	2.5	2.5
2. Free association	1	2	3	4.5	4.5
3. Physical release/activity	5	4	1	3	2
4. Punishing and rewarding	5	3	4	2	1
5. Role playing	4.5	4.5	1	2.5	2.5
6. Systematic problem solving	4.5	3	4.5	1	2
7. Structured imagery/dreams	3.5	5	1	3.5	2
C. Focus/structuring					
1. Awareness/now (1) vs Insight/then (5)	5	4	1	2.5	2.5
2. Preplanning sessions	5	3	4	1.5	1.5
3. Internal structuring/control	4.5	4.5	3 (Gestalt Only)	1.5	1.5
4. Broad band (1) vs narrow band (5) goals	1	2	3	4	5
5. Unconscious (1) vs conscious (5) awareness	1	2	3	4	5
D. Relationship					
1. Formal (1) vs informal/spontaneous (5)	2	1	5	3.5	3.5
2. Personal and self disclosing (1) vs impersonal (5)	4.5	4.5	1	3	2
3. Involvement/support giving	3	5	1	3	3

*Where not otherwise indicated, a rank of "1" is high on the dimension and a rank of "5" is low.

age of psychotherapy where certain directed strategies, developed largely in the behavioral schools, can be satisfactorily applied to certain conditions, independently of the therapist. For most, however, the therapist is more important (Frank, 1981) than the technique. Therefore, given the variety of treatment strategies possible, the well-prepared eclectic therapist will be capable of systematically altering the frequency of using certain types of therapist-evoked interventions and also be proficient in the use of a number of directed treatment strategies. It is not the intention to teach all of these procedures in this volume. Instead, the attempt has been to give a basic introduction to many of them, assuming that the well-instructed therapist will seek knowledge from other sources. The focus at this point must turn to a reformulation of these procedures, independent of their founding theories, and to the construction of guidelines for their application. The focus upon *when* rather than *how* to apply therapy procedures arises from a concern with where the deficits are in the field and does not reflect a belief that the *how* is less important than the *when*.

9

Fitting the Therapy Technique to the Patient

DIAGNOSTIC ISSUES

In Chapter 4 it was suggested that the complexity of a patient's symptoms, coping style, and interpersonal sensitivity (reactance) may be related to his response to therapeutic persuasion methods. The search for such dimensions began with the clinical and empirical observation (e.g., Cole & Magnussen, 1966; Gillis & Moran, 1981) that traditional diagnostic systems do not predict either the patient's assignment to treatment or his/her response to it. It will be no surprise to most clinicians that with few exceptions, traditional diagnostic labels are not useful in determining what type of treatment to offer a patient. When exceptions occur, they are primarily in providing indicators of medical rather than psychotherapeutic interventions (cf., Frances & Clarkin, 1981a).

The reasons for the inadequacies of diagnostic systems can be seen in two factors. First, diagnostic nomenclature is largely based upon a medical analogy that fits poorly with most psychological disturbances. Therefore, it is most easily applied to those conditions where a medical intervention is warranted. Hence, antidepressant medications are applied to major depressive disorders, Lithium Carbonate for bipolar affective disorders, Phenothiazines for thought disorders, and wars are waged over what to do with those who present less clearly defined or severe pathologies.

A second factor in predisposing the lack of correspondence between diagnostic labels and treatment assignment is the simplistic viewpoint applied in most psychiatric texts to the differentiation among psychotherapies. It is traditional (e.g., Kolb, 1968; Rowe, 1980) to differentiate among insight-oriented therapy, psychoanalysis, supportive therapy, and behavior therapy. Such global distinctions do not do justice to the complexity of the hundreds of psychotherapy theories and thousands of therapeutic practices. Nonetheless, by being aware of our inability to clearly differentiate among psychotherapies, the availability of a wide variety of highly differentiated medications and a diagnostic system that more easily lends itself to medical applications than psychological ones, the reasons why psychotherapy has failed to obtain the prescriptive specificity warranted by an eclectic orientation will be seen (Frances & Clarkin, 1981a, 1981b; Goldstein & Stein, 1976).

PATIENT DIMENSIONS AND TREATMENT HYPOTHESES

In the search for patient dimensions that might predicate the discriminant use of various psychotherapeutic procedures, the author recently compiled a list of 52 highly select, comparative psychotherapy studies (Beutler, 1979a). Selection criteria insured that only those studies that best represented good or at least "adequate" psychotherapy research would be included. The studies were then individually evaluated relative to the major comparisons among the psychotherapies investigated and the populations utilized. Following this rational approach to the problem, the clinical hypotheses developed were operationalized, and comparisons were made in order to crossvalidate the preliminary impressions. While this type of analysis can be criticized (Kazrin, Durac & Agteros, 1979) for its lack of statistical precision, it closely approximates the type of clinical decisional process frequently involved in defining both relevant patient groups and therapies.

From this review of methodologically adequate studies, the three patient-symptom dimensions described in Chapter 4 were rationally extracted because they emerged repeatedly in various of the comparisons. These dimensions—symptom complexity, coping style, and interpersonal sensitivity (i.e., reactance)—were distilled, not only on the basis of the literature reviewed, but on the basis of clinical impressions as well. For example, the dimension of symptom complexity has been discussed extensively in the literature as a potentially critical variable in determining the probable value of symptom focused treatments (e.g., Wolpe, Brady, Serber, Agras & Liberman, 1973). Likewise, the concept of coping style has been variously categorized and then applied in theoretical formulations relating to psychotherapy (e.g., Berzins, Seidman & Welch, 1970; Kipper & Ginot, 1979; Tolor & Reznikoff, 1967).

Finally, the concepts of reactance (Brehm, 1976) and locus of control (Rotter, 1966) have been applied to psychotherapy and touted as important determiners of the amount of directiveness usefully applied in the treatment process (e.g., Abramowitz et al., 1974; Baker, 1979; Tennen et al., 1981). Indeed, from a prior review of the persuasion literature it had become clear that the concepts of reactance and the dimension measured by the locus of control scale were similar in many influence situations (Beutler, 1978). Hence, when this pattern reemerged in the review of patient variables in psychotherapy outcome, the hypothesis that the patient's reactance or interpersonal sensitivity is an important dimension in differentiating treatment response again assumed relevance.

There then emerged in the earlier review a series of hypotheses about each dimension and its implications for treatment interventions. For example, an inspection of the literature led to the speculation that simple and complex symptoms would differentiate between the use of broad and narrow band treatments. It was anticipated that symptom focused (narrow band) treatments would be superior to ones devoted to global or underlying conflict change (broad band) among individuals whose symptoms were circumscribed, while the reverse would be true among individuals whose symptoms were complex. Applied in the current context, a guiding focus on the core conflictual themes of attachment, separation, ambivalence, and detachment may be more relevant than a symptomatic focus among those patients whose symptoms are broadly generalized and not isomorphically related to situation specific events.

Similarly, in the original review, it was postulated that behaviorally-oriented (externally focused) treatments would be favored over insight or experiential (internally focused) treatments among individuals who had external defensive styles. By the same token, it was proposed that internally focused treatments would be advantageous in the treatment of those who had internalized defensive styles.*

Finally, it was originally hypothesized that individuals with high levels of interpersonal reactivity would be poor responders to therapist directed treatments, while individuals with low levels of reactance would respond well to such directive interventions.

Unfortunately, the studies available at both the time of the 1979(a) writing and at present are insufficient to provide clear confirmation of all of these hypotheses. Nonetheless, the general conclusions reached in the earlier review have been partially born out by subsequent research. For example, strategies with narrowly defined objectives have been consistently found superior to broad band treatments among individuals with relatively simple, monosymptomatic or constricted symptom patterns (e.g., Hampson & Tavormina, 1980; LaPoint & Rimm, 1980). Conversely, differential outcome is not as likely to occur when comparisons are made between treatments that have similar breadths of focus (e.g., LaPointe & Rimm, 1980).

There are relatively few research studies where the targeted population manifests relatively complex symptom patterns. The predilection for psychotherapy researchers to study either constricted populations of nonpatients or those with minor forms of psychopathology (e.g., Malkiewich & Merluzzi, 1980) is a continuing drawback in the resolution of contradictory findings in psychotherapy research. Nonetheless, the original conclusion that the effec-

---

*It bears underlining that the behavioral treatments themselves vary in the band width of their impact (cf. implosive therapy). Similarly, within each of the nonbehavioral treatment groupings, different procedures vary in their band width and even in the amount of introspection or insight necessitated.

tiveness of insight-oriented treatments increases with the complexity of the symptom pattern being treated has received some supoprt (e.g., Lipsky et al., 1980).

Similarly, the original suggestion that behavioral treatments are superior to internally-oriented treatments among patients with externalized defenses has also received consistent support in the years since the initial review (e.g., Biran & Wilson, 1981; Klein et al., 1977; Olson et al., 1981). Some evidence has even accumulated to suggest that internally-oriented treatment strategies might be better than externally focused ones among patients who develop internalized coping styles (e.g., Leal et al., 1981). However, this latter finding is not yet definitive. Several studies have found effects that fail to confirm the author's predictions among individuals with internalized coping styles (e.g., Comas-Diaz, 1981; LaPointe & Rimm, 1980; Townsend et al., 1975).

Interpersonal reactance, at least as defined by scores on the locus of control scale, continues to be an area to which much investigative attention has been given. Moreover, the data continue to support the relative value of more highly directed treatments among those with low levels of interpersonal reactance (or external locus of control) and of less highly directed treatments among those with high reactance (e.g., Frances & Clarkin, 1981b; Koffman, 1977; Ollendick & Murphy, 1977; Osborn, 1981; Schwartz & Higgins, 1979).

What is lacking in this literature is an indication of how interactions among the proposed dimensions affect treatment response. Yet it is these interactions that hold the most promise in the development of a systematic eclectic psychotherapy. Studies that have focused on differences between behaviorally focused (narrow band) and insight focused (broad band) treatments (e.g., Cross, Sheehan & Khan, 1982; Sloane et al., 1975) might have obtained different results, for example, if they had not studied heterogenous groups of patients whose status on the various dimensions may have been sufficiently variable to attenuate any expected treatment effects.

In general, therefore, there seems to be continuing support for the viability of the patient dimensions extracted in the author's 1979(a) review. But without clear research on contrasting groups of homogenous patient samples, definitive conclusions cannot yet be reached. In the meantime, the dimensions have clinical appeal in suggesting that treatment dimensions can be adjusted to fit one's symptom pattern, complexity of disorder, and anticipated response to control.

SPECIFIC PROCEDURES FOR SPECIFIC PATIENTS

The previous chapter described many of the procedures and techniques on which various theories differ. Table 8.6, it will be recalled, provided a rough ranking of the various theories in terms of their reliance on the therapist's evocative, directed, and relationship-oriented behaviors. However, for application it is important to make more refined discriminations among specific procedures. To do so requires that a distinction be made between "final" and "intermediate" objectives.

Final objectives refer to the ultimate goals of psychotherapy. In the current system the ultimate goals are either symptom removal, requiring narrow band treatments, or conflict resolution, requiring broad band treatments. Moreover, it is feasible to subclassify both symptoms and conflicts into various subordinate groups.

Intermediate objectives are the short-term effects designed to be accomplished by certain therapeutic procedures in the service of final objectives. Intermediate objectives are to final objectives as instrumental values are to terminal values, utilizing Rokeach's (1973) conceptual scheme. Like final objectives, intermediate objectives can be catalogued utilizing a variety of common, short-term goals. While at different times specific techniques may be directed to different of these intermediate objectives, such a cataloguing furthers the aim of divorcing treatment techniques from their theoretical origins.

Final Objectives

An exhaustive list of the possible final treatment objectives for narrow band treatments would be unduly extensive. Since symptoms are easily recognized for the most part and bear a relatively direct relationship to patient complaints, no such listing is considered necessary. The broad band final objective of "resolving psychological conflict," however, requires a degree of extrapolation and inference which is not true of symptom specific goals. Previous chapters have identified four basic conflicts or conflictual themes whose resolution characterizes the final objectives of broad band treatments. While these core conflictual themes are inferential, they do provide an important integrative focus for guiding treatment (e.g., Malan, 1976). It is the therapist's task to keep the conflictual themes constantly in front of the patient, to utilize treatment techniques to clarify and resolve the conflicts associated with them, and to use the therapy relationship itself to illustrate the patterns (e.g., Malan, 1976; Strupp, 1981b).

In using these themes as points of focus, it is important to remember that the concepts of attachment and separation are not mutually exclusive (Millon, 1969). An individual whose life theme reflects movement toward attachments also has separation needs. That is, attachment and separation themes represent only balances in favor of one or the other, and either may be an avoidance of impulses or desires reflecting the other. The final goal of psychotherapy with the attachment prone individual is to establish a tolerance for autonomy.

Similarly, the goal in working with a separation-oriented patient is to increase tolerance for nurturance.

Ambivalent individuals are encouraged to accept and anticipate their cyclical variation through attachments and separation. To the detached individual, in contrast, the final therapeutic objective is to allow him/her to develop the skills, values, and social contacts necessary either to move towards nurturant attachments, autonomous relationships, or both.

Intermediate Objectives

Table 9.1 provides a representative but incomplete menu of evocative and directed interventions grouped in terms of their intermediate goals and rated for their breadth of impact, internal versus external focus, and the amount of therapist control required for implementation. It will be useful to refer to this table throughout this chapter as suggestions are made for tailoring psychotherapy approaches to fit the subjective or objective nature of the focus, the patient's coping and reactant styles, and the desired final objectives. The procedures outlined are clustered under six categories of intermediate goals: (1) insight enhancement, (2) emotional awareness, (3) emotional escalation, (4) emotional reduction, (5) behavioral control, and (6) perceptual change. Many procedures can be implemented with varying levels of therapist control, aimed at different intermediate objectives, and be adjusted for breadth of impact. The therapist's sensitivity to these possibilities is required for systematic and planful application. The maximally effective therapist will be skilled in utilizing several procedures from each of these groupings.

Insight Enhancement Methods. Procedures designed to facilitate the patient's cognitive understanding of either the unconscious motivations or interpersonal dynamics of behavior have largely risen from the interpersonal and psychoanalytic schools of thought. The evocative strategies of transference interpretation, reframing, and questioning that are common to most therapies are particularly used in the pursuit of insight. These strategies have been supplemented by various directed procedures. For example, free association, dream interpretation, role-playing, free fantasies, and the use of relationship sculpturing (e.g., Satir, 1964) and polarities are directed procedures used to facilitate the awareness of motivations and interpersonal patterns.

Free association (Freud, 1933, 1939) is a nonconfrontive and broad band directed procedure in which the patient is asked to report whatever crosses her awareness with a minimal amount of self-monitoring. In order to vary directive involvement and breadth of impact, the therapist questions the patient's meaning, provides a transference or resistance interpretation of the production, or places the patient's productions within a novel context. The latter method is that of *reframing* and is done in order to facilitate a reassessment of how that association belies unrecognized processes within the patient (Weakland et al., 1974). While free association may be used without any interpretation from the therapist, its maximal use as an insight facilitating procedure requires that the therapist either provide or encourage the patient to seek alternative ways of viewing the productions in terms of the so-called parent-child transference links to current behavior (Malan, 1976).

Similarly, free imagery or fantasy (e.g., Klinger, 1971; Scheidler, 1972; Shorr, 1974) is a strategy that requires the patient to create visual and auditory images. The therapist provides minimal structure for these fantasies. Occasionally, a superficial structure may be created by the therapist as, for example, when the patient is asked to imagine the face of a significant other and then to report whatever form the ensuing image takes. The fantasy is complimented with questions and interpretations in order to force the patient to place a new meaning upon the productions. Occasionally, the therapist imposes an unfamiliar context upon the fantasy as, for example, when asking the patient to imagine that an interpersonal exchange he/she has just reported has occurred with an individual from the patient's protected past. By placing the fantasy interaction in an alternative context, reframing forces the patient to recognize a primitive thematic pattern in current relationships (Goulding & Goulding, 1979).

Even more active therapeutic strategies involve feedback and role-playing. Feedback may take numerous forms, including direct interpretation by the therapist, audio or videotaped review, or feedback from groups (Alker et al., 1976; Bailey & Sowder, 1970). In some instances, the patient may be asked to seek feedback from individuals in his/her environment, family, or social group. The nature of the feedback is typically aimed at forcing the patient to develop a new perspective of his/her behavior, placing it in the context of previous experience.

Similarly, role-playing (e.g., Goldstein & Simonson, 1971; Kelley, 1955; Lazarus, 1966; Moreno, 1946) may facilitate insight by asking the patient, either within or outside of the therapy session, to engage in a new set of behaviors and to observe the consequences. Typically, role-playing either takes the form of paradoxically exaggerating certain in-place behavior patterns so that their magnified themes and dynamics can be observed more easily by the patient, or as a means of encouraging the development of a new repertoire of behavior. In the first case, historical insight is a principal focus, and the subsequent discussion may be oriented toward helping the patient understand how given behavior patterns act out life patterns and primitive conflicts. In the latter case, role-playing is designed to help the patient become aware of how altering behavior subsequently changes environmental contingencies. In either case, the methodology is frequently accompanied by the therapist's interpretations, clarifications, and questions, again varying the breadth and directiveness of the procedure (Table 9.1).

Dreams are frequently used in the same way as free fantasy. In dreams, however, the patient has created her own fantasy, largely independent of the therapist. Dreams are typically approached in one of two ways. In a traditional psychoanalytic framework, the patient reports a dream, associates to various contents in a manner similar to free association, and develops a symbolic interpretation of the dream production (Freud, 1900, 1939). An alternative method (Greenwald, 1972; Perls, 1970) assumes that each aspect of the dream represents a disenfranchised part of the individual that is seeking reintegration. The patient is asked to take on the role of each object or significant figure in the dream sequentially, reconstructing the dream from a first person perspective. In either case, the objective of dream work is to facilitate awareness of how symbols are utilized to express alternative aspects of conflicts. The language utilized and the insight obtained may differ, but the particular interpretation may be of less importance than its believability (Frank, 1973; Hobbs, 1962).

Single and two chair dialogues (Greenberg, 1979; Greenwald, 1972; Levitsky & Perls, 1969; Perls, 1970) focus directly on the patient's conflictual struggle and are active insight strategies. The methodology utilized in these procedures is to exaggerate a particular conflict that the patient seems to be experiencing, either with himself/herself. He/she is asked to alternatively take different sides of the conflict in an effort to first magnify that conflict and then to integrate the polarized viewpoints being expressed. By enacting two sides of an internal conflict or interpersonal confrontation, it is hoped that the patient will realize how these dilemmas represent a dynamic struggle between the introjected demands of significant others and his/her own strivings for attachment and/or separation.

Emotional Awareness Methods. The primary evocative strategies utilized to faciliate emotional awareness are questions, reflections, and restatements. Unlike such responses when used in the service of insight, however, evocative responses designed to enhance emotional awareness address aspects of patient feelings rather than understanding (e.g., Meara et al., 1981). These verbal processes are often used in conjunction with a variety of activity-oriented procedures, such as free association, experiential focusing, and exaggeration.

What distinguishes emotional awareness from insight enhancement methodologies is the relative balance in favor of attending to sensations and emotionally-toned words rather than historical reinterpretations. Hence, both free association strategies, free fantasy, and polarity enactment can be used as easily to facilitate emotional awareness as conceptual or historical insight. For example, in "focusing" (Gendlin, 1969) the patient is asked to concentrate attention upon present feelings and sensations and then to provide imaginal associations in the hope of increasing awareness of the affective components of current experience. In the process, the patient may also facilitate historical insight into how various emotions have developed and their relationships with past conflicts. In targeting emotional awareness, however, the therapist is often trying to assist the patient in discriminating among sensations, so that distinct emotional experiences can be defined and the range of emotional experience can be increased.

These procedures may be complimented by enacting various feeling states. For example, a patient is asked to act out the opposite of a feeling that is easily within his current awareness. Similarly, the patient may be asked to engage in some physical activity designed to increase or release those bodily sensations often associated with some negatively valued emotion.

Exaggerating gestures (Perls, 1970) or interpersonal roles (Kelley, 1955) are other methods of facilitating awareness. By directing the patient's focus during these activities and the judicious use of reflections or questions, the therapist can vary the breadth of impact of the procedure and the amount of therapist control required.

Emotional Escalation Methods. The objective of escalating emotional states is primarily to move the underaroused or compartmentalized patient toward an active resolution of emotional conflicts. However, arousal increasing methods may also be used to either inhibit undesirable behaviors or facilitate cathartic release.

On one hand, anxiety may be seen as a guiding signal of unresolved emotional conflict (e.g., Sifneos, 1979). As such, the therapist attempts to increase arousal in the pursuit of clarifying conflicting emotional experiences and discharging feelings. When used in this way, arousal methods range from directed behavior and enactment to experiments with altering the patient's language and providing confrontation.

In confrontation, the therapist may take an extreme stance which is assumed to trigger the patient's vulnerability and systematically force situations which have been protectively avoided. In this connection, silence and reflection may confront the patient's fear as easily as a verbal challenge (Brammer & Shostrum, 1960). Likewise, directing the patient to speak in the first person, present tense when discussing experience may confront a fear of individuation, producing the anxiety that signals such a conflict (Greenwald, 1972). More actively, the therapist may ask the patient to role-play or exaggerate a pattern of behavior that has been systematically avoided. If the fear is disappointing another, for example, the patient may be asked to practice doing so. The patient may also be asked to engage in or imagine an avoided activity in a remembered or expected situation. Taking this risk will often assist both the patient and therapist to see the nature of the conflict and discharge the associated feeling (e.g., Cohen & Twemlow, 1981). Physical enactment of a feeling like anger may further this cathartic discharge.

Often anxiety arises from surprising sources and can assist in the cognitive resolution of conflict. For example, paradoxical interventions and instructions

Table 9.1. Intermediate Objectives, Foci, and Breadth of Various Therapy Procedures

Intermediate Objectives	*Rating Non-Confrontive (1) to Directive and/or Confrontive (5)*	*Behavioral (B) Cognitive (C) or Affect (A) Focus*	*Rating Broad Band (5) vs Narrow Band Impact (1)*
1. Insight Enhancement			
A. Verbal/Evocative Activity by Therapist		Procedures are designed to emphasize *cognitive* experience.	
Transference Interpretation	5		4
Reframing	4		3
Questioning	2-4		2
B. Directed Activity			
Free Association	1		4
Dream Interpretation/Work	3		3
Role Playing	3		2
Free Fantasy	1		5
Single/Two Chair Dialogue	4		2-4
Audio/Video/Group Feedback	5		2-4
Sculpturing Roles	4		3
2. Emotional Awareness			
A. Verbal/Evocative Activity by Therapist		Procedures are designed to emphasize *emotional* experience.	
Reflection	1		2-4
Questioning	2-4		1
Restatement of Feelings	3		2
Reframing	4		3
B. Directed Activity			
Focusing	2		3
Free Fantasy/Imagery	1		4-5
Enactment	2		2
Single/Two Chair Dialogues	3		2-4
Playing Opposites	4		1-3
Exaggeration	3		4

Table 9.1. (Continued)

Intermediate Objectives	*Rating Non-Confrontive (1) to Directive and/or Confrontive (5)*	*Behavioral (B) Cognitive (C) or Affect (A) Focus*	*Rating Broad Band (5) vs Narrow Band Impact (1)*
3. Emotional Escalation			
A. Verbal/Evocative Activity by Therapist		Procedures are designed to emphasize *emotional* and *cognitive* experience.	
Confrontation	5		2
Paradoxical Instructions	4		2
Reframing	4		3
Questioning	2-4		2
Interpretation	5		4
Reflection	1		4
B. Directed Activity			
Verbal or Language Control	2		3
Role-playing	3		2-4
Directed Fantasy/Imagery	2-4		2-4
Implosion	5		3
Covert Avoidance/Sensitization	4		2
Aversive Conditioning	5		1
Physical/Emotional Exaggeration and Release	4		3
Free Fantasy/Imagery	1		3
4. Emotion Reduction			
A. Verbal/Evocative Activity by Therapist		Procedures are designed to emphasize *emotional* and *behavioral* experience.	
Reassurance	1		4
Teaching/Explaining	4		2-4
Giving Information	2		1
Reflection	1		2-4
B. Directed Activity			
Exposure	2-4		2-4
Counter Conditioning	2-3		2
Relaxation/Breathing	1		3
Autogenic/Biofeedback Training	2		1
Hypnosis	4		2-4
Assertive/Mastery Training	3		3
Directed Fantasy/Imagery	2-5		2

Table 9.1. (Continued)

Intermediate Objectives	*Rating Non-Confrontive (1) to Directive and/or Confrontive (5)*	*Behavioral (B) Cognitive (C) or Affect (A) Focus*	*Rating Broad Band (5) vs Narrow Band Impact (1)*
5. Behavioral Control			
A. Verbal/Evocative Activity by Therapist		Procedures are designed to emphasize *behavioral* experience.	
Information Giving	2		1-2
Teaching/Advising	4		2-4
Questioning	2-4		2
B. Directed Activity			
Graded Practice/Homework	2-4		1-3
Behavioral Contracting	1-3		2-3
Overt/Covert Reinforcement	5		2
Shaping	4		1
Discrimination Learning	3		1
Self-Monitoring/Instruction	2		2
6. Perceptual Change			
A. Verbal/Evocative Activity by Therapist		Procedures are designed to emphasize *cognitive* and *behavioral* experience.	
Questioning	2-4		2-4
Reframing	4		3
Teaching/Advising	4		4
Clarifying	1		2
B. Directed Activity			
Self-Monitoring/Instruction	2		2
Alternative Thinking	3		3-5
Evidence Gathering	1-3		2-4
Playing Opposites	4		1-3
Role-playing	3		2
Overt/Covert Reinforcement	5		2
Hypnotherapy	4		2-5
Directed Fantasy/Imagery	2-5		2-3

can frequently allow the patient to let go of the various controls that prevent emotional release (Frankl, 1960; Omer, 1981). Encouraging either the exaggeration of a symptom or a particular feeling may paradoxically produce relief and/or feeling discharge for certain patients (Weeks & L'Abate, 1982).

In those instances where anxiety induction is designed to inhibit certain impulses, a different tactic is utilized. Covert sensitization (Cautela, 1973), for example, has been successfully used in the treatment of alcoholism and other habit disorders. In these methods, the individual is asked to associate an anxiety-provoking fantasy with a behavior usually found to be gratifying. By imagining a nausea-inducing concoction intermixed with alcohol, for example, aversive associations are created which may reduce the patient's appetites. Aversive conditioning (e.g., Callahan & Leitenberg, 1973) methods serve a similar function of increasing the anxiety aroused by certain stimulus elements or activities.

It is often interesting that in the process of implementing such aversive controls the patient reports fantasies, images, and associations that serve to direct the therapist toward the source of interpersonal conflict. For example, a patient in the author's acquaintance, while engaging in the process of covert sensitization for a long-standing drinking habit reported that a scene designed to be nausea producing had pleasurable components. The level of anxiety desired was attenuated by the spontaneous report of experiencing pleasure at the image of throwing up on one of his "friends." Hence, the patient's association allowed the development of a fantasy that did not include this friend and also signalled the need to implement methods designed to increase insight into undisclosed hostile feelings toward significant others.

Emotional Reduction Methods. In order to maintain optimal arousal levels, any excessive anxiety must be reduced. Arousal reducing methods are drawn from a host of behavioral strategies, particularly those emphasizing assertive training and relaxation (e.g., Wolpe & Lazarus, 1969). The overall label of "Exposure Methods" may encapsulate much of the work done in this area. Indeed, it is possible that these are the best developed of the therapeutic strategies for very anxious patients, since in many cases they can be applied independently of the therapist (e.g., Marks, 1978).

The exposure methods typically include relaxation training, graduated exposure either in imagery or in vivo, and instruction in the development of assertive responses to replace avoidance behaviors (Marks, 1978). The evocative, verbal behaviors of the therapist are highly reliant upon information seeking, clarifying, and advice-giving. More actively, the patient is systematically taught relaxation, advised to use it periodically and in specified situations, and is rehearsed in the establishment of a systematic method of exposure to feared elements. Goldfried (1973) has successfully utilized relaxation training in a host of fear-provoking environments, encouraging the patient to employ the relaxation response as an active coping strategy, thereby reducing therapist control and broadening the potential focal impact. Likewise, autogenic training (e.g., Luthe & Schultz, 1970; Yates, 1980) and biofeedback (e.g., Benson, 1976; Brown, 1977; Katkin & Murray, 1968; Stroebel, 1978) are methods that have been largely used for reducing anxiety and can apparently do so effectively (Yates, 1980).

Since counterproductive arousal represents a major mental health concern, relaxation methods, assertive methods, and the use of therapeutic advice may be especially useful skills for therapists to develop. There are numerous relaxation methods, ranging from systematic muscle relaxation to hypnotherapy, autogenic training, and biofeedback. In each case, the patient is taught to exert some control either over cognitive activities, muscle tension, or autonomic processes. Since all of these response systems are involved in anxiety, training in any or all is useful as a method of reducing anxiety. Moreover, teaching response alternatives in the face of anxiety is often helpful. Although it is unclear whether the specific methods have differential effects (e.g., Qualls & Sheehan, 1981) some combination of the procedures appears to be helpful in treating a variety of anxiety related disorders (Thompson & Dockens, 1975; Turner, Calhoun & Adams, 1981).

Training individuals to respond assertively and aggressively when confronted with fear may be an especially important tool in their coming to feel masterful over their environment (LaPointe & Rimm, 1980; Lazarus, 1966). Instead of being immobilized by the sight of a bug, for example, developing an active response to attack and destroy the object of one's fear can produce significant decreases in anxiety and a dramatic enhancement of one's sense of power. Indeed, cognitive change is often a consequence of reducing anxiety and changing behavior (Bandura, Blanchard & Ritter, 1969).

Behavioral Control Methods. Efforts to systematically and directly control behavior have naturally enough evolved from the large group of behavioral strategies. As a consequence, they rely largely upon contingency management and extra-therapy activities (e.g., Stuart, 1971; Weathers & Liberman, 1975). Graded practice in which behaviors are systematically shaped, token economies, contingency contracting, and both covert rehearsal and overt practice are powerful methods of altering behavior (Bandura, 1969).

Behavioral control procedures are heavily reliant upon advice-giving and information-seeking, sometimes along with a paradoxical injunction (Ascher & Efran, 1978; Frankl, 1960). This latter variation allows commitment changes in both therapist control and breadth of therapeutic impact (Weeks & L'Abate, 1982). In addition, the process of implementing behavioral control methods usually includes systematically self-monitoring certain behaviors, establishing a contingency based upon the therapist's observation of the reinforcement-behavioral relationships, and modification of this contingency as its consequences are observed (Goldfried & Davison, 1976). These procedures may be used to paradoxically increase a stubborn behavior in order to bring it under control as well as to directly reduce it (Ascher & Efran, 1978).

In applying these procedures, the therapist must remain flexible and not overly committed to the patient's responding in a given way to the contingency program established. For example, it may be as important to the ultimate goals of therapy to discover that the patient does not perform his homework as to observe that he does. The patient's struggle with authority, investment in being "sick," or fear of losing interpersonal attachments may all be obscured if one allows the patient's chronic frustration of homework assignments to create a barrier in the therapy relationship. It is probably well-advised to treat behavioral control methods like experiments in which any outcome is legitimate. As a therapist becomes bent upon a single narrow band outcome, both the larger meaning of the patient's struggle and the collaborative therapeutic focus may be lost.

Perceptual Change Methods. Cognitive therapies have largely contributed to a host of methodologies designed to demonstrate that the patient's assumptions of life produce a variety of emotional and behavioral states. Accordingly, many therapeutic procedures are devoted to changing these faulty belief systems and perceptions. These strategies rely heavily upon questions, advice-giving directed practice, and clarification-seeking.

Among the directed methods utilized are teaching the patient to monitor, evaluate, and classify cognitive patterns into categories of self-destructive or depressogenic thoughts (Beck et al., 1979). He may then be taught to construct and test hypotheses about the validity of these beliefs. In order to change his/her perception, the patient may be taught to make up alternative beliefs and to rehearse these.

All of these procedures require the patient to attend to the cognitive images and verbal processes that accompany problematic feelings and behaviors (Mahoney, 1980). Providing labels for certain categories of thought assists in the monitoring process. Beck et al. (1979) utilize a set of simple rating scales as well, asking the patient to rate his belief in certain problematic attitudes or perceptions at various points in treatment.

Changes in cognitive patterns may be overtly or covertly reinforced. Finding pleasant fantasies or activities to reinforce practice in the adoption of more realistic beliefs is often helpful (Cautela, 1977; Kazdin, 1973, 1975). The focus of the cognitive or perceptual change methods, however, is not upon the behavior or even the altered social activity. These things are assumed to accompany cognitive changes. Unlike direct behavioral control or arousal management methods, perceptual change methods are primarily directed at cognitive patterns and beliefs. Whereas behavioral control methods take as a principal focus certain problematic behaviors, and anxiety-reducing methods ask patients to rate sensations, perceptual change methods judge effectiveness on the basis of alterations in cognitive functioning with a secondary emphasis placed upon emotional and behavioral changes.

Another method increasingly returning to vogue in the modification of perceptual experience is hypnosis. Hypnosis compliments cognitive therapy as a means of introducing and reinforcing perceptual changes, enhancing self-image, reinforcing new cognitive patterns, and sensitizing an individual to distorted patterns of thought. Unlike most strategies used in cognitive therapy, hypnotherapy can be used to distort experience in a selective fashion (Erickson & Rossi, 1981; Orne, 1959) and bypasses the logical, counterargument phases. It moves directly to instigate change through repetition, relaxation, and suggestion. The induction of selective, cognitive distortions may be particularly useful in helping individuals control the experience of pain, making them amenable to surgical and dental procedures, reducing scarring (Anderson, Basker & Dalton, 1975; Rock, Shipley & Campbell, 1969; Stambaugh & Howe, 1977) and perhaps producing a significant impact upon biological functions associated with chronic disease (Sarbin & Slagle, 1979; Simonton, Simonton & Creighton, 1978; Wadden & Anderson, 1982). In all of these functions, the therapeutic strategy is essentially that of reinterpreting normal experiences to reflect a different frame of reference, similar to that utilized in the method of reframing. Erickson and Rossi (1981), for example, have described methods of altering the patient's cognitive-perceptual experience through simple changes in the therapist's voice inflection which lend a different meaning to a given pattern of words.

Treatments for Monosymptomatic and Habit Patterns

The less symptoms have generalized, the fewer areas of life affected by their manifestation and the less the need to rely upon insight and introspection to effect relief (Wolpe et al., 1973). Simple phobias, habit disorders, and situational anxiety states are among the symptoms most often observed. In part, the value of symptom-focused procedures for treating such conditions represents a parsimonious application of a narrow band treatment for a focal condition. A focus on symptoms themselves provide the integrative glue for the various procedures used.

Similarly, by selecting procedures with an external (behavioral) or internal (cognitive or emotional) focus and by adjusting the degree of therapist confrontation in accordance with the patient's coping style and reactance level, respectively, an appropriate treatment regimen can be selected. Table 9.1 provides a suggested outline to which one might refer in this process.

High Reactant, Externalizing Patients. Treatment applied to the habit and phobic disorders that characterize highly reactant and externalizing monosymptomatic patients must deemphasize the therapist's control while maintaining an overt, behavioral focus (see Table 9.1) and an eye toward reducing the frequency of acting out behaviors. Referring to Table 8.6, one can see that no uniform theoretical orientation meets all of the requirements of being low in interpreting or advising, high on reflecting, low on the use of directed activity, high on punishing and rewarding, and low on internal structuring. The most desirable approach would include procedures with a narrow band impact and would not focus on unconscious material. One can see that an eclectic approach to a patient of this type will combine the expressive-evocative behaviors of the experiential or interpersonal therapist, the directed activity inherent in some combination of the experiential and cognitive therapist, the focus and structuring of the behavioral or interpersonal therapist and the type of relationship frequently observed among psychoanalytic and cognitive therapists. Referring to Table 9.1, one can select more specific procedures and guidelines that embody the low therapist control and behavioral focus required for these patients.

In developing these procedures and principles, the therapist should concentrate on avoiding interpretations and advice and emphasize clarification, questioning, and reflection. Directed activities should be those that have behavioral control objectives and in which the patient is an active participant, such as behavioral contracting. Some patients who are capable of insight or self-reflection can also utilize various of the emotion reducing and perceptual change methods described in Table 9.1, since these can also have behavioral targets. Exposure methods, self-directed desensitization, and self-monitoring of assertive behavior may be quite appropriate, therefore, depending upon the nature of the patient's symptoms. At the same time, methods aimed at emotional escalation, awareness, and insight are probably least effective.

Highly directed activities of either an overt or covert nature will probably not be tolerated well by the patient. Hence, role-playing may be quite acceptable, but implosive fantasies or covert sensitization may be expected to invoke the patient's resistance on the same basis as described by Goldstein et al. (1966).

The therapist must allow the patient to govern the internal structure of the session while maintaining a narrow band attention to behavioral goals. The patient's high degree of reactance indicates the value of remaining relatively formal, emphasizing background similarities and deemphasizing one's status.

Low Reactant, Externalizing Patients. Among this group of monosymptomatic patients, more directive treatment strategies can be utilized than is true of the foregoing group. The primary distinction between methods employed for patients in this and the preceding group is the degree of external structure imposed by the therapist, both in preplanning the sessions and in structuring the flow of each session. While the focus must remain narrow band and external, the expressive-evocative behaviors of the therapist can become questioning and analytical and include teaching and information giving. One need not be overly cautious in the use of directed activity in dealing with these patients. Hence, token economies and other overt behavioral control methods are more appropriate in this group than in the preceding one.

Emotional release, awareness, and insight activities should probably still be minimized, given the externalizing nature of the symptoms. The directed activities employed should continue to emphasize role-playing, reinforcement, behavioral extinction, and systematic problem solving. The relationship can be informal, with the therapist emphasizing rather than deemphasizing his/her status and credibility while being active in providing support. Greater amounts of therapist spontaneity are also acceptable in working with this group of patients than the former group.

Among the specific treatment strategies, behavioral contracting, assertive training, and virtually all of the behavioral control methods described in Table 9.1 can be utilized here as long as the focus is constructed to remain relatively specific and narrow. These patients are also susceptible to some arousal reducing methods, particularly in vivo exposure or desensitization. Even covert sensitization and implosive fantasies can be employed more effectively with this group than more highly reactant patients who are likely to resist the degree of therapist direction involved in these procedures.

Highly Reactant, Internally Coping Patients. High reactant, internalizing patients who fall within the monosymptomatic groups are likely to present anxiety patterns that are relatively situation specific. Some anxiety disorders and situational adjustment disorders fall in this category. Their reactant status is frequently observed in their failure to comply with homework assignments and in their chronic frustration of efforts to establish contingencies. Evocative/verbal strategies should deemphasize the therapist's power, utilize questions rather than instruction, and provide information without confrontation. Collaborative problem solving in the context of a relationship that is relatively nondemanding is also appropriate.

Unlike those who manifest their conflicts through acting out, projection, and sublimated physical activity (i.e., externalization), anxiety reducing or increasing methods that retain a narrow band impact and subjective focus are the treatments of choice for this group. Self-monitored systematic desensitization, biofeedback, and graduated exposure therapies where the control is decidedly with the patient are appropriate. These treatments, in contrast to those utilized with the externalizing patient, are more often focused upon internal than external states.

Low Reactant, Internalizing Patients. Compared to their highly reactant counterparts who present similar anxiety symptoms, patients in this group are likely to be more compliant with the therapist's directions. Because they present with situational anxiety or panic attacks, the narrow band focus must be retained. But in a manner similar to that used with low reactant patients who utilize externalized defenses, the therapist's expressive and evocative behavior can turn to analyzing, advising and teaching. These activities would be less advisable with more reactant patients. Even physical release activities, inappropriate for the externalizing patient, can now be employed. Anxiety reducing or increasing procedures now can be implemented with a relatively high degree of therapist directiveness and control. More therapist involvement in the use of systematic desensitization, along with the use of covert sensitization or implosive fantasies, may be appropriate among this group. Cognitive exercises for increasing assertiveness and developing externalizing coping strategies are also suggested.

Treatments for Complex Adjustment Patterns

Those patients who develop complex and widely generalized symptom patterns that affect numerous areas of their lives and are manifest through multiple symptoms warrant the use of broad band treatment procedures. With these complex problems, there is tolerance for discussing past events and obtaining historical information as they reflect on the current problems. The treatment procedures share a common goal of resolving dynamic or underlying conflicts and altering interpersonal values rather than simply symptom change.

High Reactant, Externalizing Patients. Patients in this category frequently manifest relatively complex counterphobic, oppositional patterns, suspicious behaviors, socially alienating compulsions, or conversion patterns. The preponderance of young patients who have anorexia nervosa may also fall into this category (Hood et al., 1982). Variations of suspiciousness, promiscuity, distrust, somatization, and projection are characteristics of individuals who frequently act out in ways that either are destructive to others or bring them into confrontation with authorities.

A treatment plan can be accomplished by extracting from Table 9.1 those behavioral and perceptual change procedures that combine low therapist control and a broad band focus. The therapist's verbal-evocative behavior should be similar to that described for use with other externalized, highly reactant patients but will focus on basic attitudes or conflicts from which symptoms are assumed to derive. Directed activity will concentrate upon systematic problem solving, given the variety of situations in which the symptoms are displayed, but will maintain both an emphasis upon establishing behavioral contingencies and role-playing. Behavioral programming is still appropriate, but the focus must extend beyond symptomatic goals to the conflicts that promote generalization and should deemphasize emotional escalation activities.

Given their highly reactant status, emphasis must be given to insuring the patient's control over his behavior. Cognitive management techniques, such as some of those described under the label of perceptual change methods, may be useful (see Table 9.1). The impulse control methods described by Meichenbaum (1977) and Finch and Kendall (1978) may be effective, given their emphasis on self-instruction. Teaching the patient to self-monitor, evaluate, and classify his/her behaviors and thoughts, while at the same time learning self-controlled relaxation procedures may be appropriate. Among the more reactant, a combination of anxiety reducing methods with perceptual management procedures, paradoxical injunctions, and verbal reframing (e.g., Weeks & L'Abate, 1982) can be anticipated to be effective.

Some very recent data from the University of Arizona psychotherapy research program (Arizmendi, 1982; Kolb, 1981) suggests that the subgroup of externalizing, reactant patients who are separation oriented, as reflected in the use of distancing or boundary defenses (e.g., projection and acting out), require even more attention to therapeutic procedures than those whose externalization is more reflective of attachment themes (e.g., phobias, conversion, or dissociative disturbances). These active externalizers have low tolerance for therapist dissimilarity, empathy, or authority. Any directive procedure is seen as threatening, suggesting that the structured programs that are symptomatically effective in treating most patients with somatic and agoraphobic symptoms will be ineffective for these patients. Not unexpectedly, these patients by description are similar to those who are considered to be unresponsive to the confrontive, insight oriented procedure advocated by Davanloo (1978). Paradoxical strategies, injunctions, and homework assignments are probably useful, while interpretations and confrontations are taken very negatively.

Low Reactant, Externalizing Patients. Patients in this category tend to develop passive, externalizing patterns of adjustment. A multitude of hysteriaform, physical symptoms, complex phobias (e.g., agoraphobia) and emotional outbursts are probably more frequently observed in low reactant than highly reactant patients. Conversely, suspiciousness, distrust, and antisocial behavior are less often seen among this group of patients than among their highly reactant counterparts. Accordingly, more therapist directed planning of the session can occur, but the emphasis upon the externally focused behavioral strategies detailed in Table 9.1 must remain realtively high. Methods aimed at changing behavior while reducing emotions that impair behavioral adjustment (Table 9.1) are appropriate with some secondary reliance on cognitive and perceptual change methods. Moreover, exposure to conflict inducing stimuli and physical release (e.g., exercise methods) may now come into play. Given the patient's relative compliance, the use of hypnosis may now also be employed to assist in reducing anxiety and increasing the patient's internal attribution of power.

Gradually, these procedures are utilized to move the patient's perception from the external to the internal with the therapist's verbal activities concomitantly becoming increasingly devoted to reframing, questioning, clarifying and interpreting, or advising. While teaching and informing by verbal exchanges are more appropriately applied to those with more constricted symptoms, the verbal activity level of the therapist can remain relatively high. The amount of therapist directed activity can also be high when working with this group of patients, and the therapist can exert an active role in structuring the patient's images and problem-solving efforts.

The therapist continues to refrain from excessive emphasis upon unconscious material among patients such as this, but relatively high levels of internal structure can be developed for the session and for the course of therapy. The therapy relationship can also be relatively informal, personal, self-disclosing, and directive in providing support.

High Reactant, Internalizing Patients. This group of patients is likely to present with obsessive, angry-depressive, and ruminative symptoms, but will avoid their own affective expressions and those of others. Concomitantly, the therapeutic focus must emphasize the patient's control over therapy but must also direct the patient to reduce emotional overcontrol by enhancing the affects that are being contained and separated from the rest of his/her experience. Emotional awareness procedures may be best used in those instances where individuals are overinclusive in their affective experience. These individuals tend to respond to environmental change with a limited affective range and poor discrimination among various feeling states. Emotional escalation and discharge methods are the treatments of choice and seem to have a significant advantage over insight enhancing methods (Beutler & Mitchell, 1981). Accordingly, reflection, clarification, questioning, and other nonconfrontive verbal activities should be employed.

The directed treatments selected may appropriately be designed to undermine the patient's constrictive, internalizing coping style. Control must be placed in the hands of the patient, however, and therapist directed role-playing or therapist guided imagery might be abrogated in favor of free fantasy and patient guided practice. Hence, covert sensitization is not a particularly useful strategy in increasing emotional experience among this group of patients. By the same token, the egalitarian and spontaneous relationship usually associated with experiential treatments must be a goal with this patient. Given his high reactance, this latter patient works best when he can see the therapist as somewhat similar to himself and nonauthoritarian. Nonetheless, emotional closeness is not initially well tolerated and should be reserved for less reactant individuals or later stages of therapy.

Low Reactant, Internalizing Patients. These individuals frequently develop depression, diffuse somataform symptoms (psychophysiological and hypochondriacal rather than the conversion symptoms seen in the externalizing patient) or chronic timidity and withdrawal. Like their more highly reactant counterparts, these patients are frequently obsessive but without the oppositionalism that would bring them into conflict with others. Helpless depression is a major feature of these individuals, although it reflects less overt anger than that present in the more highly reactive patient.

The insight enhancing, emotional escalating, and perceptual change (internally focused) methods described in Table 9.1 are probably the treatments of choice for these individuals. The patients in this group can better accept insight than those in other groups. Interpreting, teaching, and confronting are all appropriate activities (e.g., Davanloo, 1978; Sifneos, 1979). Among the more directed activities, perceptual change methods, particularly those following the structure outlined by Beck et al. (1979) are also helpful. Moreover, these individuals are susceptible to perceptual change through hypnosis, and this may be a particularly useful modality of treatment in the event that psychophysiological symptoms are present (Anderson et al., 1975; Stambaugh & Howe, 1977; Wadden & Anderton, 1982). Exploration into the historical development of a patient's conflicts and even into unconscious motivations also appears to be appropriate (Malan, 1976). While there is some evidence to suggest that even among these patients, intensive exploration of early childhood experiences may be counterproductive (Beutler & Mitchell, 1981; Beutler & Thornby, 1982), the value of these efforts cannot be discounted without more research.

Given the low reactance level of the patients in this group, positive transference is often a problem. While a personal and spontaneous relationship seems to be desirable in meeting the patient's initial expectancies and desires, increasing disengagement from the patient may be required in these circumstances.

Finally, various emotional escalation and discharge methods can also be employed among this group of patients. Directed imagery or fantasy, directed role-playing, two chair dialogues, and other experiential procedures are often quite effective.

SUMMARY AND CONCLUSIONS

Evidence continues to accumulate for the value of certain patient dimensions in dictating treatment directions. While the model presented here must remain largely hypothetical, it may not be too premature to use it in the development of treatment plans, and it may have particular value in setting research directions. There continue to be many unknowns in the manner in which the patient characteristics outlined in this volume interact with specific treatment approaches, however. In the previous pages guidance has been provided for developing treatment programs for patients representing various positions along the multiple dimensions described. Varying therapist evocative behavior, directed activity, focus, and the quality of the relationship are all seen as important variables in guiding treatment and are assumed to vary in effectiveness as a function of the type of patient seen.

Accordingly, treatment procedures have been categorized on the basis of their intermediate goals and objectives rather than on the basis of their original theoretical superstructure. Yet even within the various categories of objectives, procedures vary in terms of the amount of directiveness required by the therapist, their breadth of impact, and the emphasis upon overt and covert experience. These factors must be taken into account when selecting from the available menu the procedures to be employed with any given patient.

While the persuasion process is relatively independent of the theroretical orientation adopted, some treatment strategies provide a more direct influence upon attitude and value change than others. For example, cognitive change procedures are relatively forthright in the proposition that they seek to change attitudes and beliefs on the part of the patient through very focused and systematic procedures (e.g., Ellis & Harper, 1966). On the other end of the spectrum, treatment strategies that are designed to produce insight or emotional awareness are less obvious in their persuasive intent. Nonetheless, adequate documentation has accumulated to confirm that subtle conditioning processes take place in all therapies (Strong, 1968; Wolfe, 1978). Even techniques designed to provide behavioral control, while often considered to be value-free, have a major impact on one's values and attitudes (Bandura, Blanchard, & Ritter, 1966; Frank, 1973; Garfield, 1974; Strupp, 1974).

There is no such thing as a value-free psychotherapy. The values and beliefs taught not only characterize the broad ranging philosophy from which the techniques arise (Glad, 1959), but more importantly they characterize the idiosyncratic beliefs of the therapist who is applying these techniques (Beutler, 1979b). For all our discussions of techniques and procedures, it must be remembered that these do not constitute "psychotherapy." When techniques are applied, they must derive from within the therapeutic relationship. They evolve from an interflow of behavior between the patient and therapist and are woven together around the common objective of illustrating, highlighting, clarifying, and finally changing the patient's life. The therapist must, therefore, be concerned with what is being persuaded and to what end. Therapists must also be aware that unintentional, nontherapeutic changes might also accure when patients come to perceive the world more like the therapist does.

What is persuaded in the current scheme is dependent upon the breadth of symptom generality and complexity. Situation specific and monosymptomatic conditions are directed primarily toward the final objective of symptom removal. However, the more complex a condition is and the more its manifestations seem dependent upon idiosyncratic generalizations and conceptualizations from core conflictual themes, the more focus must be addressed to conflict resolution. Reiterating and following a patient's conflictual theme through his/her relationships with others weaves the processes of psychotherapy into an intricately patterned fabric and distinguishes it from the mere application of procedures. The contrast is like that between a colorful blanket and a pile of colored threads. This observation underlines the necessity of retaining a focus on the treatment process, not one that is blind to either the persuasive power of the therapeutic relationship or its associated techniques, but that utilizes these techniques selectively in the interest of persuasion.

An inferential substructure of using conflictual themes to direct the focus of treatment in complex adjustment conditions has been provided. Enhancing the willingness to enjoy interpersonal attachments, mobilizing contacts with others, facilitating autonomy and a tolerance for the vicissitudes of attachment and separation are suggested as final treatment goals. While these goals may be extended and made more complex with greater knowledge of the patient's idiosyncrasies, keeping in mind the final objectives will assist the therapist in focusing and integrating the various treatment procedures.

While certain procedures that seem to be most likely to produce benefit among certain patients have been specified, the patterning of these procedures is left uncertain. Unspoken in the foregoing is that various procedures place differing amounts of emphasis upon behavioral, cognitive and emotional experiences. The patterning of particular procedures may have much to do with this emphasis. Ultimately, cognitive, affective, and behavioral realms must all be affected in order to substantially impact most complex symptom patterns. Yet it is well-known that certain procedures produce change more readily in one or another of these dimensions than in others (e.g., Jesness, 1975; Leal et al., 1981). Patients may differ in the order which various cognitive, behavioral, and emotional systems are to be impacted. Attention must be turned, therefore, to the patterning of these interventions across time, both within and across sessions.

10
The Processes of Psychotherapy

While the previous chapters have described important patient dimensions on which treatment strategies can be developed, it is unlikely that patients can be neatly categorized in stable compartments along these dimensions. Indeed, most patients situationally vacillate between internal and external coping strategies or high and low reactance. Other patients erect internalized coping strategies for some sources of anxiety and are externalized in response to other sources. As a result, one must use the foregoing guidelines flexibly in developing treatment strategies. The way in which a patient is conceptualized will depend upon the topic being addressed, his/her usual method of functioning, and the process or phase of therapy. The current chapter is designed to address how therapeutic strategies change both within and across sessions.

TARGETING AREAS OF IMPACT

Research has been relatively explicit in suggesting that various types of therapy affect different aspects of one's adjustment and well being (e.g., Bandura, Blanchard & Ritter, 1969; Beutler, Oro-Beutler & Mitchell, 1979; Jessness, 1975; Leal et al., 1981). Conceptually, attitudes are composed of three components: cognitions or thoughts, affects or feelings, and overt behaviors (Middlebrook, 1974; Smith, 1969). Behavior therapies are likely to be most potent in affecting the behavioral components or manifestations of attitudes. Similarly, experiential and dynamic/interpersonal therapists seem to address more pointedly the emotional and cognitive aspects of attitudes, respectively. Since in an ideal world, all three attitudinal dimensions will ultimately come into consonance through the process of psychotherapy, various permutations of behavioral, experiential, perceptual change, and insight therapies may be required. In situation specific or monosymptomatic conditions, a single aspect of one's attitudinal systems may be out of consonance, requiring a less complex series of interventions than is needed for more complex conditions in which there is both discordance between and within attitudinal systems.

Complete attitudinal consonance and unilateral improvement infrequently occurs (e.g., Beutler & Crago, in press; Garfield, Prager & Bergin, 1971; Green et al., 1975; Mintz et al., 1973). Nonetheless, a priority for implementing initial interventions can be established by utilizing the concepts described in the previous chapters. The particular type of intervention used will be based upon the unique patterning of patient defensive style, reactance potential, and symptom complexity. Based upon these same considerations, second order interventions may be designed to further facilitate improvement once the patient begins to change. Treatment patterning ultimately depends both upon the patient's receptivity to these intermediate objectives and his/her movement along the symptom and interpersonal dimensions of reactivity and coping style.

In establishing the initial priority of interventions, it is important to underline that the initial focus must be upon either the attitudinal dimension or conflictual pattern that is most disturbing to the voluntary patient. Often these areas of first concern are represented as symptoms along the continuum of internal to external coping style. The patient's primary coping style, which is usually exacerbated in symptom development, is usually the primary determiner of where treatment begins. If the patient's symptoms represent external manifestations of internal conflict, such as projection, compulsion, phobias, or acting out behaviors, behaviorally-oriented treatments must be the level of intervention.

In contrast, if the focus of concern and/or symptomatic behavior is internal, the beginning point of therapy must be either in the cognitive or affective realms. Greenberg and Kahn (1979) have described the usefulness of differentiating between the *discovery of awareness* and the *dynamic self-understanding* processes in psychotherapy. The first process seems to correspond with the emotional awareness (affective) dimension and the latter to the insight enhancement (cognitive) dimension described in Chapter 9. To the degree that the patient's disturbing, internalized symptoms represent cognitive or ideational avoidance of emotional experience (e.g., anxiety binding obsessive thoughts), a treatment strategy designed to enhance emotional awareness and expression is most appropriate. This pattern is especially characteristic of those who have relatively high reactance potentials. Those with lower levels of reactance (i.e., feeling sensitizers) may be susceptible to perceptual change and insight enhancement procedures.

Finding a Common Focus

In all the foregoing, the final objectives of the psychotherapy process should not be lost. While situation specific and monosymptomatic conditions can usually be addressed through narrow band treatments that focus upon either specific cognitive patterns, specific behavioral changes, or reductions of specific anxieties, the more complex conditions require the integration of the attitude changes embodied within the notion of conflictual themes. Underlying conflicts, while reasonable to target and specify, are much less central to the organization of the therapeutic plan among monosymptomatic patients than is true of patients who have widely generalized symptom patterns or areas of disturbance. In these latter patients, the identified core conflicts, rather than the symptoms per se, serve as the integrating force in the application of treatment procedures. Persuasion efforts addressed to those conflicts are central. Emotional awareness procedures, insight enhancement procedures, and so on, are all constructed around the common goal of altering beliefs and values associated with attachments, separation, or interpersonal contact.

For example, if an affective escalation or facilitation procedure is called for, it can be accomplished in an ambivalent individual by images depicting either attachment or separation behaviors. The attachment oriented individual is likely to experience the greatest affective arousal when envisioning interpersonal loss or personal autonomy; anxiety facilitation is accomplished for the separation striving individual through images of increasing commitment and for the detached individual through the description of social contact and communication.

A similar use can be made of conflictual themes in constructing treatments that have other intermediate objectives as well. For example, anxiety reduction can be achieved by encouraging behaviors that gratify attachment or separation needs or provide only gradual withdrawal from such behaviors. Likewise, cognitive and behavioral change procedures may focus on the cognitive or behavioral representations of these themes in constructing interventions.

The attitudes and values represented in the core conflicts can be conceptualized as the constant objects or targets of verbal interpretations, reflections, and injunctions. To a patient whose core conflict is seen as ambivalence, the theme of the therapist's evocations will be in the dilemma of the patient's failure to decide whether to value separation or attachment more highly. The affective representation of such ambivalence is often *anger* and its relationship to this conflict must be recognized if the affective elements are being addressed.

Similarly, in the attachment-oriented patient, evocative statements of the therapist are directed to the patient's drives for nurturance and accompanying *fears* of losing emotional attachments. Concomitantly, to the patient with an interpersonal theme of separation struggle, the evocative therapeutic strategies address the patient's drive for power and an underlying sense of helplessness.

All strategies should be considered as *experiments* designed to draw the patient closer to either the affective or cognitive elements of these internal struggles. In turn, the struggles are considered to belie unrecognized incongruities among or within attitudes. The concept of being a "personal scientist" (Kelley, 1955) is stressed for both the patient and the therapist. While the type of active or evocative strategies used may change along with the patient's vacillation or change in coping strategy, interpersonal sensitivity (reactance), or even symptom complexity, the focus of both active and evocative treatment experiments remains constant, varying only as one develops a more detailed hypothetical picture of these core conflicts or themes.

In the final analysis, psychotherapy is a *cognitive dissonance inducing* process. It focuses either upon an unrecognized incongruity that exists between two attitudes in the conflictual theme, conflicts between patient and therapist views, or upon the incongruity that exists between various aspects of one's attitudes toward a given object. By inducing the patient's awareness of these incongruities, the therapist mobilizes the natural forces (i.e., arousal) of the individual to reinstate consonance. The therapeutic strategy is to force these incongruent systems to have some contact so that cognitive dissonance is induced and optimal arousal levels are maintained until the conflict is resolved through the assimilation and accommodation of one's attitudinal system. If arousal levels are too high, anxiety reduction procedures may be used to retain dissonance induced anxiety at a level that is motivational but not debilitating.

THE PHASES OF PSYCHOTHERAPY

Patterning Interventions

Because of intrapatient changes in coping styles, reactance, and expectations, some organizing principles must be maintained. The process of therapy is one of altering the patient's reaction to environmental/situational or conflictual sources of threat, resulting in change from either an extreme external coping strategy to a more internal one, or vice versa. Similarly, therapy focuses upon moving an individual from an extremely high or low reactance potential to a more moderate one and from generally complex to simple symptom patterns.

Among externally defended patients, the usual treatment proceeds from a behavioral to a subjective (i.e., either an affective or insight enhancement) focus. However, among those patients who develop primarily internalized defenses, the treatment movement is from subjective to behavioral. Similarly, in the initially high reactant patient one moves gradually from a patient-directed to a therapist-directed procedure with the reverse being true for the patient who initially has very low levels of reactance. In treating this latter patient, increasing emphasis is placed upon self-control and is the treatment goal for most patients. Likewise, concomitant with a patient's movement from complex to more simple or less generalized symptoms, one should systematically move from conflict resolution to changing socially adaptable responses.

It follows that for individuals who have both complex symptoms, internalized coping strategies, and high reactance, the therapist at once begins with a broad band treatment and proceeds to narrow band treatments, initiates insight or affect enhancement procedures and gradually moves to more externally focused ones, and maintains initially low therapist direction but employs greater direction as reactance levels change. A similar logic follows for the other possible combinations of symptom patterns. This evolution of treatment strategy, however, requires that the therapist be sensitive to changes in the various dimensions as they accrue with treatment and the natural ebb and flow of stress, coping style, and reactance level.

Since many patients routinely vacillate between the development of internal and external coping strategies or vary from moment to moment in their level of reactance, the therapist must be aware of these changes in "state." As topics are addressed that incur the patient's reactance, increasingly lower levels of therapist directiveness are required. Similarly, if one is dealing with a patient who vacillates between internalizations of guilt and/or rumination and periods of externalization (e.g., acting out), the therapeutic strategy must match these changes with shifts from an internal to an external focus and back again.

In a similar fashion, some patients maintain a basic, internalized coping style, while certain predominant symptoms and sources of conflict are expressed through external coping strategies. A good example of this latter pattern will be seen in Chapter 11. The case of Lynne illustrates a complex external condition (agoraphobia) occurring in an individual whose primary coping strategies are internal, emphasizing rumination, guilt, compartmentalization, and intellectualization. To the degree that the external symptom is a point of focus, an external treatment strategy must be employed. Exposure therapy, therefore, is seen as an appropriate treatment implementation (Marks, 1978). However, there often comes a point with such patients when their external symptoms must be set aside for the moment in order to concentrate upon their more dominant, internalizing method of dealing with their conflictual sources of stress. Managing these defensive thought patterns, perceptions, and other internalizations must be combined with the external treatment focus.

Retaining Specificity

To return to a previous point for a moment, it is important to observe that while it has been noted that the therapist may move from a broad band or conflict focus to an increasingly narrow band impact as patients change in the degree of symptom complexity, this is not to suggest that the topics of discussion should remain general rather than specific. Indeed, requiring even the patient with very complex, internalized patterns of adjustment and symptom development to be specific about events that illustrate attitudinal and value conflicts (e.g., to remain in the "I" and "here" mode of dialect) serves to provide a needed focus in treatment (Levitsky & Perls, 1969; Strupp, 1981b). While the overall goals and areas of impact remain conflict- rather than symptom-oriented, maximal power in any procedure is found in the relevance of being specific. However, to the degree that these specific situations characterize a patient's life style, generalization must still be pursued. It is best to move the patient from a general tendency to talk about things in the abstract or global to the specific and current. Only later in the session and the therapy process should the general be emphasized again.

Internal Structuring and External Processes of Therapy

Most therapists observe that there is a common pattern to the process of therapy across time. What is infrequently recognized is that there are important transition periods in therapy as well. Research suggests that the primary concerns of a patient are resolved in therapy relatively fast, usually within the first fifteen to twenty sessions (Butcher & Koss, 1978; Smith, Glass & Miller, 1980). Hence, whether the therapy is short or long does not produce major differences in symptomatic change or even patient comfort (Luborsky et al., 1975). This pattern suggests that a transition in focus normally occurs sometime between 15–20 sessions, from the problems that bring a patient to treatment (usually symptomatic and acute) to more introspective and broad band concerns. Nonetheless, not all therapy needs to proceed to the second or broad band phase, and for most individuals the initial or acute phase is sufficient. Indeed, failure to appropriately manage this transition period may account for the observation that those who terminate during this period of time tend to do less well than those who either terminate treatment before or after this time (Cartwright, 1955; Smith, Glass, & Miller, 1980; Taylor, 1956). The therapist who is overly commited to developing long-term relationships may be insensitive and even psychonoxious to the patient who has no desire to develop such long-term treatment relationships. A sensitive transition or termination at the time after which the major acute symptoms and disturbing feelings are largely resolved may help to reduce the sometimes negative impact of terminating treatment during this *critical period*.

Aside from the critical initiation period and the subsequent long-term treatment period, the phases of therapy have been conceptualized in different ways by different individuals and different theoretical orientations. What is relatively consistent across these concepts, however, is that the internal process of a therapy session seems to recapitulate both the treatment process and life long patterns (e.g., Stiles, 1979). Whatever the interpersonal patterns or conflicts that characterize external relationships, these will also be enacted with the therapist. Indeed, the therapy relationship is a micrococsum wherein the patient's interpersonal life and/or conflictual struggle can be viewed. The patient's perceptions, behaviors, and expectations toward the therapist all enact this theme, and this pattern is at least partially reciprocated by the therapist enacting his/her own interpersonal life pattern.

However, this interweaving of conflictual themes and patterns between patient and therapist is conceptualized, it is expressed within a larger treatment process that seems to be quite consistent within individual sessions and in the pattern of many sessions. That is, an introductory or low intensity period is usually observed at the beginning of each therapy session which gradually progresses in intensity and meaning as the session develops and then tapers off again toward the end (Frank et al., 1978; Pope, 1979). This pattern corresponds with treatment phases, progressing from an initial relationship-building period through the resolution of acute struggles and through a transition into less affectively arousing exploration phase before tapering off toward the end of treatment. The phases identified in the following pages may be reenacted both within a given therapy session and within the overall course of the treatment itself.

Identify. This first phase of the treatment session is where the patient and therapist collaborate to develop a mutual understanding of the issues to be addressed in the treatment to follow. During this period it is important that a collaborative relationship be maintained between the patient and therapist so that the agreed upon points of focus are in fact mutually determined. Often in the course of a treatment hour several topics are addressed, and each may be approached first through this "identify" process and with as much specificity as possible.

Similarly, the early sessions of therapy are devoted to the process of identifying the symptom or conflictual areas of concern and developing a collaborative relationship. This identifying process is repeated frequently as treatment progresses.

Comply. The comply phase of a therapy session is very critical but is frequently and unfortunately left implicit. This phase is one where the therapist obtains the patient's permission to proceed collaboratively with some evaluation, inspection, or exploration of the identified concern. Obtaining the patient's permission to do "work" is especially important in the highly reactant patient. A simple question, such as "Would it be alright if we explore that issue further?" may do much to increase the patient's sense of collaboration and participation in the treatment process. It is this type of attention to the patient in a piece of work, therapy session, and in the overall therapy process which may develop the "we" aspect of the relationship which is so predictive of therapeutic outcome (Luborsky et al., 1980).

In the overall structure of the therapy program, the comply phase is one in which systematic collaboration and an experimental attitude is erected in order to approach and experiment with the issues identified in the first phase.

Magnify. This phase of the treatment session is designed to increase the patient's awareness or the arousal of cognitions, behaviors, and emotions associated with the concern identified. The usual treatment process is to encourage emotional discharge, exaggerate some aspect of awareness, or to plumb the patient's emotional experience, in order to obtain a better picture of the way in which the patient's dynamic conflicts impact his life or paradoxically, to soften the defensive boundaries that prevent change. It is at this point that arousal levels are optimized in order to motivate movement and demystify change.

Frequently, this stimulation period of a therapy session will serve to underline previously unrecognized beliefs that influence one's disturbing feelings. Guided imagery, behavioral exaggeration, interpretation, or other strategies are frequently invoked. Depending on the type of patient, the usual procedures invoke emotional awareness, emotional escalation, or behavioral exaggeration objectives.

In the broader course of therapy this is the early midphase and "critical period" of treatment and is often seen by the patient as a phase where problems have become worse. Indeed, very often they have, at least in their overt manifestations and in the patient's awareness. This observation leads the author to emphasize to the patient that, during this period, therapy is not a process of helping people feel better, but one of making them feel worse. This is true because most human behavior is devoted to avoiding both conflict and intense emotion. The patient may be told that psychotherapy is a process of preventing such avoidance in favor of developing more direct and effective resolution procedures. The patient needs reassurance that while initially distressing, the escalated struggle and turmoil will pass as he/she moves toward his/her problems rather than away from them.

Validify. Within the therapy session, the validifying phase is devoted to analyzing the feelings, behaviors, or insights that have been exaggerated in the immediately previous phase. It is important that the patient remains in therapy during the period of magnification when emotions are high, since an escape would simply reinforce an avoidance of therapy (Stampfl & Levis, 1967). Therefore, it is important that the therapist leaves plenty of time following the period of emotional plumbing and/or behavioral exaggeration to validate, inspect, and obtain a perspective on these experiences. This, indeed, is a testing period that can vary from the formal process of rational evaluation advocated in the cognitive therapies (e.g., Beck et al., 1979) to the less systematic approaches employed by the experiential and psychoanalytic therapists. In the latter traditions, asking the person if they can agree with the observations made serves a validation function. In interpersonal therapy, this is a period of exploring reciprocal impacts of the behaviors and feelings exaggerated in the prior moments.

In the overall course of the therapy process, the validifying phase is one in which the patient begins to deepen and test out new insights or feelings through behavioral and interpersonal change. The patient experiments with new patterns of behavior. At times, this experimentation is made explicit as in fixed role therapy (Kelley, 1955) or homework assignments (Goldfried & Davison, 1976), while at other times it is allowed to occur without explicit instructions. Nonetheless, validating experience should be addressed rather explicitly as one inspects the types of changes the patient is experiencing. It is also during this phase of the therapy process that new behaviors may meet unexpected results, even at times confirming all of the patient's worst fears. Hence, continued experimentation must be encouraged even in the face of apparent failure, so that the new behaviors and feelings can be modified, modulated, and appropriately assessed relative to their long-term rather than short-term effects. Beck et al. (1979) suggest that the therapist explain that these periods provide important opportunities to practice new attitudes and then encourage the patient to treat them as further experiments.

Solidify. This phase of each individual therapy session extends the previous phases by giving the patient, either implicitly or explicitly, an alternative conception or behavior in order to understand his experience. This is the period when attitudes are most susceptible to change and insights are most easily obtained (Frank et al., 1978), coming as it does, after intensive arousal. In cognitive therapy, for example, this is the process of giving the patient an alternative thought to practice and then monitoring the change in feeling that occurs with this alternative. In psychoanalytic therapy, this is a procedure of underlining previous insights and allowing the patient to explore how these can be incorporated into daily struggles. In either case, multiple procedures can be utilized with varying breadths of impact and varying degrees of structure in order to be consistent with the patient's personality and coping styles. It is important that the therapist underline and reinforce the patient's explorations into new behaviors, feelings, and/or thoughts.

In the overall course of the treatment process, the solidifying phase of treatment is one where the therapist and patient collaborate to explore modulated methods of displaying and reacting to environmental stress. External reinforcers that might maintain change are being sought in order to begin the process of termination. Many times, these external reinforcers are sought nonexplicitly and obtained in the normal course of social exchange as the patient improves his social contacts. Whether explicit or implicit, however, this is an important phase of therapy insofar as the failure to develop appropriate social support and reinforcements predicate the probability of symptom reoccurrence (Schramski, 1981). Maintenance of therapeutic change has been shown repeatedly to be contingent upon an individual's available support systems and ability to change social environments or relationships in order to be consistent with this change.

Verify. The verification process should be completed at several points in the therapy hour, following movement through each topic of concern. The verification process is one of seeking and giving feedback. The therapist seeks to know whether the experiments and procedures employed in order to magnify, validify, and solidify experience have been helpful in clarifying or resolving the initial concern. At this point, the therapist can provide feedback to the patient about the relationship and the direction of therapy. While this latter is important to most patients and intensifies the quality of the therapeutic relationship by making patients feel accepted, the patient who is both highly reactant and externalized may not benefit greatly from such feedback from the therapist. Because these latter patients have an investment in maintaining control of the treatment process, their role in providing rather than giving feedback should be emphasized. This effort is designed to establish the patient's sense of collaboration and control and to discredit the therapist's knowledge.

During the verification phase that immediately precedes termination, it is useful to review the treatment relationship across time. An exploration of areas still in need of work prepares the patient for termination. During the verification stage, the attachment bond between the patient and therapist must be reconstructed so that the patient is willing to take the risk of giving up an important relationship in order to stand on his/her own and continue to grow.

Goodbye. In order to insure the patient's continuing sense of collaboration and to underline the fact that one session does not usually constitute the total treatment package or program, the end of each session or "work" might include a query on the part of the therapist as to whether it is acceptable to leave things at the degree of the resolution attained and, if necessary, a promise to return to the topic in the future. Providing the patient with an opportunity to express any last thoughts before the session or topic is ended helps prepare for the transition from the therapist's office to the external world.

This process of moving from *identify* to *goodbye* may be repeated several times in the course of a single session and across time in the therapy process. In the latter regard, the final stages of therapy are designed to allow the patient to say any last words or provide any last thoughts to the therapist before treatment is completed. It is also a time when the therapist can help the patient make plans for the future and work on leaving the door to therapy partially open, though sufficiently closed to encourage his continued growth toward independence. Final needs to either please the therapist or please the patient must be addressed. It is also a time when the therapist might suggest areas in need of future and continued attention. One of the most important aspects of this phase of the therapy relationship is the therapist's encouragement and reinforcement of the patient's continued growth.

SPECIAL ISSUES

The Resistant Patient. It is the concept of reactance that identifies resistance in the interpersonal influence process. It should also be understood that the concept of "low reactance" does not mean "no reactance." Reactance is a concept that is common to all individuals and specifies not only a tendency to avoid interpersonal influence but to react in a manner opposite to that advocated. While all people have this tendency, the latitudes of external control in which it is invoked characterize one's resistance. The struggle, therefore, is to become tolerant of whatever latitudes of interpersonal control produce anxiety.

The highly resistant patient requires less in the way of external, authoritative structure and more opportunity to develop and reassure himself of his own autonomy than the less resistant patient. The use of paradoxical interventions (Omer, 1981) as well as emphasis on the experimental nature of any directed activity are appropriate for these purposes. Special attention must be given to maintaining the patient's permission. Therapeutic vacations might even be considered (Brehm, 1976).

A general rule of thumb is: "Never fight with your patient." Fights are seldom productive and cast the relationship into a one winner/one loser conceptualization. While the patient's reactance may be therapeutically stirred, as in paradoxical interventions, the therapist must always be willing to back down or assume the role of loser in favor of the patient's sense of autonomy and power. The "psychonoxious" therapist described by Bergin (1971) and Ricks (1974) is one who attempts to defeat the patient through caustic remarks, shame, or ridicule. Fighting, unfortunately, frequently has that character, and competition between patient and therapist can produce a deterioration effect in the treatment process (Bergin, 1971; Strupp, Hadley & Gomes-Schwartz, 1977). Therefore, if a therapist has a hypothesis about an underlying attitude or insight that is necessary to the patient, it should be approached carefully and interpretations offered only when they are ready to be accepted or when the therapist is willing to back down. An intermediate position is to deal with such insights with questions so that the patient has the opportunity to reject them. Alternatively, the patient can be asked to engage in a fantasy that such an interpretation is correct. The patient would be asked to play a role and imagine how he/she would be if the interpretations were correct (Kelley, 1955).

Within therapy sessions, an impasse is frequently reached when important insights or emotions seem close to the surface, but the patient seems unable to penetrate the last barrier to them. In this kind of context, setting explicit time limits for the patient to continue the struggle may provide sufficient reassurance to allow him/her to go through the impasse. Similarly, paradoxical injunctions frequently help resistant response.

Again, the distinction between *states* of impasse or resistance and *traits* of resistance must be underlined, not because they will be dealt with differently as they occur, but so that the therapist will be able to change his/her therapeutic stance. State reactions diminish from moment to moment, and trait reactances or resistances change only with considerable time. The therapeutic stance adopted must parallel these superimposed functions.

Working With Reoccurring Patterns of Behavior. All behavior occurs within some context and pattern. This has been described as life themes by many authors (e.g., Dreikurs, 1964). There are also certain types of symptoms that impose their own patterns upon the patient's adjustment or mood. Depression, for example, usually is a self-limiting condition and passes through phases. Reassuring and educating the patient of these phases is highly touted as a method of assisting the patient in expecting and thereby controlling his reactions (Beck et al., 1979; Klerman & Weissman, 1982; Weekes, 1976; Weissman & Paykel, 1974). Patients with anxiety disorders are particularly in need of reassurance of the cycle these patterns take, since they almost uniformly are concerned that each anxiety episode will bring their final destruction. Waiting through the intense affect and anticipating the well-rehearsed and systematic changes in affect and behavior that sequentially occur is important. Depression, anxiety attacks, the experience of pain, as well as certain habit patterns are susceptible to these types of reassurances.

Frequently, the therapist observes a pattern developing in the patient's behavior but feels unable to prevent the cycle. Efforts to help the patient see this cycle may not be successful, and even if they are, may not stop the cycle from occurring. In these cases, particularly with the highly reactant and resistant patient, some explicit prediction of the next stage of the cycle may be helpful. If the therapist makes this prediction, it has a paradoxical influence with the highly reactant patient, tending to break the cycle simply by the patient's investment in being free of the therapist's control. In less reactant cases, the cycle might in fact be predicted by the patient, giving a sense of control over the process even if the cycle continues. The point to be emphasized with the latter type of patient is that prediction equals control—if one can predict behavior one is in control of it. This type of prediction is especially helpful in the development of pain control and to some degree in the control of anxiety or phobia attacks (Weekes, 1976).

Transference and Countertransference. Issues of transference and countertransference have been addressed by many authors in great detail, and not much in the way of additional information can be provided here. However, it bears stressing that positive transference and countertransference are most likely to become issues among patients with low levels of reactance. Conversely, negative transference and countertransference may be most likely to develop as issues among patients with high levels of reactance. Therapists are drawn into the helping professions in part because of a desire to be of service, and they are likely to be caught in a transference trap when they treat patients who are most openly in need of this help and most receptive to it. It is important to be aware of the trap of dependency and to remember that the therapy relationship is built upon weakness and/or pain. The attachment striving patient establishes an important relationship on the basis of pain, and giving up pain or weakness in favor of strength and confidence threatens the maintenance of this important relationship. This contradiction must be addressed directly in the treatment process. It is frequently helpful for the therapist to reassure the patient that therapy can even be continued if he/she becomes well. The paradoxical effect is that if he/she becomes strong and free of pain, he/she will not need the relationship anymore and will be less drawn to it. Nonetheless, the assurance that therapy is not simply maintained on the basis of pain and weakness is often helpful.

From the standpoint of positive countertransference, it is frequently important for the therapist and, perhaps, even the patient to keep in mind that anyone can be kind, benevolent, sweet, and understanding for one or two hours a week if paid sufficiently well for it. The therapist's rescue fantasies can frequently be aborted by reminding himself that he is, as one patient has expressed, "a highly paid prostitute." While this analogy may be rather exaggerated, it is nonetheless applicable. It may serve as a reminder of the demand characteristics in the environment that foster positive transference and countertransference and that lead patient or therapist to exaggerate feelings in this very unrealistic environment of psychotherapy. Storr (1980) has aptly pointed out how the expectancies and behaviors appropriate in therapy often depart from those usually considered to be socially appropriate or adaptive.

Negative transference issues are more difficult to handle. Evidence is increasingly accumulating that the patient's negative reactions to the therapist bode poorly for the success of the treatment. Appropriate matching on the basis of belief systems and treatment orientations may reduce the likelihood of such reactions but will not eliminate them. Given its dire implications, however, the old doctrine that one must see such reactions through may now be inappropriate (Luborsky et al., 1980; Strupp, 1981b). If a patient is unable to develop a positive feeling about the helpfulness of the therapist within the first few sessions, the likelihood of positive gain is reduced markedly, and it may be wise to suggest that the patient seek treatment with a therapist about whom he is able to develop more positive feelings.

The therapist's negative countertransference is a more difficult issue to address from the standpoint of current research. It does not appear to be necessary that the therapist like the patient. In fact, several studies have suggested that therapists do best with those patients who they find least attractive and with whom they enjoy working the least (Bednar & Mobley,

1971; Shows & Carson, 1966). What does seem to be important is that a patient perceive the therapist as helpful and understanding. Given the degree that patients may distort the therapist's behavior, such perceptions may not be based upon any actual incongruence or falsity on the part of the therapist. Observe for example, the wide discrepancy that exists between external ratings of therapist offered conditions and those provided by the patient (Gurman, 1977).

Termination Issues. Termination is frequently perceived as a negative consequence of getting better. Thereby, it is not a pathological phenomenon to observe that any patient who likes the therapist and the therapy relationship (not necessarily transference in the classical sense) will have some degree of investment in hanging on to his/her conflicts and difficulties. It is unrealistic to expect that all conflicts, problems, turmoils, and other difficulties will be resolved with psychotherapy. As one patient has expressed in Chapter 14, psychotherapy and life beyond it is a process of hatching from an egg to explore a bright new world, only to discover that you have been hatched into a larger egg. Experiential therapists define this as the "getting there is being there" phenomenon. That is, an important part of termination is teaching the patient that the process is more important than the outcome—the process of solving problems and coping, of terminating and initiating relationships, and of emotional pain may be more important than the exact way in which these issues are resolved.

The same holds true for the therapy relationship itself. The process of ending relationships is as important as beginning them. Even the experience of pain is not a negative sign that one has learned and developed poorly; it is only an indication of being human and able to feel. Fear of abandonment, in other words, is realistic, understandable, and important, but should not be equated with the actuality of abandonment. Encouraging the patient to face fears of abandonment, lack of support, or lack of closeness (whichever may be the case) just as other risks in psychotherapy have been faced, is critical. Facing fears rather than avoiding them should be taught during this period of treatment.

Nonetheless, in order to assist the patient in breaking the bonds of treatment, it may be valuable with many to develop a systematic slowdown in the frequency of therapeutic contacts. This fading out process may be used to emphasize that the things learned in therapy and even the therapist's presence itself can still be maintained without face to face contact. Giving the patient a time when support systems derived from therapy can be counted on may assist in the termination process. Typically, in the author's experience, such scheduled sessions are frequently cancelled as the patient learns that it is possible to function well independently. Periodic booster sessions may be especially planned to maintain gains.

It is also important to assure the patient that termination can occur even though he/she continues to be in some distress. Indeed, termination is frequently preceded by a crisis, but this should not deter the therapist from going ahead with such termination plans in concert with the patient's planning efforts. As Beck et al. (1979) have suggested, these periods of crisis can be seen as important opportunities to practice new ways of responding and testing out one's new feelings. In most therapy, patients continue to progress and grow even beyond therapy termination (Schramski, 1981; Sloane et al., 1975).

Another important termination strategy is to recognize that termination begins the very moment that treatment starts. From that moment, the therapist begins preparing the patient for termination, autonomy, and self-sufficiency. Particularly through the stages of solidifying and verifying one's experience, efforts are made to alter external systems, provide support for the patient, and encourage his continued growth. It is also during these stages that the therapist can provide reading materials (bibliotherapy) or reminders of important ways that the patient has developed to cope with stress.

As an example of the foregoing, the author recently worked with a patient who had morbid obsessions of stabbing his wife. During the course of the successful treatment regimen, we found ways that he could cope with various fears by utilizing cognitive strategies, making interpersonal approaches, expressing his feelings, or utilizing relaxation. During the final stages of therapy, we compiled these strategies for dealing with various feelings in a small notebook. The patient took it upon himself to tabulate the notebook and make it into an explicit self-help manual. Each troublesome feeling or impulse was tabulated in the margin with helpful hints and reminders on the following pages. Some of these reminders were of active interventions that he could employ alone, others involved contact between him and his wife, and still others were reminders of insights that he had acquired. Two years after the end of treatment, the patient was still utilizing this notebook during periods of recurrent crisis or anxiety, even though the original obsessions had long since dissipated.

SUMMARY AND CONCLUSIONS

The current chapter is a reminder that patients are individuals, and no set of conceptualizations or dimensions will uniformly capture any one of them. Patients move from coping strategy to coping strategy and from reaction to reaction. It is the therapist's task to stay with the patient rather than expecting the patient to stay with him. Through the course of implementing a variety of procedures individually determined by the patient's place in therapy and response to the treatment relationship, the therapy designs to systematically impact the cognitive, affective, and behavioral components of troublesome attitudes and values. The process of therapy is to systematically move the patient toward greater autonomy, greater social sensitivity without reactivity, and fewer areas of negative and pervasive life disturbance. The internal structure of therapy recapitulates the overall therapy process and moves from relationship development and commitment through a process of letting go and disengagement. This process is facilitated by the quality of the collaborative relationship established between patient and therapist, as well as the specific techniques employed.

The therapist can anticipate that troublesome issues will arise during the course of the treatment process, but some reassurance that both therapist and patient can see the process through typically provides the structure needed to give the patient permission to explore and grow by this exploration. While patients must be handled differently, there is also a great deal of uniformity in the quality of the relationship that will support therapeutic change. Openness on the part of therapist, flexibility, and a willingness to avoid competition and criticism are all important. It is through these kinds of therapeutic processes that one sees a patient change and grow while, perhaps, changing and growing oneself.

In order to clarify these issues, the concluding five chapters of this book will present clinical examples of patients who vary in conflictual themes, defensive styles, levels of reactance, and to some degree, symptom complexity. In each of these presentations, an attempt will be made to provide a running dialogue of what interventions and procedures are most appropriate. The patients whose stories are presented were asked simply to describe a little of their own history as it applied to their seeking treatment, and to detail as much as possible the things they found to be helpful, ineffective, or even harmful in the course of their treatment. Each patient was selected because he or she had received a variety of treatments varying in effectiveness. All represent a unique view of the therapist's role from the other side of the dyad.

11
Clinical Applications: I

PREFACE

The concepts that are necessary for applying a systematic eclectic psychotherapy have now been explored. The efficacy of these concepts, however, can only be fully appreciated in the context of the patient's experience. This chapter and the ones to follow describe the personal experiences of particular patients in psychotherapy. These patients were asked to describe those things that they found to be effective and ineffective. Before approaching the following chapters, it is important to observe that there is little direct information available on how good the fit was in each patient and therapist dyad. Hence, the focus of the presentations will be on the development of the treatment relationship without the knowledge of the closeness of value/belief system match. Some of the positive or negative impact of psychotherapy, therefore, may have been decided before the patient entered into the specific relationship with the specific therapist discussed.

LYNNE

My name is Lynne Ellen Stanley, and I was born 31 years ago. In the first 20 years of my life, I was a Brownie, a Girl Scout, and a sorority member. I was a beauty contest winner, an honor roll student, and a campus officer. I am a daughter, a sister, a lover, and a friend. I am tall, selfish, slender, happy, generous, sad, and agoraphobic.

Agoraphobia is a fear of traveling any distance from the safety of home and a fear of crowded places. That is the definition, but that does not describe what being agoraphobic is.

At my worst, I had trouble getting up the courage to walk out the door of my house. I can remember when a walk to the corner (about eight houses from mine) was an ordeal, and a walk around the block was not only impossible but unthinkable. Just thinking about those feats produces tension, tears, shaking, knots in my stomach. In the doing, I experience all those things plus rubbery legs and a feeling that I can't breathe. Rather than subject my body and my mind to all those feelings, I prefer to stay home.

I have not traveled more than 20 miles from my home in the past ten years. The last football game I attended in a stadium was over five years ago. The last time I rode in an elevator was three years ago. The last time I was downtown (eight miles and 20 minutes by freeway) was nine years ago. The last time I flew in a plane was 12 years ago, and the last time I rode in a bus was over 13 years ago. You name it, I haven't done it in the last ten years.

I read once that by admitting you had an emotional problem you had licked 50% of the problem. If that is the case, I have been 50% cured from the very first. Admitting I had a problem was relatively easy in comparison to getting help for my particular affliction.

My problem is not unique. I understand that it is quite common. I have read that there are two million agoraphobics in the United States alone and many more world-wide. The reason no one knows about us is that we stay home—we're afraid to go out. We are ashamed and embarrassed about our problem because it is so difficult to explain and to understand.

In my senior year of college, I experienced an emotional upheaval which left me ten pounds lighter, continually tearful, and fearful of traveling any distance at all. I know now that what I had was a severe anxiety attack, coming several months after my grandmother died, my boyfriend entered the Army, my parent's marriage collapsed, and my family transferred to another city. I didn't know then what an anxiety attack was, and it scared me.

Neither my parents nor I had any idea what had happened, but we agreed that I was ill. The family physician diagnosed my trouble as mononucleosis and prescribed bed rest and Librium. I felt that there was something else wrong, but he never said anything about an emotional problem.

None of the medical doctors I have seen have been impressed with my mental state. Each doctor had one diagnosis for why I was afraid of everything. I was tested for sugar diabetes, hypoglycemia, thyroid imbalance, smallpox, heart irregularities, inner-ear imbalances, polio. When the test results came back and there was nothing physically wrong with me, then the physician dismissed me. Of the seven physicians I have seen, only one referred me to a psychiatrist. I received diagnoses like: "You worry too much." "It's a phase you're going through." "Everyone has to do things they don't like to do." Who was I to question a *DOCTOR*? I was only 21 years old, just out of college.

I would take a new prescription for tranquilizers or sedatives and be sent on my way. I seemed to be the only one who thought that a 21-year-old woman who needed to take four Valium a day to function was a little strange.

It was several years before I realized that I know my own body and mind better than anyone else, that it is my business to be an informed patient and to question and to try to understand why a particular treatment or test is being used.

Commentary

This patient's onset of agoraphobia is not atypical. It began during a period of environmental upheaval, emotional loss, and crisis. The first indication was in the form of an anxiety attack. The very nature of the anxiety attack, juxtaposed with the loss of a grandmother, a boyfriend, and the decay of her parents' marriage stresses the significance of emotional attachments in the patient's history. Confronted with the threat of separation, she felt helpless and inadequate with the anxiety attack following shortly thereafter.

The fact that the patient's initial loss was redirected into a fear of an external event suggests the dominance of an externalizing coping style in this symptom development. Rather than confronting her own fear of loss, however, the process was extended and generalized to external and nondangerous events, representing broad ranging fears of things outside herself.

In this initial section, there is also some indication of the patient's tendency to willingly comply with external control or directives. Her tendency to defer to authority and experience suggests a relatively low level of reactance. Indeed, as she suggests, it took several years before she began to emerge somewhat from this reliance upon medical authority and to assert herself relative to her own treatment.

Lynne. After two years of coping with fear of everything, I contacted a psychiatrist myself. I think I looked in the yellow pages of the phone book. Unfortunately, the man I chose turned out to be weirder than I thought I was. In his waiting room, he had a group of humanoid figures in purple, orange, white, yellow, and blue. These figures were grouped in a circle staring down at an egg in the center of the circle. That should have given me a clue of some kind.

The decoration of any room reflects the personality of its owner. (If you could see my living room right now, you would probably laugh.) This psychiatrist's waiting room was paneled in dark wood and not well lit. My mind was also dark and not well illuminated. Was his mind also? And who were those egg figures? I couldn't identify with them. Could I identify with the man who allowed them in his waiting room?

The only session with the "egg-figures psychiatrist" I remember was about my handwriting which is very large. I understood him to say that I might change my personality and thus my life if I could make my handwriting smaller. I sure tried for a week and all I got was a cramp in my hand and no great changes in my life. Meanwhile, I trudged five flights of stairs once a week to his office because I was afraid to ride the elevator. I don't know if I told him that or not, but I did tell his receptionist, a chubby, bespeckled, grandmotherly sort who did me more good than he did. She served me hot coffee or tea when I came in upset, and she put her arm around me and showed me warmth and affection. She seemed to care. I never felt he did.

The doctor and I never achieved anything resembling rapport and I decided for the money, I could do without him and his egg people. I still didn't know what was wrong with me.

In the course of consulting a physician for a very bad cold, I told him I had developed a fear of rain and was very depressed.

"Oh!" Dr. M. exclaimed, "My ex-wife was just like you!"

Anyway, he gave me a prescription for Sinequan and told me it took the place of electro-shock therapy. His verbal prescription was to make no big decisions for the next two weeks. Within two weeks, I had put on ten pounds, stopped shaking as much as I had been, gave up my apartment and moved back home with my mother.

Commentary

In this section, we begin to see the patient's response to interpersonal relationships further evolve. Her negative reaction to Dr. M, for example, whose wife was seen to be just like the patient, suggests an unwillingness to be too similar to others in spite of her felt need for closeness. Likewise, doctors did not seem able to establish with the patient the sense of collaboration and involvement required for therapeutic gain. The movement from an attachment to an ambivalent conflictual theme is suggested in these patterns.

As a bright, articulate, psychologically minded and motivated individual, Lynne was acutely but negatively sensitive to her environment. Her reaction to the "egg figure psychiatrist" is particularly striking. Even in the waiting room, before meeting her doctor she perceived or inferred certain attitudes and beliefs that fostered a sense of distance from her doctor and predicted her failure to establish a compatible relationship with him. The importance of meeting certain of the patients' initial expectations and the value of having some characteristics in common with a patient in regard to social and philosophical outlooks, underlines the value of demographic and social similarities presented in Chapter 5.

Lynne. Within the year, I felt that I needed some professional counseling again, and Dr. M. recommended Dr. T, a calm, soft-spoken psychiatrist.

I talked to Dr. T. and he listened for one hour a week for a whole year. He prescribed tranquilizers which I took religiously. I remember telling him that I understood how the whole thing was supposed to work: I talked, he listened, and somewhere in there I was to come to some conclusions about myself and my life and with new understanding make the necessary changes. However, I didn't seem to be doing that; none of what I was saying and feeling was making much sense to me; no pattern was apparent to me. I felt I needed some guidance, a more directional approach. I do not remember his response, but nothing changed.

I was not getting better or even different. I was getting worse. The tranquilizers—Librium, Valium, Sinequan—which had enabled me to function enough to teach school for four years, to live by myself in an apartment for a year, and to attempt and sometimes achieve something of a social life were no longer effective. Eventually, the five mg. of Valium that I was taking four times a day did nothing but dissolve me into tears. So, Dr. T. changed my tranquilizers to Mellaril.

I took a pill in the morning and fainted. I took a pill after lunch and fainted. I called the pharmacist who suggested that I not take any more and call my doctor. Dr. T. suggested that instead of continuing with the Mellaril I should start taking eight Valium a day. I was in a very poor mental and physical condition, but I had enough presence of mind to say, "Dr. T, I am 24 years old. If I have to take eight tranquilizers a day to function, then I won't function!"

I stopped taking any medication, and I stopped going. I took a leave of absence from my teaching position and took to my bed where I remained for several weeks, afraid to leave it to do more than go to the bathroom. At night, I couldn't sleep and would cry until the early hours of the morning when I fell asleep through sheer exhaustion. In the mornings when I opened my eyes, my whole body would tense, my stomach would contract. Tears formed in my eyes and I would lie there afraid, pulling the covers over my head. I lived in fear this way for the better part of two months.

I talked to Dr. T. on the phone once more during this time—I couldn't travel to his office now. He said that I had quit my job so that I wouldn't have any money to pay him so that I wouldn't be able to see him any more and then I wouldn't have to talk about sex. That may or may not have been the case with my subconscious, but sex was the furthest thing from my conscious mind. And I still didn't know what was wrong with me.

Commentary

The patient's consistent tendency to comply with even ineffective treatment bespeaks her relatively low reactance levels. While she relied upon medications, even passively taking them, she felt no great benefit from the intervention. Still, she continued to persist. Yet one also sees that this compliance is not uniform. Oppositionalism is suggested in her final defiance of Dr. T.

Moreover, Lynne's reaction to her therapist's nondirective style and its lack of impact begins to draw attention to the potential value of more directive and structured approaches in working with an individual who has developed externalizing (phobic) coping strategies. Nonetheless, while her primary symptoms represent externalized defenses, her withdrawal, hesitancy, and retreat carries with it a marked internalizing quality. This pattern suggests an inconsistent coping style. She vacillates between a pattern of externalization and a more subtle pattern of internalization and compartmentalization.

Lynne. One morning, although I still woke up tense and afraid, I decided I did not want to spend the rest of my life in my nightgown in my bed in my room in my mother's house. I knew that even if I were afraid to go out of the house, I ought to be able to do something in the house. So that morning I made myself some rules. I moved my television out of my bedroom and into the den. I told myself that I could watch as much television (the plug-in drug) as I wanted but not in my bedroom where I would be tempted to stay in bed. I told myself that I would get up every morning, wash my face, brush my teeth, get dressed, and eat breakfast. Those were simple enough rules, and I had some activities to occupy my mind the first moments of the day. Whatever else happened during the day, I had accomplished those few tasks, and that made me feel good.

As time passed, I created other rules for myself and began to set small goals. Some were more difficult than others for me to achieve, but I kept trying. I tried to read something inspiring or uplifting every day which led me to some fine books.

I tried to keep a journal of my feelings and thoughts which led to my writing some poetry which I had never done before. I still amuse my friends and relatives with my verse.

I also figured that if I couldn't quite get my emotions in shape, I could get my body in shape. I started doing four simple exercises every evening before I went to bed. I began to sleep better and I began to look better and to develop some stamina. Once I felt better physically, I volunteered to keep the house clean and cook the evening meals for Mother and me.

Once I began to feel comfortable in the house, I set my sights and goals outside the house. A small task again was the beginning: walk to the corner of the street and back. I took it literally and figuratively in small steps. Not only did I make it to the corner, but working at it the same way, I made it around the block!

My dearest friend gave me a bicycle for Christmas and I rode it every day. I mean, I rode it *every* day in all kinds of weather—sun, rain, and once even in sleet! I rode it all over the neighborhood and worked towards and accomplished a bicycle trip to the store.

Then, I found the courage to drive my car again and I told myself that I would drive to a store every day and get out and go inside. I didn't have to buy anything; I just had to make myself go inside and I did.

The hardest continuous thing I did was go grocery shopping. I chose a small grocery store and I elected to go on Thursdays. Every Thursday, I would wake up with tears in my eyes, knowing that this was the day I made the trip to the grocery store. I would pace around the house and cry, trying to get up the courage to go out the door, get in the car, and drive down the street to the store. I would not give up on myself and eventually I would make the move out the door and into the car. I would cry all the way to the store. Once inside, I would stop crying, but while I was shopping, I would get scared and want to rush out of the store and race home. I never did, though. I just kept telling myself to keep shopping, slowly and steadily. I was always very pleased with myself when I returned home with the groceries, and I was always exhausted. I went through the same routine many, many weeks before I started taking grocery shopping as a matter of course.

Commentary

The value of an externally-oriented treatment for an externally-oriented coping style is seen in the patient's self-directed treatment efforts. Exposure, external structuring, setting behavioral goals are seen in her own successful efforts. In this, she developed and then directed her own treatment program in a manner not unlike that described by Marks (1978) and Weekes (1976).

Lynne. Families sometimes do not understand an emotional illness and mine is no exception. My parent's marriage was falling apart when I arrived home from college in the throes of emotional trauma, and I was overlooked. If either of my folks had taken me in tow and found the help I needed then, I wouldn't be writing all of this now. I am bitter about the lack of support from them, but as my mother so often told me, they did what they thought was best at the time.

Mother, at least, put me in touch with her lawyer who in addition to handling messy divorce cases and working with alcoholics, did psychological counseling. It was a strange arrangement from the beginning.

Because I was relatively homebound, Dr. (of what I don't know) G. said he would come out to the house. He came by or called on an irregular basis. I never knew when to expect him. More often than not, he would arrive in the middle of the day when I was alone, on his way to some place else, or he would call me at 10:30 at night to talk to me. He loaded me down with mimeographed sheets listing his rules for living and told me to read and study them. He refused to set any fees for his counseling.

I so desperately wanted help that I went along with this unorthodox method of treatment. I figured that my strange affliction required strange treatment. It made me uneasy for him to arrive without prior notice when I was alone, and it made me uneasy when he hugged me before he left. He encouraged me to lean on him, to trust him. He explained that because he wasn't charging me for his services, he couldn't come out on a regular basis and I couldn't get in touch with him. I thought I needed to see someone more regularly, and I was getting suspicious of his treatment methods, which I told him. He was surprised at my suspicions and suggested that I was reading something into his good intentions that wasn't there. I went along with the arrangement for a while longer, but as badly as I wanted and needed help, I was uncomfortable in his presence. I eventually decided that he was interested in more than the state of my mental health, and I put an end to his visits. I still did not know what was wrong with me.

After Dr. G, I sought help through the Jewish Family Service, a United Fund Agency. The Service at first refused to allow me the privilege of their counseling service because I was not Jewish. When I told the voice on the phone that my father's mother was Jewish (true), I was informed that the board would meet and determine whether that Jewish relationship would suffice or not. It seems that it did because they did take me on.

At the Jewish Family Service, I met with a social worker once a week. The charge for the service was determined by my income. I think I paid $8.00 a session. J., the social worker, was younger than I and was a very kind, caring person. The meetings were good practice for us both: he was just making practical application of his recent schooling and I was beginning to learn more about myself. When I became afraid to travel to his office, he politely explained that part of the cure was coming to get it. Never mind that fear of traveling from my home was a chronic problem for me. So, I quit going to see him. I never heard from him again. I still didn't know what was wrong with me.

Commentary

As with Dr. T., the patient's negative reaction to the absence of external structure is seen in her response to Dr. G. His inconsistent schedule of attendance produced an uncomfortable amount of distress and anxiety for the patient. This negative reaction to such lack of external structure is probably quite typical of an individual with a usually low level of reactance and an underlying need for attachment. However, it now becomes increasingly apparent that attachment needs alone do not represent the core conflictual theme. While most would agree that Dr. G.'s affectionate overtures were inappropriate and unusual, one would also expect that an individual with clear and more consistent needs for attachment and closeness would have gravitated more readily toward them. The patient's suspicions, her tendency to pull away, and her resentment of his approach, while appropriate, suggests a core conflict in the area of ambivalence.

This ambivalence becomes even clearer as Lynne describes J. While making active efforts to receive help and support from others, her approach is uniformly followed by withdrawal and separation. This pattern is seen consistently in each of the patient's therapeutic relationships thus far described. Each relationship begins with her seeking and striving for closeness and ends with her initiating separation and disengagement. This pattern seems also to be reflected in her familial conflicts. In her family, Lynne apparently learned to expect that any close relationships might be followed by abandonment and separation. Thus, one sees the patient's struggle between moving too close and moving too far away. A stable emotional equilibrium between need for love and need for separation characterized most of her relationships. This pattern was most clearly observed in the unchanging but nonintimate relationships with parents and boyfriend.

> ***Lynne.*** I had been at home, unemployed, for the better part of the year when a friend offered me a job at a neighborhood swimming pool working in the concession stand for $1.00 an hour. With a B.A. in English, some graduate hours in English grammar, and four years of teaching experience, I was overqualified and improperly trained for the job, but I had to start somewhere. By the end of the summer, I had been promoted to assistant manager of the pool and received a raise in salary to $1.25 an hour! That little job gave me courage to enter the working world again.
>
> Another friend offered me a position as a leasing agent at an apartment property near my home. That was six years ago, and I am now the construction coordinator for the conversion of the property from rental units to condominiums.
>
> Getting back to work was one of the best things that happened to me. Having a job gave me the opportunity to be with people every day instead of brooding alone at home over my problems. The salary I receive at work tells me that what I do is valuable and worthwhile and thus, I reason, so am I. It gives me the courage and makes me feel more "normal".
>
> After my first year of employment, I was entitled to a week's vacation which I elected to spend at home (where else?). A well-meaning friend who knew I wouldn't be traveling to Tahiti loaned me some books to occupy my time. By the time I finished reading them, I was so depressed I didn't know what to do. That week my father called me and told me he was going to file for divorce from my mother. I was ready to kill myself.

My good friend suggested that instead of killing myself I should sit down and make a list of all the places I thought I might be able to get some help and call them. So, I dried my eyes and did just that.

One of the places I called was the Mental Health Authority. I had seen advertisements on television and I thought they might be able to refer me to someone or to treat me themselves. I find what I am about to relate is comical now, but at the time it was a very frustrating experience. I had already determined that not traveling was my biggest problem and that in order to get help I had to travel. It was a "Catch 22" situation. If I could travel to get help then I wouldn't need to get help. As I explained it to various people I spoke with by phone at the Mental Health Authority, "If I could come to you, I wouldn't need to come to you." I felt like some kind of nut saying that, but then I figured they were used to dealing with nuts. Wrong. I called expecting someone to say that they had heard of a problem similar to mine and that if they couldn't help me, then they might refer me to someone who could. When someone finally did talk to me, she said she was sorry but there was no way I could be helped by them unless I could get there (which, may I remind you is my problem). Nothing else. No referral.

Commentary

We see in the foregoing more evidence of the patient's internalizing defenses. Her tendency to pull back on herself and retreat to her home and aloneness, her depression and self-derogation, and her use of fantasy and books for gratification are important indices of this process. Overall, while this vacillation between externalizing and internalizing coping strategies underlines the importance of focusing first upon the coping strategy utilized in the most destructive symptom, it also underlines the importance of seeing beyond those reflected just in primary symptom development.

Lynne. Another place I called on my list of places to get help was Baylor College of Medicine, Psychology Department. The man whom I spoke with on the phone was very kind, not at all shocked or surprised by what I told him about myself. He said he would see what he could do and someone would return my call.

That was on Friday. On Monday, Larry E. Beutler, Ph.D. called me. I understand from him that I became a note on a bulletin board which intrigued him.

I had to accept certain conditions before he would take me on as a patient. He requested that we meet somewhere other than my home (my sister had an apartment nearby and agreed to let me use it every Monday at 6:00 p.m.); I had to have someone else present—not in the same room during our meetings, but at the same abode (this was to protect both of us, and my good friend agreed to spend an hour of his time each week that way); and he had to charge me a little bit more than his regular fee to make up for traveling time and expenses.

As I waited for Larry to arrive for the first meeting, I was telling myself that I wanted to get well, that I wanted to cooperate, only please (powers that be?) don't let him have a mustache and a goatee. Guess what. Oh well. . . . That was almost five years ago. In those five years, I have had my greatest successes and my greatest failures. Neither were achieved easily; I had to work hard at both.

My progress has been rather irregular. Some things Larry and I try work, and others don't (just exactly like life—isn't that strange?). One of the most successful techniques for me is hypnosis. It is a state of total relaxation and, as Larry has told me, I cannot have a relaxed body and a tensed mind at the same time. For me, hypnosis is better than any tranquilizer or sedative I have ever taken because I feel I can control it. Larry made a tape for me and thus I was able to practice hypnosis at home as well as at our meetings until I was able to hypnotize myself.

I use hypnosis to give myself a break from the tension which I also create myself. In combination with other techniques, I have used hypnosis to travel outside my territory more comfortably, to be the maid of honor in my sister's wedding, to have surgery several times, to cope with ordinary situations which I perceive as threatening (i.e., a thunderstorm) and with extraordinary situations such as two large fires (really!) where I work.

In some ways, hypnosis is a retreat for me. I just relax and let feelings wash over me while I float along. I can function fine but in a relaxed state. The *magic* of it appeals to me. It is not a cure-all for me, because if it were my problem would be solved. It is one of the many tools or aids Larry has introduced to help me cope with being agoraphobic. When we first started meeting, I was an absolutely miserable being. Larry started right there, working to help me accept myself as I was right then and moving forward from there.

Another tool I have found helpful is physical exercise. It gives me a sense of control, of power (those two statements are really something coming from someone who managed to graduate from high school without setting a sneaker in a gym class—and that took some fancy footwork on my part—and who took folk dancing to meet college physical education requirements). Starting with the four simple exercises and the bicycling I did when I was homebound, I have enlarged my repertoire to become an avid walker, on-again-off-again jogger, tennis player, and swimmer. I have even taken ballet and exercise classes. None of these activities (except swimming) were especially enjoyable at first. Now, I look forward to even jogging. Somehow stretching and straining and loosening my body does the same for my mind (is exercise a form of hypnosis?). Larry recently *prescribed* that I start jogging or solo dancing again at least three times a week. I have, and it does make a difference in my general mental attitude. It's doing something.

Obviously, being able to talk and consult with Larry is a help to me. He provides me with an opportunity to try out different points of view, different emotions, different approaches to my problem. I look upon Larry in several different ways. He is a mental therapist who helps to exercise my injured emotions in the same way a physical therapist exercises an injured body. He is a consultant to whom I can bring my questions and comments. He is a resource person who can suggest books or tapes or observations on agoraphobia. He is a teacher who assigns me lessons. He is a student who, with me, is learning about me. Most important, he is a friend who accepts me as I am. He neither approves nor disapproves of me; he just lets me be.

Reading and studying about agoraphobia and general psychology are yet other tools I use. I feel that even when I am not making physical progress (enlarging my territory), I am making mental progress by reading and studying about coping.

Commentary

The patient's reliance upon both external structure and self-enhancement activities, as well as the amount of benefit received from them, are reiterated in the foregoing comments. The structure of therapy seemed to assist her in developing a relationship with me that was relatively safe. Moreover, the structure provided an opportunity for her to develop strength and confidence in her own abilities. Indeed, perhaps because of the safety found in structuring treatment, we readily and easily developed a sense of initial compatibility in working on her problems. However, it seemed important, in those early sessions especially, for Lynne to retain a sense of interpersonal distance. While we worked together for five years, it was well past twelve months before she would ever call me by my first name. Her need to keep me at a stable emotional distance underlined and highlighted the ambivalence of her attachment needs. The need to obtain support and nurturance only from a safe distance was frequently reiterated as treatment progressed.

One sees indications of the collaborative nature of the therapeutic relationship with Lynne as she talks about working on things together and the experimental nature of much we do. Her ready acceptance of directive procedures also indexes the dominance of her low level of reactance. By the same token, the patient's reliance upon external structures and activities underline the compatibility of external symptoms to an external treatment focus.

Lynne. Some people collect stamps or matchbook covers or coins. I have become a collector of information on agoraphobia. Each piece of information helps me to understand my illness and myself a bit more. Collecting and reading the information is one way of coping with it. I then must face it, accept it. In some ways, agoraphobia is easy to ignore. I have reached the point where I can pretend I am not agoraphobic. I have a job which I have held for six years, I now live in my own apartment, I shop in the stores in the area and have everything else delivered. I could let that be my life, and sometimes I do. But if I continue to read about agoraphobia, to talk about it, study it, and think about it, then I am facing it. In fact, I have developed an interest in my illness. My tendency is to shrink from it. Instead I am attempting to embrace it mentally, and sporadically I embrace it physically by putting myself in situations which create anxiety for me. A lot of times, something I have read inspires me to try once again.

Two other aids I employ are Valium and a notecard. I have a bottle of Valium in my purse and carry it wherever I go. It is like a lot of ex-smokers I know who still carry an unopened package of cigarettes around with them to remind them that they can have a cigarette any time they want one. The prescription for Valium is over two years old (my physician assures me they are still good). I think that if I get in a situation that I think is unbearable, I can always take a Valium and, if worse came to worse, I could take them all. You know, I have been through some rocky times but have never taken a one. I know I would never take one and yet they are there if I want one.

The notecard has ten rules for coping with panic typed on it which I found in my reading. I keep it in my billfold and pull it out and read it when the going gets rough for me. Reading those rules is some sort of signal for me to relax, to let the feelings come without fighting them or running away. I recently had to have some minor surgery done in my doctor's office, and I was in the midst of a full-blown panic attack over it. Plus, I had to wait over two hours before he could see me. I wanted to run away, but instead I pulled out that card and kept reading it over and over. I even carried it into the examining room and kept it clutched in my sweaty palms during the entire procedure. I know that I got myself through that and that the card is not magic, but it helped.

Another thing I do for myself is talk to myself. I use this tool in several ways. Larry first suggested that I sit in front of a mirror and debate a question with myself, taking as many sides of the question as I could. He also suggested that I tape-record some of these encounters. Listening to these tapes is a revelation. At first, I was extremely self-conscious about it. Then I began to feel more at ease with the various aspects of my personality that emerged.

I then began to realize that I talk to myself quite often. For example, when I say "RUN!" then I say to myself, "Why don't you wait five more minutes?" Myself says, "Okay, but I am leaving in five minutes." I have stayed literally hours that way. I also say things like, "Lynne, there are nine million Chinese who don't give a damn about what is happening to you, so why should you?" And, "A hundred years from now this won't make any difference, so just cool it." And, "An hour from now this will all be over so stick it out." And, "Think how good you will feel about yourself if you do this and how badly you will feel about yourself if you run away."

Writing about agoraphobia or writing about a specific problem I am having is helpful. It is a distillation process. My emotions are sometimes so distorted that I cannot determine, for example, why I am angry or at whom. By sitting down at my typewriter which becomes rather an automatic writer for me, I can distill my jumbled feelings to the pure emotion and then deal with it.

Most of the hindrances to my progress have been inside me. I am both my curse and my salvation. I hear Larry's observations of me as criticism. Or I hear those observations as a command to change, and I become very frustrated when I don't change.

I have a problem with motivation. If going places and doing things were reward enough in themselves then I would probably try harder to get there. I think I am distinctly not self-motivated. I require an outside incentive. I am working on that though.

I have difficulty making decisions. I constantly second guess myself. I want some direction from outside, some reassurance that I am doing well. I wasted a lot of time with therapists and counselors I didn't like—the egg psychiatrist, Dr. G.—simply because I thought whether I like them or not as people didn't matter. But it does. I like Larry as a person.

Commentary

With much of the patient's initial crisis passed, we now begin to see the strength of her intellectual resources in her report. The reliance on data gathering, information seeking, and other intellectualizing patterns index the aforementioned internalizing defense process that compliments her externalized symptoms. Indeed, the strength of this internalization and the quality of her intellectual resources can be seen throughout her writings and point toward the value of capitalizing upon these resources in her treatment. Concomitantly, the utilization of perceptual change and cognitive management procedures, ranging from hypnosis to cognitive rehearsal, is seen as a viable treatment focus. Because of her internalizing tendency, much of her direct symptomatic treatment was directed toward anxiety management rather than strictly behavior control. Hypnosis, for example, was designed to reduce anxiety and was complemented by other anxiety management and relaxation training procedures to assist in this process. The compatibility of this anxiety reduction procedure, the behavioral control procedures, and the perceptual change procedures, as well as their sequencing, can be seen in the patient's report.

Likewise, one can see in the patient's description the beginning use of emotional enhancement or awareness procedures. With an awareness of her internalizing processes which seemed designed to compartmentalize and control her affects, the use of two-chair dialogues and both mirror and focusing procedures emerged. These, as one can see from the patient's descriptions, were used concomitantly with cognitive retraining wherein the patient constructed arguments against her own impulses.

Lynne. I tend to unrealistically divide my life into two parts: my life and my meetings with Larry. My meetings with Larry are just as much a part of my life and just as real as anything else. In real life, I spend time with people I like. So it stands to reason that therapy would be much better and more productive if it were done between two people who liked each other.

I also feel that Larry cares about me. Some of the other therapists were so impersonal. Whether this is true or not, I feel that if I all of a sudden stopped going to see Larry that he would call me and encourage me to come back and try again. I say that, whether it is true or not doesn't matter because that's the way I feel. There have been times when I took a break for a month or cancelled appointments on a regular basis, and yet I have always returned. As I said earlier, the others made no attempt to find out why I really quit going to the sessions or to encourage me, ever so gently, to return.

Rapport was an overused word among educators when I was a teacher, and I hesitate to use it even once more. But that is what Larry and I have achieved because of the kinds of people we are and through many hours of both joyful and heart-wrenching work.

Commentary

The patient's tendency to utilize internalizing defensive strategies, such as compartmentalization, is seen in her separation of her outside life from her life in therapy. The need to break down these barriers through the use of procedures that allow her to release these intellectualizing processes is important. A major feature of these procedures involves the use of the therapeutic relationship itself. It is no accident that the patient talks about this compartmentalization process in juxtaposition with a description of her feelings of fondness toward her therapist. The establishment of a productive, collaborative relationship was very much dependent upon her developing ability to care about me and my ability to care about her. Encouragement, exploration, support, and a genuine sense of caring and regard does much to facilitate emotional awareness and to allow one to release the internalizing controls that block one's life. When coupled with emotional enhancement and emotional awareness procedures, a satisfactory therapeutic result can be obtained.

> ***Lynne.*** I want to define agoraphobia again in the way I tell others in conversation about me. I am basically a quiet, home-body type. I enjoy being alone, and I amuse myself fairly well. I am better on a one-to-one basis with people than I am with a crowd. Agoraphobia is a distortion of that. It is an emotional distortion or dysfunction. It is like looking in one of those funny mirrors at the fair and seeing yourself all fat and wavy. You are still basically there, but what you see is distorted. If you met me at work or in a situation where I felt comfortable, you would never believe that all the foregoing is true abou tme. But it is. As my dad always says, "That's part of my charm."
>
> I have mentioned earlier that a very good friend gave me a bicycle for Christmas, and a very good friend hired me as an employee at a swimming pool, and a very good friend suggested I make a list of places to get help instead of killing myself, and a very good friend gave up an hour of his time a week to sit by himself while I met with Larry. That very good friend has stood by me through the past ten years. He has taken me on drives, he has held my hand, he has cried with me, and he has rejoiced with me. I am fortunate to have such a friend.
>
> I talk about what I have accomplished, and I have come a long way from where I started. No one else could have done it except me; but, like the people who accept the Academy Award, I have not done it alone. I may win the award for the leading role, but the supporting cast—Larry, my friend, my co-workers, my family—deserve awards, too. I am living proof that you are not alone, and there is someone out there who can help you if you just look hard and long enough.
>
> I am not cured. I have more hard work ahead of me. But, then doesn't everyone? "Lynne Stanley, THIS IS YOUR LIFE!"

CONCLUSIONS

Even while describing Lynne as having an "ambivalent" conflictual theme, one is struck with how this theme evolved from an earlier one of attachment. Lynne developed her initial relationships on the basis of maintaining attachments, and by her own description, may have been overly involved in issues having to do with retaining the love of her parents and the relationship with her grandmother. Indeed, her primary symptoms began developing at the point when these attachments were threatened. When the external environment no longer supports the intensity of one's attachment needs, such problems arise.

In her later development the primary theme was clearly one of ambivalence between attachment or nurturance needs on one hand and autonomy and separation needs on the other. Her "good friend" is a case in point. With him she was able to establish some sense of attachment but did not proceed to the point of making a final, love commitment. At the same time, she was not willing to retreat from the security provided by this relationship; it remained in a stable equilibrium characteristic of low reactant ambivalence. The same pattern characterized her relationship with her mother and all of her therapists. Even when a satisfactory treatment relationship developed, she seemed to need periodic "treatment vacations," perhaps to keep the relationship from becoming too confining.

Agoraphobia is not like a simple phobia. It represents a more dynamic interference with life, as well as being less susceptible to change through behavioral methods (Gelder, Marks, Wolff & Clark, 1967; Marks & Gelder, 1965; Weekes, 1976). Hence, treatment needs to be directed to more than symptom removal. While systematic exposure was valuable, both in her own self-directed treatment and in that provided by trained therapists, more broadly based treatment procedures were also required. Perceptual change methods, including hypnosis and self-instruction, were particularly valuable in addressing value/belief conflicts. Hypnotic induction combined suggestions for self-image enhancement with Systematic Desensitization procedures designed to facilitate anxiety reduction. In this case, the initial concern was with symptom reduction and then with perceptual change. The value of perceptual change efforts are seen in the patient's description of how cue cards and self-talk helped her control her symptoms and how she needed to learn to define herself in some "normal" way.

The magic of hypnosis appealed to Lynne's desire for external structure. The increased self-acceptance coming through mastering work, exercise, and graded exposure was also important but was facilitated by contact with others who had similar conditions. It was in this context of interpersonal warmth that Lynne was ultimately able to gain some sensitivity of her own anger and her own resentment toward those who placed demands upon her. Her role as "glue" for her parents' marriage and her struggles to take possession of herself without losing the support and warmth of others is partially seen in her own writings.

Therapeutic Process

As the patient's external symptoms decreased, there emerged a more subtle but dominant internalizing strategy of coping with life's stress. Her tendency to compartmentalize affect became more apparent as a life style of coping. Her self-criticism and need to control her anger through constricting her social contacts, mobility, and emotional ties also became apparent. Therefore, as therapy proceeded, many therapeutic procedures began to attend to exaggerating emotional awareness and insight. Two-chair dialogues and even some direct confrontation with her mother was possible, although immediately following the latter contact, she underwent a significant regression for a period of time.

By way of postscript, several observations are important. The treatment relationship described by the patient ended when the author took a new position in another city. The patient has continued to make significant positive changes by involving herself with a structural treatment program for agoraphobia. In this program she found group support and external structure. She has expressed the impression that she has been able to utilize and integrate many of the things that were discussed in individual therapy into this group focused program. Since beginning therapy, she has been able to travel on freeways, appear on television, change apartments, and both begin and end emotional relationships. The progress of therapy has been one of moving through external symptom management procedures to internal struggles and dynamic conflicts, only to return to the specifics and external concerns of everyday life. Her experience with the symptom focused group treatment which followed her therapy with the author has provided a satisfactory completion to this cycle.

12

Clinical Applications: II

BILL

I am 45, white, male. Divorced, remarried, 6 children—2 hers and 4 mine.

My experiences in therapy bridge more than half of my life. The first when I was 18 in college, and the last terminated a few months ago.

I have been asked to write about the "therapeutic experience" and its influence on my life. It's a difficult assignment, and I find it difficult to begin. Do you want to know about all of my therapists? Hell, I don't remember much about most of them! How many? Nine—more or less. Were there any mileposts? Not until recently.

I feel that a brief history is in order, and I will keep it brief. Deep south background. Dominant mother, passive and often distant father (no, homosexuality is not my problem though I have had two post-adolescent experiences, and I have wondered and occasionally worried about it over the years). Withdrawn and isolated childhood, few friends, sense of alienation, exceptionally "bright." Considered myself ugly and uninteresting as far back as I can remember. Was told by mother that I was just that through adolescence. Erratic, given to extremes of mood (manic-depressive?). Became adventurous early in life to escape. Took off for Alaska to fly bush in early 20's (after B.A.). Wandered about the world some. Married the first time at 27. Wrote. Worked. Went back to school for Ph.D. Made it through. Went into business where I had lots of highs and lows. Big house. Lousy marriage. Divorce. Bankruptcy. Middle aged hippy. Love. Marriage. Where I am now is a successful businessman again, but determined to stay reasonably sane and maintain a sense of proportion and balance in the world in which I live.

What has therapy done for, to, with, against me during this time? As I said, the first time was in college. I knew I was fucked-up, but not sure why. I made a few "suicide attempts" (in quotes because I knew even at the time that they were phony). Thus, therapy. A kindly old man who sat quietly, read some of my poetry, said little, and was, I suspect, as bored as was I. His contribution to my life was, at best, that I didn't pretend suicide anymore—but I thought about it a lot—a hell of lot—and talked about it occasionally when I was in deep depressions. That man was the sort, though, who gives therapy a bad name (to me, at lesat). I really wanted to work at it, but he was bored, boring, and plain disinterested. I gave up.

Commentary

Even early in Bill's description, one can see the development of strong needs for emotional attachment, based upon a long history of deprivation. Similarly, one sees an investment in his own autonomy and an effort to separate from painful emotional commitments. Bill describes what is probably an overprotective mother and a distant, detached father. The struggle between the attachment needs of his mother and his father's separation characteristics are, not surprisingly, recapitulated in Bill's ambivalence. He grew up as a frightened and isolated child with a very poor self-image and a drive to escape from painful contacts through the relatively inconsistent behaviors of both nondirected world travel and highly directed academic achievement. From these polarities an ambivalent life theme emerges. On one hand, he is driven toward affection and nurturance and on the other, toward independence and separation. Having never achieved a gratifying emotional attachment, it is not unsurprising that Bill should devote much of his life to seeking one. However, he also finds emotional attachments relatively dangerous, provoking him to a pattern of unfulfilling distance and separation. He married, but found it difficult and traumatic; he involved himself in therapy, but found it difficult and unrewarding. In neither case did he achieve the closeness or separation he sought. The conformity of marriage and school contrasts with the individuation of hippyhood.

Also in Bill's early report one can begin to see basic characterological defenses. Running away, excitement seeking, and even "phony" suicide attempts all represent externalization of anxiety. Similarly, his tendency to look at the therapist instead of himself as the source of the relationship problems encountered in therapy suggests this externalization. Nonetheless, his report of periodic depression and erratic vacillation of mood raises the possibility that even though externalization may be his dominant mode of defense, it was not his only one. Even in the early descriptions, there are obvious periods of internalization that may have involved guilt, certainly invoked anxiety, and were representative of depression, all of which have significance for his treatment.

Bill. The next experience was a few years into a crazy marriage that managed to limp along for more than 14 years. Many of my peers have admired me during my life, and in many instances envied me. I could never understand why. I decided to give therapy another shot. Why did I always feel so badly about myself? Why were my choices so limited, and all bad (depression?)? Why could I never do anything right? Why couldn't I be a "success" and maintain? What the hell, maybe a shrink could help me find the way. No, that's not what I wanted. Maybe a therapist could *show* me the way. I checked around and chose one. What a bummer. A one visit trip. A mental crook. I walked out before the session was finished and didn't go back. I'd heard those platitudes and the shit from Sunday School on. "If you do the right things everything will be O.K."

Meanwhile the marriage went through ups and downs and I went along for the ride. It was a poorly put together vehicle in the best of circumstances, and riding on the roller coaster was too much for the lousy construction to stand. It really started falling apart. We finally agreed on something. "Let's try marriage counseling." What we got was a water soluble glue to temporarily hold the thing together. Another inept therapist. But I think he really wanted to help. The problem with him, in retrospect, was that he let his two crazy patients control the therapy. He couldn't or wouldn't offer any direction, and was obviously overwhelmed by the complex and deepseated hostilities, hurts and irrationalities. Two people babbling at each other. He gave up after a couple of months and suggested an "exceptionally good" psychiatrist.

We went together for a few sessions, then separately. Interesting bit—I guess we were both really boring because the quack literally slept through most of our sessions. Complete, on occasion, with snoring. He was totally unresponsive to our problems, and our stumbling attempts to make some sense of the mess we were in. Prescribed antidepressants for her and suggested she accept her "proper role" as a wife and mother. Basically ignored me.

By now determined, I tried another psychiatrist. She gave up. Actually he wasn't bad. A cross between Norman Vincent Peale, Buddah, and KierKeggard. At least he responded. More pat answers. "You aren't listening to her." Shit, man I want someone to listen to *me*! What about where I am? But is sounded authentic, and we got another paste job on the creaky old marriage machine. I got little or nothing for me.

Commentary

As Bill continues his story, the vacillation between subtle internalizing and more dominant externalizing defenses is more clearly evident. Poor self-concept, depression, self-criticism about his lack of success, all of these things suggest the internalization process. Yet in each of the experiences described in therapy, the final act of Bill's scenario requires the blame to be established somewhere external to himself. It's as if bad experience gives rise to the need to blame someone but he vacillates between intropunitive and extrapunitive blame. Nonetheless, the relatively strong flavor of the anger and externalization that most dominantly characterized Bill's view of therapists is apparent here.

In the foregoing, the ambivalence conflictual themes also emerge more clearly. His sense of loss at being "ignored" and his resentment at someone paying more attention to his wife than to him all indicate his strivings for attachment and intimacy. However, the clear vacillation of his efforts to satisfy his dependency, and the chronic tendency to break off attachments also continue to suggest an equal investment in separation and autonomy. He finds comfort in neither autonomy or individuality. One notices in Bill's description of his marriage and therapy equally salient needs to establish boundaries and to individuate himself from others when they do not provide nurturance.

Finally, one can now begin to see some indication of high levels of reactance in Bill's response. Suicidal attempts, recognized as efforts to communicate and engender support rather than to die, are especially observable as possible counterphobic movements away from closeness. His response to authorities, both his own parents and to his therapists, portrays a certain competitiveness and active resistance that defies any efforts to invoke controls or establish a direction for the treatment process. Yet while resisting external control, he also asks for greater direction, establishing the double bind characteristic of a reactive, passive-aggressive response to authorities.

Bill. Finally the marriage collapsed. Divorce and bankruptcy within six months of each other. She got the kids, though I wanted them desperately. About as total a failure as anyone could be. Soon back into therapy.

And it couldn't have been better.

This is an experience that really helped, and the contrast between it and what had happened before was like the proverbial difference between day and night. It took time (1½ years). It wasn't a bed of roses, but it worked.

Actually this experience consisted of working with two separate therapists. The first was one of the most gentle men I have ever met, and the other a considerate, challenging, and responsive woman.

Prior to beginning this journey I spent a lot of time thinking about what I wanted to accomplish, where I thought I was, and where I wanted to be. I had evolved an image which seemed to best describe how I saw my life, and an extension of that image which described where I wanted to go. My life and situation at the time appeared to me to be a gigantic mass of tangled rope—all sizes, colors, lengths, and materials. Each piece of this rope represents a single facet of my personality, environment and experience. There were thousands. I defined my problem as a feeling of near hopelessness in trying to untangle the rope and make some sense of things. I felt that in order to do this one needed to be able to take each length of rope and be able to trace it from beginning to end. I couldn't do this, and the result, in my mind at the time, was that I was stymied and basically immobilized. What I thought I wanted (no, really wanted) was to separate the labyrinth and lay all of the pieces neatly in rows, side by side, then connect them into a "practical," "useful," continuous, single rope, albeit varied and irregular.

The gentle man worked patiently with me, moving through a variety of exercises which we worked out, session after session. He listened, and he responded. He asked questions and listened to my responses. He suggested exercise and helped me begin to gain some insights into me. If he had a major, identifiable fault it was in letting me control too often, to go off on apparently meaningless flights which pretended to have a destination, but were, in reality, ways in which I was avoiding dealing with some basic problems. Such a small fault when I consider that he gained my respect and my attention and guided me into an even greater determination to work things out.

There were, in all of our sessions, no great moments of insight. But there were many small steps which he helped me to see as such. He helped me find a path through a sometimes chaotic, always transitional period of my life. I think now, again in retrospect, that he was perhaps less than satisfied with his dealings with me. In fact, it was for me as perfect a beginning as I can imagine. I needed that and would probably have responded very badly to a firmer approach. I suspect that I would have viewed a more controlling person as another combatant whom I had to outwit. Someone else to whom I had to prove my intellectual superiority while I continued to come apart inside. He gained my confidence and helped me to become more confident. He worked skillfully, remembering what had gone on in previous sessions, referring to my obviously contradictory feelings, and moving slowly along.

When, after a few months of therapy, he told me that he would be leaving the city but would line me up with another therapist I had mixed emotions. In a way I felt a sense of desertion, but it was not strong. I knew that I wanted to go on, but was worried about the possible new therapist (after so many negative experiences, I had to believe that the norm was about third grade level). When I received word that my new therapist was to be a woman, my internal response was mixed. On the one hand I was, and am, a firm, adamant supporter of female equality, but on the other I questioned how a woman could possibly deal with *my* problems—a male's problems. Would she be prejudiced by my frequent resort to profanity? Could I discuss sexual feelings, fantasies and problems openly with a woman? How much could she possibly know about the problems that a man faces in business (as though a woman in business or a profession doen't have all of the same problems—in spades!)?

Commentary

As the reader will recall, the combination of high reactance and external defense is a unique one and predisposes a negative response to a credible, authoritative expert as a therapist (Kolb, 1981). Such patients resist external control and have a major investment in establishing a therapeutic relationship in which they are equal or superior, even at the sacrifice of therapeutic gain. We can see this pattern to some degree in Bill's previous struggles with therapists. Perhaps, the fact that the therapist described in the previous paragraphs and the one whose description is to follow were relatively naive students instead of seasoned practitioners and were younger and less knowledgeable than the patient provided an atmosphere in which he could relate without having to defend his own excellence. Moreover, the man who Bill describes as a "gentle person" was characterized as unable to establish close relationships, as being frequently rejecting, and as struggling with issues of anger and emotional distance by supervisory faculty. Indeed, among themselves the faculty expressed concern about whether this man had the requisite level of interpersonal skills to function professionally. Perhaps the combination of this therapist's lack of expertise, unwillingness to establish close relationships, and Bill's own intolerance for authority, competence, and expertise in others was the very reason that he was able to manage Bill's perceptions of the therapeutic alliance satisfactorily when others had not.

Not to minimize the importance and skill of the therapist, however, it is important to observe that Bill's fledgling therapist began by concentrating upon some of the areas of relevance to an externally defended individual. He not only listened, but he responded and provided structure. Together, they developed "exercises," which included contingency contracts, and moved through the therapeutic resistances gradually. While Bill continues to express a desire for therapist control, it is unlikely that he would have responded satisfactorily to it. Indeed, his need to outwit others underlines his reactance potential and low tolerance for placing control of his life in others' hands.

Bill. The first session was an airing of these feelings and the decision to give it a try. Used to the soft, gentle moving around that had been the pattern till now, we continued along that way for a few sessions. Much of these initial meetings was a recapitulation of what had happened before. But it didn't seem to be working. I remember well the pivotal session—primarily bullshit. We both chatted amiably about irrelevant matters, then I got up to leave and said something like, "I enjoyed the visit." I wasn't looking forward to going back again, but I knew that I had work to do. Evidently we were both aware of the drifting because in our next meeting we addressed the problem. From that time on I made, with her help, the most significant strides toward mental health in my life. We worked together for almost a year after that.

She became more and more confident and challenged me to deeper and deeper levels of insight—often with the opening of long ignored sores and hurts which had been festering well below the surface. She took control and let me know that she knew when I was playing a game (often when even I was not aware of it). She contradicted many of my concepts of the stereotypical therapist. She talked a lot. She related experiences. She treated me as a peer. She helped me dig into areas of myself that were not pleasant.

More and more during these months I had a greater sense of well being—of being well. So many things were happening. My relationship with my new wife was getting better and better. My sense of balance and perspective with the children was improving. I was making enormous strides in my comeback from bankruptcy. I was examining my relationships with friends and acquaintances. I was developing a feeling of confidence. I could see alternatives and make decisions.

Then one day in a session during which I was feeling particularly good I said something that I had, to the best of my recollection, never even dared think before. I said something like, "I really am doing a great job in this new project!?" She picked up on it and pointed it out. My usual mode of thought and expression was quite different. When things were going badly I would feel and say, "I really fucked that up," but when I was doing well it was, "It worked itself out" never, "I worked it out." Now I had felt it and said it! That was one of the most significant days of my life. I should have marked the date and proclaimed it a personal holiday.

From that point, I was on the road to termination—though I didn't think of it in those terms.

There were many other matters to deal with, and we began to work on a support system for this new self-concept. Later I began to talk about termination. I was ready to try my new wings (to be trite), but there was still the nagging doubts about my ability to make it without the weekly feeding.

The last session was short. I cried, but it was a healthy cry and one of thanks. I told her about the knotted rope image, but now I knew that I could never lay the various ropes out side by side, nor would I want to. The ropes are knotted and tangled because that's the way my life and relationships have developed, and, like macrame, the whole can be viewed as a design—pleasing to some and forbidding and hopeless to others. I expect that I will be in therapy again from time to time. I will use it when I feel the need for it.

Commentary

Bill's attachment to his first therapist is seen in his sense of loss when anticipating the man's departure. Such feelings are important to address in therapy since they characterize and represent the patient's life-long struggle. In this case, Bill's ambivalence is noted again when he approaches the potentiality of a new therapist—a woman. The fact that his second therapist was a younger woman who lacked experience and provided self-disclosure may have allowed the same safety to exist in this relationship as it had in the first.

In response to both of his therapists, one can see that Bill's investment in the therapeutic alliance was facilitated by the therapists' willingness to be active and involved and to establish some external structure without predisposing control. Struggles with authority and adequacy, a drive to compete and to show superiority, his contrasting sense of inadequacy, his dependence on his "weekly feeding," and his sense of failure, illustrate the contradictory demands placed upon the therapist. Being both needy of support and unsure of his ability to separate, Bill responded with strong competitiveness, projections of ineptness, and efforts to establish boundaries between himself and others. In this pattern, one sees the interaction among Bill's reactance, style of defense, and core conflictual theme.

Bill. I have four basic observations in rereading this:

1. Too many therapists, in my experience, assume a condescending attitude which establishes yet another barrier for the patient. Little or no work can be done until I have proved my intellectual equality at least (and usual superiority), and by that time the whole experience has been strained beyond recovery,
2. When I sought therapeutic help I was in pain—a pain much deeper and inexplicable than mere physical hurting (though it often manifest itself in physical hurting). Too often in my experience the therapist either didn't care or confused the maintenance of objectivity with aloof detachment. Maybe therapists need more training in "chairside" manner.

3. It would have been most helpful if, somewhere along the way, someone had offered me a diagnosis—had said, "You know, one of the symptoms of depression is the feeling that you have no alternatives, or that all of your alternatives are negative." That would have provided me some basis for emotional and intellectual thought and, perhaps, action.
4. I often had the feeling that a lot of the mystical double-talk mumbo-jumbo that so many therapists blabber was just a cover-up for a gross lack of competency. The therapist was just stumbling around trying to find his way at the expense of my time and effort. I still believe this to have been the case. I am not certain that I have done my assigned task in this. If so, and if it's helpful to another person, so much the better. If not, at least it has been helpful to me.

CONCLUSIONS

Therapeutic Process

In sum, the therapeutic strategy selected for working with Bill had to be: (1) focused upon resolving core conflicts rather than simply removing symptoms, (2) behaviorally oriented, and (3) low in therapist control. The development of "exercises" (in fact, "experiments" and "behavioral contracts") met some of these requirements. The experiments carried some of the topics discussed in therapy back into Bill's environment. The focus of therapy, true to his conflictual theme, was to persuade Bill toward increasing both autonomy and intimacy. The establishment of a "we" in therapy was done only after the therapist became involved and was defrocked of authority and superiority. His second therapist's willingness to directly confront negative feelings and the lack of progress was, in fact, a turning point to him. In spite of his resistance to directiveness, therefore, the active involvement of the therapist promoted persuasive power and this was done successfully through the therapist's self-disclosure, gentle confrontation, and acknowledgement of frustration and lack of expertise. The real task of therapy, however, was to move Bill back to an acknowledgement and acceptance of his own weaknesses and power. The acceptance of the "knotted rope" and the "I have done a good job" represents this type of movement. Therapeutic experiments and experiences were constructed to enhance this sense of separation from the therapist without sacrificing the relationship.

Giving Bill new perceptions of his behavior, including the conceptual underpinning or structure by which to understand it, was important. Combination of broad band, low directive procedures designed to induce both perceptual change and behavioral control were, therefore, dominant in the treatment. The initial steps, however, were oriented around behavioral control, in order to reduce the dominant attention seeking but self-destructive behaviors. Once the initial relationship was established, therefore, these interpersonal experiments assisted Bill to control the extremes of both his internalizing and externalizing coping styles. The perceptual change procedures were particularly effective in assisting him in controlling his angry depression. Cognitive change procedures, role rehearsal, and assertiveness training were seen, from my role as supervisor, as especially valuable.

As treatment proceeded, it became increasingly insight oriented, particularly as the extreme externalizing defenses became less extreme and his attention became more directed at emotional awareness and self-responsibility. Cutting off avenues of escape, as he describes, was useful in the process of redirecting him toward an internalized focus.

In short, the therapy process was one of reducing external behaviors through behavioral and perceptual control procedures and then developing emotional awareness through reflection, reframing, and belief validation. The concentration of activities was initially directed at current patterns in which ambivalent internal drives were in evidence (e.g., his marriage) and later progressed to explorations of transference-parental links.

Among highly reactant, externalizing patients emotional awareness procedures seem to be of less value than more behaviorally and cognitively oriented ones. Only when behavioral controls and emotional stability are developed can emotional awareness procedures be successfully employed. While research has indicated that emotional release and awareness procedures are sometimes more effective than insight oriented ones in this group of patients (Beutler & Mitchell, 1981), when used on individuals who are moving from crisis to crisis as this patient seemed to be, such procedures are problematic. When in crisis, such individuals deteriorate if presented with emotional escalating procedures early in their treatment (Liberman et al., 1973) and without opportunity to "work through" their use.

Finally, Bill provides therapists with several profound and fundamental suggestions for dealing with highly reactant, ambivalent, and externalizing patients with relatively complex and long standing symptoms. Namely, don't control too much, too fast, too long, or too directly. Moreover, do not provide the degree of directiveness that may sometimes be overtly expressed or sought but do provide involvement, interest, and relatively high levels of therapist activity. It is clear in Bill's portrayal that the therapist has to be willing to lose before he can win. The competition that exists between patient and therapist, at least from the patient's perspective, must be one in which the patient wins and the therapist deemphasizes his own status, credibility, authority, and expertise in the interest of allowing the patient freedom to develop. It is only here that the patient can accept improvement. To Bill, improvement was the ability to accept the "knotted rope" rather than to perennially attempt to undo the knots and lay the pieces side by side. Tolerance for ambiguity and the acceptance of seemingly opposed needs for attachment and separation are seen as therapeutic movement and change.

13
Clinical Applications: III

D.W.

Everyone likes to talk about himself, and I'm certainly no exception. Thus, on the event of being asked to write a family history and a little something on my treatments, I jumped at the chance—having no idea at the time of what exactly a family history consisted of (I had the vague impression it was whether or not my grandparents were hemophiliacs). If I had known, I might have reconsidered.

This, then, is my family history. Some points may seem unimportant, but they stand out in my memory and for that reason I have included them.

I love my family. That's one feeling I'm sure of. It would certainly be easier to pinpoint the basis of my anorexia if I had a family whom I absolutely despise. I guess I'm happier to find I don't.

My mother and father are bestowed with three daughters. R., my oldest sister, moved into college dorms when I was still in junior high, long before I conscientiously worried about anything. When I look back on those times, I think of some of her "daring feats," which hardly seem so daring now; she got drunk, "tee-peed" houses, argued with dad, and dealt with all the problems of boyfriends. Yes, R. was my image of the typical teenager. This was what life was going to be like at sixteen. Yet I also remember the quarrels she'd have with my other sister, L. These were terrible ordeals; hair pulling, punching. (I usually remained noncommittal and as inconspicuous as possible. My turn came later with L.) R. liked me, though. I was included in many of her daring feats and was introduced to each new boyfriend. This was neat, especially since R. was one of those busy teenagers and almost an adult. She's in California now, and we're in Oklahoma. I think of her as often as I think of anyone else in the family, and I miss her probably more than she knows.

L. and I were more competitive. We're three years apart, so I wasn't the neat little sister that I was with R. We didn't do a whole lot together in our earliest years. I played mostly with my friends or alone. In fact, my family often hassled me for being in my own world, which is probably still true of me. When R. left, L. and I relied on each other more. These are happy memories; like sneaking peanut-butter and crackers in bed late at night, and giggling over scary stories and the crumbs between our sheets, or staging a formal wedding ceremony for my Barbie and Ken dolls, complete with an illegitimate child. We also fought, as sisters do. L. always claimed great height and certainly didn't need to overlook her strength. I was consistently the losing party. Mother offered no sympathy, only "Don't come to me with your difficulties." No matter how dramatically hurt I could act, I was always met with this same response. (One day I finally punched L. back. She was stunned, so was I. "Mom, did you see that?" she cried. But mom simply said: "Don't come to me with your difficulties." My joy was only short lived, however.) L. can be critical and stubborn at times. Her personality has always dominated me. In return, I put her on a small pedestal; I bought only the record albums she approved of, I was never seen again in an outfit she verbally disliked on the first occasion. I even followed every new diet she attempted.

Commentary

D.W.'s expression of competitiveness with her siblings and her oppositionalism to external structures and rules, ranging all the way from sneaking peanut butter at night to investing her dolls with an illegitimate child, indicate a moderate reactance potential. At the same time, dependency and attachment striving are consistently emphasized in her efforts to engender approval and love at a level that would surpass or match those of her sisters.

D.W. Before high school started, I suffered a drastic change. Our family moved from California to Oklahoma. My life was wrapped around my friends, and it was incomprehensible to consider myself away from them, or so I thought. On the other hand, it was a new experience and very exciting. L. left for school. Our house was great, even without the requested swimming pool: a two-story colonial place, 1½ acres of land, and few neighbors. Sophomore year was great too. I was the new girl, enthusiastic, not bad looking, and certainly willing to date. At home, there was just Mom, Dad, and me with all that attention. But the attention never came. My parents weren't used to me depending on them. Mom never wanted to go shopping or into town, so I often rode the five miles alone on my bike. My friends called but few drove so we didn't get together much after school.

The girls were more competitive than I was used to. My friends in California were different. I wrote them continuously, missed them, and cried about them. My bike rides after school became 20 miles long instead of five. Looking back, I see Mom and she's vacuuming. I don't know why I picture her that way, except that it must have been her common occupation, and for me it prevented any sort of discussion and any means of transportation.

L. visited us again that second summer. This time she, Mom, and I discovered Dr. Atkin's "no-carbohydrate diet." L. left in September, but I thought of her constantly. She was dieting and I was going to keep up—maybe to impress her, maybe to compete, I don't know. Soon Dr. Atkin's diet didn't work fast enough when I discovered that just plain not eating did. At times I threw up to make things faster. These times gradually increased along with weeklong fasts. Eating binges were my downfall. They scared me. I knew, even if no one else did, that I was actually an obese person inside a skinny body. Most of my friends stopped calling.

The few I went to lunch with said little about my meal of Fresca. Dinner was more of a challenge with Mom and Dad there. I snuck saccarin in my tea, and low-cal dressing on my salad. My dog grew fatter at each meal as I slid T-bones and pork chops below the table. I enjoyed the feeling of sneaking things around my parents. It provided some excitement. My dog was my real friend. I grew up with that beagle, babied him, slept next to him, taught him to jump over broom handles, and loved him very much. He knew every fear, secret, and thought. Unfortunately, he couldn't tell anyone else.

Commentary

With the patient's evolving life, a break occurred in what security and attachment she had with early friends and siblings. Moreover, as her sisters began moving out of the home, the patient's expectations for increased parental attention were not realized and she felt more alone than ever. While initially acclimating well to the move, not being allowed access to important social groups frustrated her now dominant nurturance needs. She was isolated geographically from her friends and was isolated emotionally from her mother and father.

Food seems to have taken the place of love in the patient's search for approval among her family members, but dieting was also reinforced since it was consistently juxtaposed with a meaningful involvement with her mother and sister. Meanwhile, the counterphobic, extreme reaction to usual social conventions is seen in the increasing severity of her diet and her oppositional seeking of new ways to reduce her calorie intake. The very act of sneaking things around her parents had some reinforcing properties, underlining her now high reactance potential.

Severe dieting and weight loss can be seen as an external representation of internal conflict, designed to provoke and express anger. Certainly, it also seems to have some reinforcing properties in terms of fostering social contact and communication with family members who were otherwise distant and aloof. However, one begins to see an internalizing process with which this patient dealt with her symptoms as well. In one sense, dieting provoked the same kind of intropunitive self-depreciation as her withdrawal into isolated activities.

D.W. My mother is one of the hardest persons in the world to describe. I'm so close to her that anything I say won't give you a full picture of her. In the beginning, I considered her to be devotedly loving, generous and trusting, a perfect mother. She made great egg-salad sandwiches, felt warm foreheads, gave advice on boys, and worried about my feet in platform shoes. I wanted to be just like her when I had kids—without all the selfishness I see in myself. Now I am able to see faults in my mother, but they still don't seem all that bad. I still want to be like her.

Seeing so much good in this woman, it hurt me deeply whenever my father yelled or was stern with her. He was often that way. I don't know him very well, even now, but as I grew up, the encounters I had with him were usually a physical kick in the seat for getting caught or a pat on the head for getting an "A" in every class at school. Work kept his mind totally occupied. I remember a six-month silence he went through over an insurance loss. I did not know how to comfort my mother at these times. My sisters hated him. He would not compromise when it came to arguments. He saw his side and "that was final." I say that in past tense, but it still holds true much of the time today. Sometimes, if I dare say so, I dislike him. I see traits of his that I hope I never acquire. I don't believe he's happy often. He's also harsh, critical, and cruel sometimes.

I now realize that my mother often plays the martyr and that my father is sometimes given little chance to act cordially. Actually he can be a likeable guy, almost human at times. Not only can he be cheerful and happy, but he can also worry, have faults, and be hurt. In fact, sometimes I relate to him better than anyone else in the family. We can be much alike in our thinking (however unreasonable it may be). When I was younger I only respected and feared him. He was the one authority I tried my hardest to impress. I wanted him to love me. This was a productive, prominent businessman and even a "great guy" to all his friends. My sisters no longer hate him. It was a stage they went through, a time when they wanted to be out and doing things but still had parents to confront.

I believe Dad gave me one very positive feeling. He alone distinguished me as unique and above average. That's beneficial in some ways, yet, I find it very hard to accept criticism and my own failures, and even just being purely average. I like to excel. I like to feel important and needed, either for a cause or a person. In effect, I seldom criticize others. I do not feel I have enough insight into their thoughts or their past that I can judge them. Because of this, and because I was so hurt at my sister's judgments, I never went through a stage of hating my parents. They only gradually regressed from heroes to human beings, and I still find myself expecting far too much of them. During dieting, I expected even more. I was extremely sensitive and argumentative. Nothing they did was right, and I lashed out at everything. I know I looked for arguments. I was frustrated with a fear, but couldn't talk about it, so I yelled about something else.

Commentary

In her descriptions of her parents, one sees the degree to which D.W. felt frustrated and isolated. While desiring so intensely to have affection, support, approval, and love, the sense of distance and frustration she felt is clearly portrayed. While she seemed to feel immense anger and hurt at her parents' lack of nurturing support, she also found it almost impossible to either accept criticism of them or to express criticism to them. When she did, she apparently did so explosively and then felt obliged to deny the anger and resentment that she felt. While acknowledging her sister's "hate," for example, she first expressed and then denied her own. This pattern underlines both the intensity of her attachment needs and her high reactance.

D. W. At school, dates no longer interested me. Dieting was a new obtainable goal. I could actually measure progress. I could be individual and unique. I could compete with the other girls. My body seemed to have a new purpose. It expressed my worth. I'm embarrassed now at these feelings, but I cherished thin thighs, and I checked them very often. They constantly felt heavier than I wanted them to be. Every weight loss goal I set wasn't enough. I enjoyed not eating. Suffering was making me a worthy person. Yet I was never happy or content, never suffering enough. I was capable of much more. I kept active all day, working after school, bicycling after work, jogging after that. I did not think. I don't believe I wanted to think. I had gone too far to discover this was a bad decision.

The third summer that L. came back, I looked like a magazine photo of a prisoner of war—or so I was told. Personally, I thought I looked quite trim and slim. My thighs were certainly thin, since my knees now stuck out further. In one way I was happy. I was secure about myself and my worth. I was reaching goals all the time and being thrilled, yet always setting new goals. I didn't want to bother anyone or attract attention; I just wanted to answer this drive I had within me.

When L. came back a fourth time, she was shocked, and Mom and Dad were forced to notice. So was I. I was nearly sixteen, five foot seven and weighed less than 90 pounds.

I agreed I needed help. I didn't want to be afraid anymore. We tried everything. Mom fixed favorite dishes and took me places at my request. I loved it. But I also lost more weight. With Mom's pleading, I was finally sent to my dad's doctor. This man was overweight and a chain smoker. He boomed forth his life's moral at every opportunity. I saw him as a hypocrite, hated him when he made my mother cry. This problem, he insisted was purely physical and simply a case of an active youth. I left his office three hours later with a high-protein, high-calorie diet, and the knowledge that I would never follow it.

I went on a tour that summer, spending $400 dollars of my hard earned money to backpack around the southwest with kids I'd never met. The exercise was to be vigorous, though, so I signed up. I think those were two of the most miserable weeks of my life. The other kids laughed about me, poked fun at me, yet always ate the food I gave away. I had eating binges, and found I was quite adept at ripping off grocery stores. Not only would I take candy bars, but I could even steal the purse I put them in. At one time, I was extremely hungry in the afternoon. I'll never forget swallowing a half a gallon of apricots smeared with peanut butter, and I really despise apricots. Definitely, my appetite was out of my control.

When I came home, I weighed 72 pounds. Dad came to get me and was more than startled. At home, Mom babied me. I was given my food I asked for. I think I ate nothing but ice cream, Campbell's soups, and Mom's eggnogs, all favorites. I did eat though, and kept it down. This was the first real move I made to gain weight. I liked the attention, the mothering. I felt loved, like a sick child. I didn't want to be responsible for myself any longer. I wanted to give it over to someone else. We went back to the doctor with the "ice cream diet" a week later. He blew up, insisting I needed six ounces of steak and four potatoes at every meal. Then he recommended a psychiatrist. I was scared, but I wanted to go.

Commentary

One can see more clearly than ever the effect both of D.W.'s reactance potential and her intropunitive character style. Her dieting, weight loss, and even physical activity clearly represent a rebellion against parental demands rather than simply a static disregard of parental authority. The enjoyment of both the rebellion ("I enjoyed not eating") and the suffering involved tell me she was rejecting herself and others. The involvement of her sisters, along with increasing parental demands seemed only to intensify the dieting.

The patient's response to authority is another indication of her reactance potential. Her father's doctor invoked only a stronger commitment to her self-imposed diet and self-abusive exercise. Even her exercise, once enjoyed, became misery and a way of imposing punishment upon herself and inviting the punishment of others.

D.W. Dr. M. was a quiet, kind, and very proper woman. I could fool her. I didn't intend to fool her, I was just ashamed at some things I did, so I lied. Group therapy was even less effective. No one else was under twenty-five, and all had problems dealing with sexual incapabilities. I didn't try to get involved with guys because it would inhibit my goals, and besides, if the boy liked me as I looked, then I could hardly respect him. Dr. M., my psychiatrist's husband and coworker, began needling me during group therapy, insulting Dad, claiming I saw him in every man and was submissive. He even scolded me for not paying the bills. I rapidly left their mini-mansion. I did not need to have my parents put down. Nothing was wrong with them. I was the one needing treatment.

I was a senior at school by now, not necessarily unpopular. I was on student council and the powder-puff football team and even managed to hook a date for the prom, although I looked something less than elegant in a long gown. I planned to eat and gain weight that year. I did eat too . . . a little. I maintained my weight at 78 pounds with fewer eating binges. A very good friend of mine was probably the best therapist I had. He kidded me and accepted me as always but never stopped asking me when I was going to gain back all that good weight. At home, I loved to do crafts. I could get thoroughly involved in such. I was encouraged and admired, and finally, recognized by my family for my art works. I really feel this alternative recognition was helpful. Later, it became one of the most important parts of my therapy, whether or not anyone knew it at the time.

Commentary

The patient's strong reaction to authority is seen in her response to Dr. M., a kind and proper woman who could be fooled, opposed, and beaten. Even what may have been an accurate interpretation of the patient's transference was handled negatively, in the absence of a stable and supportive therapeutic alliance. These reactions indicate the level of the patient's reactance.

Happily, the patient was able to achieve some gratification of her attachment needs by a degree of popularity in school by the time she was a senior. She also had a good friend who seemed to provide the kindness and affection that therapists, to this point, had lacked. Indeed, the patient's response to such a kind, accepting, and nurturing recognition emphasizes her dependency and nurturance striving.

D. W. When my senior year was over I went immediately into Children's Memorial Hospital research ward. Everything happened so fast and without my involvement or approval. Dad was no longer speaking to me. Mom was terribly upset, and I felt nothing but guilt. I hated myself, and my weight showed it—66 pounds.

I entered Children's Hopsital unwillingly but determined to cooperate fully. I enjoyed the new company of the people here—those that treated me as an equal, were open, and liked me for my good points. Insults and restrictions were not helpful. They gave me a sense of sneakiness. Strict rules were made to be broken. With them I was not responsible for my actions. Only when I was myself as an individual in charge of my own being did I really desire to gain the weight. A dietician came in to take down my preferences. The portions were small, however, and I always felt the need to leave some on my plate so that even with eating, I did not gain much. The doctors immediately assumed I was throwing up, and they locked my bathroom door. I was terribly frustrated at their unfounded mistrust. Yet I derived great satisfaction in picking the door lock on boring days.

At times I wasn't allowed to wander as punishment for not gaining weight. I then either sneaked out or got angry and read diet magazines and simply had more time to dwell on my problem (not a good idea). I asked for a job at the hospital, something to keep my mind occupied and make me feel useful. Since I had already been doing crafts, I was allowed to help the occupational therapist in making things for the younger children. This was extremely beneficial in my overall feelings about myself, but it lasted only a short while.

My mother, without my knowledge, had been searching for doctors and hospitals that knew about Anorexia Nervosa. She'd found a psychologist in Texas who said he would treat me. I feel very proud of her. She did not fall apart, instead she took a real decisive action. Never before had I thought of her as making decisions apart from my father. I also feared that, in the turmoil, there would be a divorce; yet, I found my parents' marriage was a lot stronger than I'd ever assumed. All those childhood ideas about my parents were beginning to change.

I entered Methodist Hospital a little excited. I don't think I've ever entered into a new situation without some excitement. I also vowed total cooperation and honesty. Honesty can be difficult for me. I find it almost automatic to make lies, in the form of excuses, for the things I do. I also don't always apply rules to myself. I wish I found it easier to go along with the rules like everyone else.

Mom and Dad left me at the hospital with my roommate, an 80 year old woman who slept with her eyes open. I discovered this after ten minutes of one-sided conversation. But I grew very fond of this woman. Sure, I was scared at first, but during her wakeful moments she was a real nut . . . or rather a lot less of a nut than I'd predicted. She too, was a conniving soul and a manipulator. The nurses claimed

I helped her too much, making her dependent on me. We helped each other. She was very good for my self-confidence. She liked my personality.

The nurses were there. I've been puzzling for a long time now over how to describe them, and I finally came up with that fantastic line. In general, they were the best thing that happened to me. The doctors I saw for only one to two hours a day, but the nurses were there, always. My first incident with them came in the morning after arrival. At 6:30 a.m. I was bombarded with three women and a huge scale. While weighing, one nurse suddenly grabbed my gown and yanked. She obviously had the idea that I would try stuffing weights in my sleepwear, to fool the doctors (I did that only once, at Children's Hospital). After deciding to cooperate with these people, this degrading event made me very angry.

Yet, the nurses were excellent in that they never mothered me or voiced their personal opinions on how I should gain weight. They treated me as a responsible person. They talked and they listened. They were also firm. Oh god, were they firm, like granite cliffs. There was no way around the restrictions. I wanted these restrictions enforced, however. There were other patients in the same predicament so this lack of privileges did not limit my social contact as it had at Children's Hospital. Privileges were something to look forward to.

More than just company, I had friends who liked and respected me. I even had a "gang" at times. This was a group of patients who dominated the back corner table at meal times. There is confidence in belonging. I don't believe the nurses were too fond of the situation, however. We all tended to get a bit bolder. Once, some of us took off to a nightclub, munching marijuana cookies in the car. This was fun, and it took away all thoughts of diet.

Among the group was a good friend named J. She was another anorexic who lived on a different floor but came up with her I.V. pole to the occupational therapy room. I loved J. She was so passive, so quiet and sweet. She helped more than anyone my age in reassuring me. Yes, she said she'd felt like this too, but these feelings change. She now felt good gaining weight. We renamed her pole "Ivan the terrible" and joked about his close attachment to J. Inside, this contraption scared me. I would never allow myself to be hooked to an I.V.—I would no longer be in control. I never experienced it, and I wonder how different my therapy would've been, had I.

Occupational therapy at the hospital included a craft room and a kitchen. These were some of my greatest aids. I would spend every hour possible creating and putting myself into my work (as I tend to do, obviously). I was complimented on my work, yet even without these comments, I was confident with my ability. I was pleasing myself. However, most projects were gifts for my parents—I still felt guilty for what I had done to myself and them. My father is the ultimate penny pincher, and I couldn't even imagine the bill I was running up.

In the kitchen, we whipped up Wednesday lunches and a weekly batch of cookies. I was not nervous. I was surrounded by hungry people who tasted often, but also laughed and enjoyed each other. This was more important to me than the actual cooking or eating.

If I worried, had any slight doubt, I had the nurses or other patients to run to. Their comfort and reassurance, at moments of fear, were so important to me.

Other helpful activities included my being secretary of the floor meetings. These were nothing more than complaints of broken washing machines, and announcements of field trips, even weddings between patients. I often had to stifle my chuckles while note taking. But this job was a responsibility. It gave me a purpose and a feeling of worth.

The field trips were great fun, and they always ended with an ice cream cone. Again, I was part of the whole group to get one. To have people join me, not watch me, while eating was very helpful. Meals, at the hospital, were ordered, and of a limited quantity which made me feel more in control. Snacks were helpful, with some encouragement from the nurses. I was still a little scared to indulge.

Commentary

The patient's neediness for people and the emotional support she derives from them are very clear. The loneliness at Children's Hospital contrasts with the group feeling the patient had with her roommate and her "gang" at Methodist Hospital. The reliance upon emotional support from such sources produced help that far outweighed any technical activities involved in the "treatment program." Yet even here there was danger of provoking the patient's reactance. One of the most salient ingredients in engendering D.W.'s reactance was a sense that others did not trust her. The very indication that she was not trusted provoked an eruption of untrustworthy behavior.

Consistent with many externalizing coping strategies, behaviorally oriented treatments were appropriate, especially those that involved a low level of authoritative direction. Art, occupational therapy, and even cooking provided some sense of relief and hope. Yet the internalizing aspect of the patient's symptoms were not handled by these programs, as attested by her repeated sense of guilt and shame.

D.W. My psychologist was the most compassionate, understanding man I've ever known. I can't help but miss him now. Without him, I would not have recovered to the point I have today. He could say more in fewer words than any other doctor I met, without being vague. I didn't feel he'd tell me just what I wanted to hear either, but would be honest with me even in saying "I don't know" if that was the case. One incident in particular was extremely important to me. It may seem ridiculously stupid, but I had, and still have, some mental conflict in choosing between diet and regular sodas. I know I'm not feeling quite right with myself when I reach for a sugar-free Dr. Pepper. My other doctor shrugged and said it didn't matter. Dr. Beutler, however, stated simply that if I couldn't drink regular soda, I shouldn't drink any. This removed all conflict for me. It gave me a guideline to follow. Using a diet product totally influences my attitude. It makes me feel very hypocritical, and I more easily fall back into old habits of dieting.

Dr. Beutler and I also tried hypnotism. It was an interesting experiment but gave no results, mainly because I never used the cues given to build up my self-confidence. I suppose there was no single program we tried. It was just a good feeling to be treated as an adult, to be listened to, and have my worries and complaints not ignored.

This was also true in group therapy. I had never before been able to discuss my problem with others my age, but since they too had problems, usually alien to me, I felt no insecurity.

I left the hospital when I reached 80 pounds. I went back home with the plan of going to school and staying out of family turmoil. I see a doctor now, about once a month. This is vital. I need someone to listen. I still never talk about this neurosis with my school friends.

Now I live in college dorms. Often I feel very insecure, very "Gooney" and self-conscious around other girls. In some ways the conflict in my mind is even stronger now. I want to gain more weight and yet I'm skeptical of myself and my ability to do this. Self-respect is an important part of my weight level. I find myself in a downward weight trend the minute I lose it. I do get called "skinny," and am sometimes avoided by people because of my appearance, and yes, occasionally throw-up, making self-respect difficult at times. Therapy even today is devoted to building self-confidence and self-respect. These are really the things I need.

My present psychologist and I have tried a reward system for weight gain and, like restrictions, it is too short term of a goal to have any real benefit. I do not want to gain weight for any reason besides gaining weight, and I want to do it to benefit myself, not to please others, as I have a tendency to do.

We're now involved in a program of counting bites. I'm thrilled with this new idea because I feel it may actually help. My biggest worry is still my appetite. Do I have control of it? By counting bites, I know the amount of food I feel comfortable with. I can add or subtract bites to control my calorie intake. Thus it's a reassurance that I do have control, and a self-confidence builder.

Commentary

Consistent with the patient's attachment needs and her high level of reactance, the expression of an "I don't know" enhanced the quality of the therapeutic relationship and had a significantly positive meaning. Providing a nonauthoritarian structure that still allowed choice partially defused the patient's level of reactance. Hypnotism, however, was not well-received. This is not surprising in terms of her dynamics, most notably the level of reactance and the degree of internalization present in her coping style. Her investment in resisting external control is seen in her failure to utilize the cues given in the hypnotic experiment. More important to her treatment was the sense of equality that she was able to establish with the author, partly through an expression of therapist ignorance and partly through a sense that she was trusted as a responsible individual.

CONCLUSION

D.W.'s case represents contrasts with the previous examples. Unlike the previous two illustrations, she displays a consistent emphasis upon the importance of obtaining and maintaining approval and love attachments with peers, authorities, and family members. It is when these attachment needs are no longer being met in the patient's environment that her problems develop. Her behavior vacillates between externalized and internalizing coping strategies, coupled with relatively high levels of reactance.

To some degree an act of self-starvation is an externalized representation of interpersonal conflict, but it is often accompanied by an even more pervasive, internalized coping style. While starvation is uniformly a manipulation of interpersonal relationships, it can also serve the joint purposes of controlling impulses, distracting oneself from conflict, and of self-punishment. In D.W.'s case, there are many indications of fear of her own impulses, self-punishment, and an effort to achieve love and nurturance in the face of emotional starvation. Being fed by her parents, establishing contacts with groups, testing relationships, and competing for parental affection are all apparent in her story.

The significance of the patient's anger toward her father and her fear that she provided the glue that held their marriage together are important issues. She tended to withdraw in the face of conflict and became more intropunitive and increasingly sensitive to bodily processes and to escape through idealistic fantasies. All of these patterns including her development of psychophysiological symptoms suggest an internalizing coping style (Welsh, 1952).

Like most anorexics, D.W. was highly reactant (Hood, Moore & Garner, 1982). However, most are also described as having ambivalent attachments (Bruch, 1978). D.W.'s story defines an attachment orientation. With the foregoing pattern, one sees a degree of hostile-dependence in her relationship to her parents and other authorities.

Accordingly, the treatment of choice is one that combines a broad band focus upon the conflictual theme of ungratified attachment needs, concentrates upon releasing constraints on internal experience, and minimizes the therapist's direction while emphasizing the therapeutic nurturance of the relationship. D.W.'s experience illustrates the failure of therapist controlled behavioral methods observed by Bruch (1974). Because of the medical implications of severe weight loss, behavioral structuring was necessary in this case, but it was most appropriate when emphasizing self-control and when the treatment focus was allowed to move from behavioral to subjective in concert with the patient's vacillating internal/external defensive style.

The most effective intermediate focus in the initial phases of treatment might have been affective awareness and emotional escalation. Even physical discharge of affect may have been appropriate. Two-chair dialogues with parental figures may also have clarified sources of anxiety. D.W. responded well to the emotional qualities of the therapy relationship but without these qualities, insight, perceptual change or behavioral change methods did not work well. Restricting herself from access to her feelings was an important function of her symptoms, and addressing these feelings in therapy was important before issues outside of treatment could be broached.

Therapeutic Process

One sees in the foregoing process that the treatment moved from an emotional enhancement perspective with the intermediate goal of heightening D.W.'s awareness of her feelings to efforts to increase her awareness of the dynamics that characterized her condition. While she continued throughout therapy to have a low tolerance for external structure as entailed in most behaviorally based programs, she was able to accept some contingency contracts whose focus was more internal. A bite counting system, for example, that required self-monitoring and internal rather than external control was approached with some degree of excitement.

It is important to avoid becoming an external advocate for such patients and to avoid involvement in the external management of the patient's caloric intake. While medical conditions dictate that weight be increased, it is often wise to keep the therapeutic relationship separate from any external contingencies in working with the highly reactant individual. This approach allows the patient to develop a therapeutic attachment based upon equality rather than control and is especially useful when the patient has high needs for nurturance.

D.W.'s response to the nurturing elements of treatment allowed her to continue her growth after she left the Methodist Hospital treatment program, when she was forced to separate from nurturing others. As observed in her report, this continued growth was supported through another positive therapeutic alliance. Nonetheless, she continued to have a difficult time whenever externally controlled behavioral programs were imposed, underlining the dominance of her reactance and internal defenses. As such a patient's feelings are increased, explored, and accepted, an increasingly behavioral focus emphasizing personal control can often be utilized in order to assist her in developing self-regard and more direct external coping strategies.

14
Clinical Applications: IV

PREFACE

The prior two clinical examples have represented individuals with moderate to high levels of reactance. Attention is now turned to a patient whose reactance level is relatively low. However, to suggest that an individual has *low reactance* is not to suggest that there is *no reactance*. It will be no surprise, therefore, to observe in the following example that even a patient who is relatively low on the reactance dimension expresses dislike for external controls and authoritative demands. The distinguishing feature of the patient with low reactance is a tendency to comply with external persuasive efforts in spite of his/her dislike. The following clinical example is of an individual who anchored her life by complying with circumstantial requirements and by becoming very concerned with her own responsibility, competence, and achievements.

JANET

I grew up in the home of a minister/teacher, the youngest of three children. My brother is eleven and my sister seven years older than I, so by the age of twelve, I was the only child at home. My parents were married in 1933, and their whole approach to life was molded by the Great Depression. Even after they were fairly comfortable financially, their attitudes toward material possessions remained, "use it up, wear it out, make do, or do without." This was very difficult for me to accept, particularly in high school when I felt that having clothes like my classmates would make me more readily accepted as part of the group. I believe that part of the snobbish, stand-off behavior I have to this day is a result of that. I gained recognition by being "smart," and that wasn't very satisfying.

My father was the absolute authority in our home. A court from which there was no appeal. My choice was to accept the situation as it was or try to manipulate it to get what I wanted. I learned very early that in order to even get heard during a disagreement with my father I had to be able to present my side of the argument logically, rationally, intellectually, and without visible emotion. Feelings were never discussed, never verbalized, and never a factor in reaching a decision. I learned to regard anger as cold silence in my father and as tears in my mother. "Getting upset" put me in a one-down position, and I did everything I could to avoid that. It was impossible for me to please my father and very easy for me to disappoint him. In his effort to make me constantly strive to do my best, he made me feel as though nothing I did was good enough.

My mother was the model of submissive wife who would never confront my father directly, but usually managed to get what she wanted by behind-the-scenes manipulation. I learned to be devious from her, and I learned to lie and manipulate with a guileless expression. When I was thirteen, my mother began having periods of illness. It wasn't until I was sixteen that my parents told me she was going through menopause, and it wasn't until she had a hysterectomy when I was eighteen, that they finally told me the details and just how ill she had been. So for five years I took care of both my mother and father without really knowing why. My mother is not a person who handles illness gracefully, and my father did not lower his expectations as to housekeeping even though I had the demands of school which my mother did not have while she kept house. Since she did not feel badly all of the time, I was constantly having to step into the middle of a chore and finish it. More difficult than the work was not being able to choose when I would do it. She would start the laundry and not be able to finish it, and I would be faced with cooking dinner and finishing the laundry when I got home from school. It made no difference if I had a test or project due the next day. The thing that annoyed me the most was not getting credit for all that I was doing. When guests were invited to our house, I would do all the cleaning, shopping and cooking, and then my mother would come out at the last moment to play hostess. I was expected to fade into the background, keep everything running smoothly, anticipate the needs of both my mother and the guests, so that no one would realize that my mother was not doing anything. All of my anger and resentment became focused on my mother. Since I had no experience or model for expressing my anger and thereby getting rid of it, I turned it in on myself and became more and more depressed.

By the time I was 18 I was having severe anxiety attacks, although at the time I didn't know what was happening to me. It seemed that for no reason I would occasionally be overwhelmed with stomach cramps, a cold sweat, and uncontrollable shaking. This never happened around my parents, and since I was embarrassed and scared, I never talked to anyone about it.

Commentary

From the beginning of her description, one begins to see an emphasis upon achievement, care-giving, and sacrifice emerge in Janet's story. While circumstances and relationships predicated the development of intense anger, it was controlled, contained, and redirected into depression, guilt, and intellectualized pursuits. Psychophysiological symptoms, characteristic of such severe internalization, increased to the point of anxiety attacks.

At this point, it is difficult to gain a clear grasp of the dynamics that characterize Janet's life theme. While there is ample evidence of unfulfilled nurturance and dependency needs, there is no evidence of an attachment pattern. Instead, one sees a gradual withdrawal from people. To the degree that her parental relationships were inconsistent and unpredictable, it may be anticipated that this withdrawal represents the emergence of separation strivings, avoidance in the face of her own anger.

> ***Janet.*** Almost without exception, the only times I got the emotional support I needed from my parents were when I was ill. This was quite reinforcing, and it took many years after I had left my parents' home for me to acknowledge my behavior pattern of "getting sick" when I needed emotional support—and even longer to develop other ways of getting what I needed. One of the hardest discriminations for me to make was seeing that the need for financial support was different from the need for emotional support.
>
> While I was in high school, I spent a lot of time talking to a minister about the problems I was having with my parents, but I never got over my fear that something I said would get back to my father. This perpetuated my habit of previewing everything in my mind before actually saying or doing it.
>
> I married at 19, and the marriage was a disaster from the beginning. It took a year for me to decide that no matter what price I had to pay for the failure of my marriage, I could no longer maintain it, and I filed for divorce.
>
> The price was high. I had cut myself off from almost all support, both emotional and financial. Part of my feelings came out of my own shame at the failure I was and the mess I had made of my life. Another part of my feelings was a reflection of my parents' attitudes and obvious disappointment. Divorce was not an acceptable alternative in solving problems, and since I was unable to talk to my parents about what I had been going through, they saw no reason why I had not been able to work things out. One of the turning points in my relationship with my parents was when my first husband died following surgery for a brain tumor. This provided my parents with a "reason," and therefore they could begin to believe what I had told them about his irrational behavior and violence. But that was two years after my divorce—two years of ever deepening depression.
>
> The only thing I was sure of immediately after my divorce was that I was not going to go back to living with my parents. My anxiety and depression nearly paralyzed me. I was unable to hold a job, and there was no one I felt I could turn to for help. I began drinking heavily and went through several brief, physical relationships that not only didn't help but also increased my feelings of guilt and worthlessness. I was dependent on anybody who could pay for something I needed and constantly compromised myself in order to survive. I found out it was a lot easier to get someone to buy me a drink than a sandwich; the liquor numbed my feelings and gave me an excuse for my behavior.

Commentary

As the patient's story unfolds, her separation drives can be seen more clearly. While she initially made efforts to obtain nurturance and support by "getting sick," a more dominant separation pattern was being developed in which she stressed the need to maintain emotional distance from other people. A marriage designed to escape the family involvement was never allowed to develop warmth or closeness. Cutting herself off from all emotional support and financial assistance also indicates the presence of a dominant separation theme. Nonetheless, the effort to stay distant from her parents coupled with her obvious longings suggest that her avoidance was an apparent counterphobic response to ungratified attachment and dependency needs.

This account further highlights the patient's internalizing coping style. Self-imposed isolation, depression, self-criticism, guilt, and a final retreat to alcoholic withdrawal underline this pattern.

Janet was now cut off from everyone, paralyzed by her own intropunitiveness, and unwilling to allow emotional support from others. Hence, a series of brief, physical relationships that substituted for needed love now became the focus of her life.

Janet. During this time I started seeing a psychiatrist. I didn't trust the idea of psychiatry. As miserable as I was, I feared that change would destroy the things in me which I valued. I saw no hope for gaining anything and did not believe I could survive if I lost anything else. The psychiatrist was a patient man. At the beginning of my treatment, my father was paying him. My father became quite provoked when the doctor told him I had a "neurotic guilt complex" and stopped paying him. I only learned of this several months later when I discovered that the doctor had been seeing me without charge. The doctor expressed enough interest in me that I kept going back every week, and having that one expectation (all I had to do was show up) that I could meet, kept me from committing suicide. In spite of the fact that I later was quite angry at other things he did in the course of my treatment, I had to admit that staying alive was a positive gain.

About a year after I starting seeing this doctor, he asked me to take a personality test for him. When the results came back, we went over them together. He asked me to explain every "key" question the computer had pulled out. Although he tried to make me feel that the test was biased and not accurate, the results were so negative and so official-looking that it further undermined my self-confidence and reconfirmed my fear of "going crazy." The other thing he did that was damaging to me was to prescribe a hypnotic sedative when I complained of having nightmares. He continued to approve refills of the prescription long after I stopped seeing him, and I became quite dependent on the drug. Although I wasn't able to verbalize it at the time, I felt that my dreams were terribly "bad" if he put me on medicine that either kept me from dreaming or kept me from remembering what I dreamed.

I don't recall anything dramatic about leaving treatment with him. I think I just got bored and quit going. Since I didn't solve any problems or come to any better understanding of myself during the two years I saw him, I can say with some assurance that I didn't leave therapy to avoid dealing with specific issues. I was nearly as depressed at the end of the two years as I had been at the beginning, but I had figured out that I could survive.

Commentary

Little can be added to the preceding account to clarify the patient's self-directed anger and sense of defeat. Though she had negative reactions to the treatments prescribed, she continued to comply. This compliant or static resistant pattern illustrates the patient's low level of reactance.

Meanwhile, the patient seems to have been unwilling to get very close to anyone, including the doctor who was treating her. Still, by her report, there is no persuasive evidence to suggest a rebellious or reactant quality to this behavior.

Janet. About a year after I stopped seeing the psychiatrist, I starting dating my present husband. He was in therapy at a clinic that later became a community mental health center. I read every book he had by modern psychologists and psychiatrists—Lowen, Laing, Harris, Bach, Goodman, Jung, Perls, May—and three months later I applied at the center. I was still depressed, but I believed that there was a way out of my morass.

The first thing I did after I got into treatment at the clinic was to get off all the medication I had been taking. I would have been depressed without the medication, but it added to the problem and prevented me from finding any solution.

I also changed jobs and went back to school—made changes faster than I could consolidate them. My husband was "ahead" of me in therapy and gave me constant support and encouragement. I don't think I would have continued treatment during the hard times if it hadn't been for his understanding and willingness to tolerate me "trying my wings." However, since he had been through what I was facing, there were times when it seemed like I was "in therapy" every day instead of once a week.

I learned about three different kinds of therapeutic techniques over the five years I was in treatment at the center. All of them helped me to some extent. The first one I was introduced to, and the one that had the most profound effect on me, was Gestalt Therapy.

It took me a long time and a lot of practice to get much out of "talking to empty chairs," but some aspects of Gestalt Therapy had immediate, beneficial results. The catch words of Gestalt were like handles on a lifeboat to me. Concepts like "here and now" and "what do you feel?" and "flow with it" were like a foreign language to me—a language spoken by "strangers in a strange land." A land that both frightened and fascinated me. It is said that when a person is totally immersed in a foreign language that is one of the signs of beginning to think and dream in that language. As it turned out, "dreaming in Gestalt" was the most singularly important thing that has happened to me in my therapy experience.

I had always had a vibrant and active dream life, and, for the first time, I was able to accept my dreams as an existential statement—they were no longer shameful or frightening or morbid, but a treasure map leading me to the riches of my Self. Sometimes the clues were obscure, but they were always there, luring me forward in an exploration that was seldom what I expected, often unpleasant, but never unsatisfying.

The dreams I worked on in group always brought me a greater understanding of where I was at that moment, and most of them also related to how I had gotten there. In one dream I was escaping from a building along air conditioning ducts that were at an angle and I kept slipping, almost falling off. My therapist had me pretend to be the ducts and then to talk to them. Finally, in frustration, I said, "You aren't supporting me like you should." At that moment in time, my feelings related to my expectations of my husband which I didn't feel he was meeting. That was enough for me to know then. Later the same dream gave me insight into the relationship I had had with my father, how he had never given me the kind of support I needed, and my fear of losing what I needed to survive.

For years I had seen myself as a fragmented person and had been terrified to let go of the scraps of "sanity" I thought I had. Slowly the Biblical injunction that one must die to be born again had meaning. I had to let go of my sanity—if only for a few brief moments—to find the parts of me that I had lost. I had to learn that every thought and feeling I had were mine—to accept them, then to own them, and finally to rejoice in having them. My dreams led me unerringly into one conflict after another. Little by little I worked through ambiguous feelings about my parents, conflicting expectations of my husband, restraints I had placed on myself. My terrors lost their power when exposed to my group-friends. I found that nothing is as shameful in the telling as in the hiding.

As I played all the roles and parts of my dreams, I learned to accept my feelings without judging them. I was so full of "shoulds" and "oughts"—parental injunctions and judgments—that I almost couldn't function for worrying. My husband used to complain that I wasn't spontaneous—but how could I be spontaneous if I had to figure out what I *ought* to do in every situation? I had to learn that my feelings were just feelings; that anger didn't kill. Knowing how I felt truly gave me control over my actions, whereas not knowing left me at the mercy of overwhelming emotions.

Commentary

As would be expected in an internalizing, emotionally constricted patient, therapy procedures that were devoted to emotional escalation and awareness seemed to trigger a good deal of emotional relief. Given her relatively low level of reactance, she tolerated a fair amount of therapist involvement and guidance in the utilization of Gestalt methodologies. Yet it is intriguing that, unlike those described earlier, this patient focused upon the therapeutic procedures rather than upon the treatment relationship. This focus upon strategy and activity rather than upon quality of interpersonal contact probably underlines again her intellectualized defenses and investment in maintaining distance from her therapist. Yet the experiential procedures were designed to make her aware of and to intensify her feelings. These highly directed procedures seem to have provoked satisfying movement. Along the way, she was apparently able to develop a satisfying and gratifying relationship with her husband, quite unlike any achieved before.

Janet. During my first year in therapy, my therapist also introduced me to Transactional Analysis (TA). The biggest advantage to TA is an easily understood language. It is clear what Berne (1961) and Harris (1967) meant by the Parent-Adult-Child terminology. While Gestalt therapy opened upon all of my "child" feelings—both the o.k. kid and the not-o.k. kid—TA taught me how to express those feelings in an adult mode. Understanding the basic TA definitions let me look at my relationships with other people and to figure out what they were doing and how I was reacting that got us at cross purposes.

I was having a lot of difficulty getting along with one of my bosses at this time. I decided to put our interactions into a TA framework. I realized that we both bounced back and forth between our parent and not-o.k. kid ego states, and did so in perfect counterpoint. One day I went to the office determined that no matter what he said or did, I was going to "stay in my adult." The results were fantastic. Within a week all the relationships within the office were smooth and mellow, and this boss and I developed a friendship that went beyond a good working relationship. I also learned a lesson that has served me well in every job I've had since then.

After this major success, I decided to put all I had learned about trusting my feelings and acting out of an adult position into relating to my father. The first disagreement we had after I had determined that I did not have to react to him as a not-o.k. kid was nearly a disaster. The strain left me physically exhausted. I maintained my position, however, and every small indication that our relationship was changing for the better encouraged me to pursue it a little further. Along the way I had had some insights into my feelings about my father that helped me when I doubted that changing our relationships was worth the effort. Once I had anticipated a conflict (which never materialized) and had been working on it in group one evening. I wasn't getting very far talking to my father in the empty chair, when my therapist sat down in the chair holding a folded mat in front of him. He told me to "hit my father." I really fought with my avoidance and finally struck the mat. I was gritting my teeth, punching at the mat, when tears started running down my cheeks, and I realized that while I was hitting the mat away from me with the right hand, I was pulling it toward me with my left hand. My anger and my longing were inseparable.

Years later, after working to develop an open and adult relationship with my father, all of my defenses dissolved, and I crawled into his lap like a helpless two-year-old and, crying, told him that my husband and I had separated. I had doubted his love; I had hated him for the way he made me be to please him; but as he rocked and comforted me, I knew I could never doubt his intentions, and I cried for all the years of our ignorance.

We still have disagreements, and situations come up that trigger old bitter feelings in me, but I usually am aware of what is happening and can let the feelings pass without acting on them. It has been hard for me to accept my father as he is. My expectations of who he should be cloud our relationship, and I don't know if I'll ever resolve that conflict.

When my husband and I reconciled, my parents were the first to know and share our joy. They had changed over the years too, and were able to accept us both for the poeple we were. I feel quite close to both of my parents now, and writing this has been very difficult for me. It is unpleasant for me to go back in my thoughts and feelings to the anger and bitterness of my childhood. It makes me uncomfortable to realize that after all these years and all the changes, I still act in many ways out of my need to be different from them.

Commentary

As would be predicted from our model for this patient, therapist directed emotional escalation and awareness procedures seem to have been satisfactorily followed by a cognitive and perceptual change methodology in the form of Transactional Analysis (T.A.). T.A. is largely a therapist-directed cognitive change procedure designed to instill new "tapes" or programs for the patient to rehearse and practice in order to combat old learning. Beyond this reprogramming goal, T.A. is an insight and awareness procedure, both components of which the patient found effective and helpful in coping with her interpersonal relationships. The conceptual awareness and perceptual change procedure provided the patient with a means of establishing interpersonal contact without threatening identity diffusion. In this process, significant changes occurred in her parental relationships, and she began investing less energy in being different.

Janet. I changed from a male to a female therapist, still at the clinic, and both the one I left and the one I went to were experimenting with "bioenergetic" techniques. I have strongly mixed feelings about this method of therapy. The good things I got from it are easy for me to see. It helped me use my body to express my feelings—particularly anger, which was very difficult for me. I became aware of my body and gained a great deal of confidence about my appearance. The breathing exercises and relaxation techniques led me to a feeling that is difficult to describe, of being centered within myself. I don't think, however, that any of this would have been possible without the years of Gestalt work that preceded. My "being in my head" was my weakness, but it was also my strength, and affective expression without cognitive understanding is useless to me. If I had not come to a complete acceptance of the Gestalt position that feelings are just feelings and are not good or bad, I would have never allowed myself to express my anger, fear, and sorrow in a bioenergetic setting.

I think one of the dangers that a therapist should avoid is becoming too personally involved with his patients in a social way. And I think this is more likely to happen with the more dedicated and sensitive therapist. I was particularly close to my first therapist—he had dinner with my husband and me almost every week after group. I was flattered by his attention, and I honestly think he found us to be interesting people. We were both excited about therapy and read the same books he did. And we looked up to him as a guide and mentor. The closeness of our social relationship, however, grew to the point that he "eased up" on me in groups and didn't really push me when a shove would have been beneficial. He came to trust my insights into other people, and I moved into the role of a sort of "junior" therapist in my group. This caused two major problems—one, I became more interested in looking at other people than at myself which significantly slowed down my progress in dealing with my own problems, and, two, it set me apart from the group in a way that was not helpful since one of my biggest problems was in relating to other people as an equal.

Commentary

In the foregoing one continues to see the patient's focus upon therapeutic strategy rather than therapeutic relationship. She responded poorly to an externally focused treatment procedure in the form of bioenergetic massage. This response could be anticipated in view of her internalizing coping strategy. By the same token, her drives for separation led her to have a negative reaction to a therapist who made efforts to become personally involved. While one may criticize the degree of involvement that the therapist imposed on the relationship, the incident, nonetheless, underscores this patient's inability to pursue therapeutic work under conditions that don't allow separation.

Janet. For the most part, my years at the clinic were very good for me. I learned to identify my feelings and trust what I felt. I learned to express my feelings in a way that was both acceptable and got me what I needed. When my husband and I moved to a larger city for the opportunities it offered in jobs and schooling, we were fairly well able to make it on our own. We still missed having someone to talk to and the community of friends we had developed, but our relationship was such that we could work out our differences and function in our new location.

Then one morning I left the house to walk to the bus stop as I did every morning to go to work, and a man ran up behind me, attacked me, and raped me in our neighbor's front yard. No one word can describe the experience, although devastating probably comes closest. When I was asked if I wanted to join a therapy group of other women who had been raped, I accepted. I had known the feelings of fear and helplessness, but never with such intensity. And for the first time in my life, I've had to learn to live with my blinding rage.

The greatest insight for me relating to this experience is the discovery that there are many ways of being "raped." Every experience I have had of being used against my will, although there were not the sexual implications, had the same affective components. The fear I felt was a magnification of every time I had been afraid. My feelings of anxiety and anger opened old wounds that I thought had healed. I questioned my entire way of living, trying to figure out why this had happened to me. So, added to my terror were tormenting feelings of self-doubt.

It has been six months now since I was attacked, and it is still very difficult to write about it. Particularly when I am alone in the house, the fear and anxiety swell up in my chest and I get up and pace the floor trying to release some of the tension. I have worked through most of my doubts about myself and have arrived at some convictions about how I believe I would act if I am ever threatened in that way again. I take my greatest comfort from knowing that even this horrible experience has not been without positive side effects. My husband and I have become much closer. Our surviving this extreme disruption in our lives by sharing our feelings about what happened and the ways in which we reacted to it has deepened our understanding and commitment. My co-workers have been very understanding and supportive, which has been important to me in rebuilding my sense of self-esteem. And the therapy group has been very good for me. I have come to appreciate how much strength is generated in a group of people who are willing to relate on the most intimate level. I am aware that it is very important to me to have a group of people to whom I can relate in this way. I know that it doesn't have to be a large group, and I know it doesn't have to be a "therapy" group, but I hope I never again underestimate my need for friends with whom I can share both my joy and my sorrow and fear.

Commentary

In Janet's final crisis, the distinction between complex adjustment patterns and habit patterns are clear. The treatment described by the patient thus far had approached issues that evolved from nuclear conflicts in her early life and had pervaded two marriages and many social relationships. However, the response to her rape experience remained more constricted. While clearly personally involving to the point of reengendering many early conflicts, the impact of the crisis was primarily in terms of its threat to the patient's sense of separation and autonomy. Unlike many rape victims, for example, this patient did not go through withdrawal of any sexual contact, break up with her sexual partner, or subsequently undermine her job or interpersonal relationships. While many individuals engage in self-destructive behavior patterns after a rape experience, this patient did not. Her ability to keep the reaction relatively confined to the situation specific cues suggests that this reaction was quite different from those that previously pervaded her life. Indeed, the experience allowed her to move even closer to her husband and to establish greater and more mature attachments.

Janet. Looking back over the time I have spent in therapy, the best analogy I can think of to describe my experiences is that of a chick trying to break out of his egg. I reached the point where my "egg" was cramped instead of cozy, stifling instead of secure. My therapists gave me the tools to break the shell, the encouragement to look around in my brand new, scary, enormous world, and the often-repeated statement that I had done it myself.

I did a lot of chirping and ran around exploring and testing my new environment. After a while, however, I made the inevitable and discouraging discovery that all I had been "born" into was a larger "egg." And the whole process of change started over again. I was anxious, tried to shore up my defenses, convincing myself that what I had found in my new way of living was really all there was, all I needed. But the feeling that there was something more persisted, and the frustration and curiosity in me built to the point where I looked for new tools and chipped away at my new "shell." I don't know how many times I went through this during my years of therapy, but I am finally at the point of accepting the limits of the "egg" I live in, and the changes have become modifications instead of "breaking out" experiences.

I was 20 years old when I first saw a psychiatrist, and now I'm 31. I feel like I've been a long time on the road of self-exploration. The differences in the way I feel now and how I felt a few years ago, is that I no longer want the road to end. I hope that I continue to grow in self-awareness, self-contentment, and self-esteem.

CONCLUSIONS

Janet represents the manner in which a person might develop internalized and compartmentalized defenses against emotional stress. Instead of adopting a pattern of hypersensitivity to physical functioning and then emotionally separating herself from her feelings, Janet utilized more intellectualizing defenses to build impermeable walls around her emotions. In this, she is similar to D.W. but without the degree of vacillation between these internalized coping strategies and the development of externalized ones. In Janet's case, the number of external coping strategies was relatively small, being best represented by momentary excursions into alcoholic indulgence and transient sexual relationships.

One can see the dominant striving for separation from others that characterized this patient. Her effort to be different from her parents illustrates this kind of movement away from people. This movement was far from being detached, however, as can be seen by the tremendous amount of emotion that was stirred in response to others. Indeed, she was capable of establishing reasonably warm relationships as long as they were not too close, nurturing, or overwhelming. Attachments were apparently "dangerous." Hence, there are many examples in her presentation where she sought separation even while expressing the desire for support. "Support," however, implies considerably less intimacy and closeness than nurturance.

There are additional evidences of Janet's struggle for separation in her relationships with others. The situation at home was difficult. Her response was to separate from family but to move into a relationship that still provided little in the way of nurturance. She subsequently separated from her therapist, her first husband, and even underwent a temporary separation with her second husband. The process of therapy tended to bring her closer to nurturant relationships, as one can see in her sudden flow of feeling toward her father at a later point in treatment. Indeed, her emerging acceptance of the denied attachment need is a signal characteristic of her treatment process. Her ability to recognize the combination and juxtaposition of anger and longing indicates significant movement from a dominant theme of separateness to one which healthily recognizes both strivings toward and away from people.

Finally, there is little to suggest more than momentary expressions of high reactance. She complied with medical regimens even when she saw them as doing little good; she complied with psychotherapeutic strategies (bioenergetics) when it made little sense, and only once when withdrawn from medication did she show rebellion to those rules governing her treatment. Parental rules were internalized self-punitively and led her to become guilt-ridden and depressive in her striving for perfection and equality. This intropunitive style, coupled with her relatively low level of reactance made her a prime candidate for self-defeating behavior. Any effort to externalize anxiety through acting out (alcohol abuse or sexual behavior) simply renewed her sense of guilt and shame, driving her ever inward in a depressogenic fashion.

Treatment Process

The patient makes very clear that she had a negative reaction to a number of efforts to provide attachment. More importantly, however, externally focused procedures did not serve the needs of this patient. Even the use of an external agent such as medication was received without benefit. She had an excessively strong reaction to the medication, feeling that it numbed her intellectual processes (especially important in view of her investment in intellectual endeavors) and prevented adequate problem solving. Not only did it encourage her habit of substance abuse, but it communicated that she was sick and out of control—another indication of how her intropunitive attributions produced further guilt.

Finally, the patient was able to get into an ongoing treatment program and was able to get off medications. Her initial contact with Gestalt Therapy produced substantial improvement. Gestalt Therapy entails a great deal of therapist involvement and direction, albeit with an internal focus and a devotion to affective awareness rather than behavioral control. The acts of allowing, knowing, and exaggerating feelings were appropriate and produced substantial change. Affective escalation methods as well as feeling awareness procedures were valuable. The use of dreamwork moved the patient through the barriers she had erected against her own angry feelings. The insight producing nature of this dream work was also helpful. The task of letting go of emotional control was facilitated by both feeling awareness and insight forces which were at work. Group support facilitated her letting go of rules and increasing her feeling awareness and self-acceptance.

The affective awareness and escalation procedures were followed by a cognitive insight and perceptual change procedure in the form of Transactional Analysis. This system seems to have given the patient a conceptual framework by which to understand her feelings while also providing insight into how relationships with her parents had been brought into the present. While the affective enhancement and release procedures opened the patient to her feelings, the cognitive training procedures brought skills for facilitating impulse control. These procedures also changed her perceptions of both her role with her parents and her own self-worth. Ultimately, they resulted in behavior changes being manifest toward her employer and her parents, the third step in the affective to cognitive to behavioral change sequence.

The patient's reaction to her rape experience illustrates the importance of adopting a narrow band treatment strategy for situational reactions. The fact that her anxiety attacks were confined to the situation in which the rape occurred rather than broadly impacting and reinstituting the totality of her previous difficulties, may clarify why she did not respond as well as some others to the experiential treatment procedures that had affected her positively in her previous experience (see Cryer & Beutler, 1980). A symptom focused anxiety management procedure would have been appropriate at that point. In most respects, the patient underwent the normal course of grief, using what she had obtained in her previous therapy to help her keep the symptoms and behaviors from generalizing and from reengendering the self-destructive forces that had earlier characterized her pattern of adjustment. She emerged a stronger, more capable woman who still retained her valued intellectual growth but without sacrificing emotional closeness and support as well.

The patient's analogy of hatching into every increasing eggs is of particular note. Treatment is a process not an end point, and one moves from one stage of life to another. Similarly, therapy moves from one stage to another, accommodating as the patient changes from an internal to a more flexible, external coping strategy.

15

Clinical Applications: V

PREFACE

The final clinical example emphasizes the necessity of intertwining broad and narrow band treatments. When specific symptoms become so overwhelming as to mitigate against the patient's successful adjustment in a variety of situations, narrow band treatments must be implemented in spite of the dynamic conflicts that may be represented. Until such symptoms can be controlled, they may prevent fruitful development of thematic approaches.

The patient to be described presents pronounced psychophysiological symptoms. Such symptoms represent a dilemma in psychosomatic theory. The traditional distinction between conversion symptoms, hypochondriacal patterns, and other psychophysiological patterns is difficult to make in contemporary thought (Kimball, 1970; Pilowsky, 1969). A determination of the defensive style represented by such a patient, therefore, must reside on a broad constellation of information pertaining to habitual ways of coping with stress.

M.A.

The aroma of roasting turkey filled the house and the sounds of family and friends talking and laughing created the festive holiday feeling that is common for Thanksgiving Day. I lay on my bed, feeling the throbbing of my head with each beat of my heart. The blinds were closed in an attempt to darken the room and ease the pain of the light of day. I was experiencing the first of a great number of migraine headaches. I had just recently turned nine years old. From that day to the present I have dragged myself through hundreds of migraines, ranging in severity from terrible to totally incapacitating. If I were to enumerate the medications I have taken it would read like the inventory of the corner pharmacy.

I was the fifth of seven children, born to parents who were emotionally unstable, bad tempered, and impossible both to live with and to please. My older brother (S.) and two older sisters (K. and J.) were my mother's favorites. My father had no favorites. My younger sister (C.) and I were both "unplanned" and consequently suffered with our parents' inability to accept us. My childhood was traumatic, to say the least.

My parents were probably the most mismatched couple in history. Neither of them was a particularly good role model for how to cope. Mom was a high strung, emotionally unstable, demanding, perfectionist, who was prone to migraine headaches and various other physical difficulties. She was well-read, educated, intellectual, and outgoing. I'm quite sure there were few women who could match her skill as a Registered Nurse. However, when it came to understanding a little girl's needs, she came up short. I was physically and emotionally abused by her throughout my childhood and teenage years. When we finally came to a rewarding relationship, I was in my early twenties, and it was over too soon. She died at the age of fifty-eight. I was only twenty-seven years old.

For many years Dad was a theater manager and also worked in copper mining. His excessive drinking interfered with and ultimately cost him both of these jobs. Dad was a one-of-a-kind combination of brains, sharp wit, and explosive temper. It was always easy for him, even in his state of drunkenness, to reduce me to a shivering, weeping "good for nothing" with his volatile temper, bombastic voice, and hands of steel. I lived in dread fear of him. Today he is a vegetating alcoholic with precious little awareness of the present. However, even now I am grossly uncomfortable when I am with him. We had no relationship in the past, so I suppose it's fruitless either to bemoan the lack of friendship now or to begrudge the fact that we will have none in the future.

In my childhood, the relationship with my parents was, at best, strained. It seems to me that my fruitless struggle to please them, coupled with regular emotional and physical abuse led to and fed my childhood headaches. During their temper outbursts they nearly always hit me in the face and head. I suffered an inferiority complex and poor self-image. I was constantly compared to my older sisters and brother. It was as if I had no personal identity at all. How I hated it! But I never stopped striving to be loved by them, accepted by them, and to meet their seemingly insurmountable standards. I lived in a constant state of guilt—guilt both because I wasn't capable of living up to their expectations and because I was never good enough for them.

Commentary

One begins to see in M.A.'s description of her family a strong and punitive mother and a clearly abusive and detached father. In this, one notes her hunger for attachment and nurturance. The inconsistency of her mother may have been particularly seductive in reinforcing the patient's nurturance and dependency needs. Her sense of inadequacy was clearly reinforced in the face of intense external expectations coupled with physical and emotional abuse.

M.A. Most of the women in my family have suffered with migraines to a greater or lesser degree. At least during those times of my pain, Mom was somewhat understanding, probably because she too suffered severe emotional stress, intense marital difficulties, and unbearable migraine pain. I'm sure she understood the severity of the pain. When my headaches were very severe, she would give me an Empirin #3. If she wasn't home and I was at the peak, I would take one myself.

In my childhood, the headaches were few and far between, However, puberty, menstruation, and the struggles of adolescence accelerated them. By the time I was fourteen, my oldest sister, K., who was my sounding board and shoulder to cry on, got married and moved away. J., my model and closest companion, was away in a convent. S. went to high school and worked outside the home and studied at the library as often as possible to escape the wrath at home. Mom worked full time. Dad worked at the mine. By the process of elimination, guess who was left to care for my invalid brother and to be mother and protector of C.? I never knew when Dad would come home late for dinner, drunk, irritable, and violent. I can vividly recall the pain creep up the back of my neck as the anxiety peaked and as I worried whether or not he would beat me or the others. I took innumerable APCs in those traumatic days. I just wanted to cope. I was convinced that I was inferior and incapable of being worthwhile. They had taught me well, and I reacted like putty, always soft and easily manipulated.

When I was eighteen, I became ill and had my appendix removed. I awoke with a terrible headache that didn't subside for several days. It was during this time that I was introduced to Demerol, both as a post-operative analgesic and as ammunition to combat the throbbing in my head. I discovered that a migraine which would normally last 6–24 hours without this superdrug, could be controlled with it. It seemed all too natural and easy to call for Demerol rather than to fight it out on aspirin-based remedies. There were always pain meds in the house, usually codeine. It was easily accessible and neither Mom, Dad, nor I seemed to care if I took it.

I trod through my teenage years battling the nightmare of several severe migraines per month while quietly putting up with an irrational, abusive father and a demanding mother whom I was convinced didn't love me. I wasn't a particularly good student. I believe I could have done better had I received encouragement or a demonstration of love and faith. But it was not there, so I existed by creating a fantasy of being loved, being worthwhile to someone, and living a pain-free life. The natural course of events led to rebelling as I grew older. If they told me to be home at a certain time, I would be fifteen minutes late. I would dawdle over simple household chores for three to five times longer than necessary. In spite of the beatings and constant criticism, at least I received some kind of attention. My final reaction was despair. Perhaps the numerous headaches were an escape from the reality around me. Time does pass, thank God, and through it all I remained optimistic that sooner or later my life would get better.

Commentary

By now the patient's intense need to please was becoming more dominant, but with it came a sense of total futility and failure. The patient turned increasingly toward emotional withdrawal and fantasy. Ample models of physical pain were available in family members, and it was apparently through pain that the patient was able to avoid conflict and engender some nurturance.

Finally, one observes in M.A.'s adolescence a period of what may have been relatively high reactance. She reports that during this period she did the opposite of what was advocated by her parents. This pattern stands at some contrast to her earlier descriptions of herself as "putty."

M.A. I graduated from high school and stepped out boldly to face the world. I was undecided as to what job or career I wanted. I knew a lot of typical women's jobs that I didn't want. My parents convinced me that I wasn't smart enough to go to college. Five months after graduation a friend of mine talked a dentist friend of his into training me as a Dental Assistant.

I will never forget that cold rainy day when I arrived on the scene knowing absolutely nothing about dentistry. I had only been to a dentist as a patient twice in my life. But oh, what a challenge! I loved it from the start and discovered I was good with my hands, plus I loved the people. Finding myself and liking my job as a dental assistant did not, however, put an end to my migraines. If anything, they just grew up along with me. I soon found myself caught in a two-way trap. I didn't want anyone to know I was plagued by headaches and neither did I want to lose time from work because of them. Consequently, I began reaching for pain medications more and more of the time. It was via the ever-abundant supply of pharmaceuticals that I got used to taking Darvon Compound 65.

It never dawned on me that I was growing dependent on pain pills. All I knew was that I was in pain a great deal of the time and I needed and wanted to work, regardless. I joined the Dental Assistant's Association and moved rapidly up the ladder of professional and political success. I drove myself physically and emotionally to be the best. I revelled in the accomplishments, the never-ending stream of interesting and intelligent people, and the fast-paced, ever changing world of new ideas and exciting people who treated me as an equal, a professional—one of them. I finally fit in. I was accepted, I belonged and was appreciated and rewarded as me for me; not as a "dummy" and for once in my life, I was not compared to my siblings.

Commentary

In M.A.'s description of her life to this point, the striving for excellence as a reflection of her need for approval and nurturance is clear. In her work, however, she found more suitable means for approval than she had previously. In spite of her continuing reliance upon medication, it did not unduly interfere with her professional development. It is here that the best historical indications of the patient's low level of reactance are observed. She was driven to success and the acceptance it brought. The rebelliousness which may have temporarily characterized her adolescence disappeared.

M.A. I married my high school sweetheart. I knew that I was not totally in love with H. but hoped I would grow to love him. I was sure H. loved me but I had never really been loved before, so I didn't actually know how to respond. Our life together was far from what I had expected it to be. We were fairly compatible on a day-to-day basis but had little in common as far as lifetime goals or achievements were concerned. I lived in a world of migraine headaches. I worked full time or part time depending on whether or not I was pregnant or taking care of our little children.

The pride and joy and love of my life, K.M., arrived in 1966. It was then that life really began anew for me. I poured all of myself and every ounce of love I could muster into that little girl. Needless to say, the arrival of J.W. in 1968 was the next brightest star. There was never a more perfect little boy born. He was fulfilling to a mama who desperately needed someone on which to shower all the love, happiness and excitement of life; all these things I never received.

Both of my pregnancies were plagued with incapacitating migraines. Fortunately for both of my lovely children, I never hurt either of them during pregnancy by the scores of Fiorinal with codeine I took.

Commentary

With her marriage and birth of two children, the patient's needs for belonging and attachment at last began to be gratified. Still, the psychophysiological symptoms persisted and with them the use of numerous medications. Nevertheless, she apparently still functioned adequately in work and marriage.

M.A. During my marriage and early motherhood, neither my husband nor I understood why I practically lived with a migraine. On the outside I was a normal, healthy, physically active, mentally strong young woman. I still looked and felt like a teenager. The doctors in my life had no answer for my pain, and since there was no obvious cause, they just kept me supplied with pain medication. I was never at a loss for something strong for the pain.

Meanwhile, my husband and I grew steadily apart. My husband's attitude was that our problems were all my fault. True to my routine of "accepting the guilt" I took him at his word, decided to leave and moved out, partially to get a fresh start, and partially to escape from my father's threat to kill me if I broke up my family.

A fresh start is an understatement. I was really green, but I decided I had to be in charge of myself. The kids were 4 and 2; now that's nearly babies! I recall facing myself in the mirror early one morning and giving myself a pep talk. I convinced myself that win or lose, it would very definitely be my responsibility; this time I was on my own!

At the outset the kids stayed with H. At the least I needed to land a secure, full-time job in order to provide a roof over our heads. I interviewed for jobs until my resume was dog-eared and tired and so was I. But it had its rewards. I was hired to work in the dental department of a hospital.

Well, rewarding job or no, my home life crumbled. In spite of numerous tries at reconciliation, our marriage was ended. With the dissolution of my marriage, a custody battle over the kids, a new job, finances tighter than skin on a grape, and assuming the role of single parent; I had headaches! Big ones, little ones, daily ones, and occasionally knock-me-down-go-to-bed ones. For the most part, my behavior for coping remained much the same. I lived on Darvon much of the time, with an occasional injection of Demerol that would wipe me out for 24 hours. We managed though, thanks to good neighbors and terrific friends who would take over where I left off.

All things considered, I was at last free and for the most part happy. I spent most of my waking, non-working hours with the children. We read and sang, learned new prayers, went on picnics, listened to classical music, and played tickle on the bed. We grew as a little family, the three of us, into a close-knit, marvelous relationship of friend-to-friend which added to the conventional parent/child relationship. I wanted to give and share and be all the parental goodies for my kids that I so desperately wanted, obviously needed, and sorely lacked. I never wanted my kids to grow up with a giant gaping hole in their hearts and a constant question: "Am I OK?" "Do you really love me?"

Commentary

The patient's struggle with her first marriage and her emphasis on her children underlines again her need for attachment and belonging. Her frustrations and efforts to reinstigate a life of her own were approached with renewed commitment but were met with frustration. By this point, the pattern of feeling abused and rejected was probably well-established and was again pervading much of her life. In spite of her continuing efforts to establish an attachment relationship with others, few were successful. Consequently, she withdrew again as she had in childhood, pulling back and investing her energies in fertilizing the relationships with her children. Meanwhile, her use of medication and the intensity of migraine headaches and other psychophysiological symptoms remained and perhaps even increased with the stress. Conflicts were dealt with, it seems, by internalizations of guilt, resulting in depression and anxiety, as well as emotional and social constriction.

M.A. Then one day, just as I was beginning to work, I received the blow of my life. My sister called me to tell me that Mom had died. I picked up the loose ends, gathered the kids and told them what had happened, and headed for home. Those were probably the worst five days of my life. I was met by a barrage of "You killed her!" from my Dad to "I hope you're happy" and "see what you've done!" from my brother. I was absolutely unprepared for this reaction and suffered severe migraines and a deep emotional hurt. The shock and frustration they put me through made me shut off my grief. I never let loose and cried over Mom. I locked away both positive and negative attitudes toward my family and suffered 4 or 5 migraines a week for nearly nine months. I took Darvon Compound like shelled peanuts to control the pain and help me through this nightmare.

A dulling of the sense of loss finally came after nearly a year. I kept on with my job and was grateful for work to bury myself in. My job suffered though, and my caring attitude did too. The area of my life that suffered the least during this time, as always, was the love of and caring for and happiness I derived from the children.

In nearly three years of living alone my love life sagged. I was too devoted to the kids to leave them with babysitters any more than necessary. Besides, I wasn't in a mood to get romantically involved. I was convinced I didn't want to get married again. Then I met A. At first I held him, and the whole world for that matter, at arm's length. A. turned out to be the best thing that ever happened to me. We dated for about a year and a half before getting married. We had long talks, discussed the world, and everything imaginable. We faced every issue that came to mind and, of course, that included my eight- and ten-year-old children.

The first two years were not bad at all. There were good times, and we all adjusted quite well together. The kids blossomed and changed in a positive way, having a full-time, stay-at-home Mom. During those fun and changing two years, I had fewer migraines than at any other time in my adult life. A lot of pressures were off of me; I felt loved and was happy and fulfilled.

Commentary

The patient's emotional and social withdrawal is seen more clearly as the difficulties with her parents re-emerged. Her tendency to turn inward, internalize stress, and pull back on her impulses continued to dominate her, while her need for close attachments solidified as a thematic pattern. Her sexual attachments apparently declined with ever-increasing emphasis placed upon obtaining gratification through the children.

Finally, M.A. was able to develop a love relationship. By this point, her internalizing stance in dealing with problems was well-developed, the psychophysiological reactions were clearly established, her reliance on pain medications was long-standing, and her tendency to become compliant in an effort to obtain external reassurance had returned to baseline. Nonetheless, stress was lessened with the presence of a nurturing relationship, and she noted a decline in the severity and frequency of her headaches.

M.A. Deep down inside my psyche was changing. For the first time in my life, I had time to face myself and realize more of the intricacies that made me tick. One thing which I had a very hard time adjusting to was having physical and material needs met without having to shed blood, sweat and tears, in return. The headaches began to return more frequently and more severe than ever before. I began a merry-go-round of daily Tylenol with codeine and frequent trips to the doctor's office or to the Emergency Room for shots of Demerol and Phenergan. I began feeling useless, lethargic, and frustrated. In May, 1979 I was diagnosed as having two large ulcers, one gastric and one duodenal. I was hospitalized for seven weeks. The anger I felt at being sick accentuated my migraines. I took enormous amounts of Demerol.

At the end of the hospital stay I was ready to come home, but I was despondent and depressed. I went through weeks of feeling inadequate and useless. I developed Pyloric Valve Dumping Syndrome and was hospitalized more times than I can remember for nausea, vomiting, diarrhea, and dehydration, along with nearly uncontrollable migraines. The doctors who cared for me were afraid that I might become emotionally or physically addicted to Demerol. All I knew was I had the pain and I needed relief. Migraines were now controlling almost 50 percent of my life. I was miserable, the kids were confused and unhappy, and A. turned into an overprotective parent. I lost my drive, my independence, and my zest for life.

Commentary

The patient's internalization of stress is now clearly seen. She had learned that attachment, nurturance and love were to be purchased with later suffering and pain. At this point, when her life should have been comfortable and settled, her pain increased, other psychophysiological symptoms developed, and she became aware that she was emotionally dependent on Demerol. While the pain and agony gave her a reason for receiving nurturance, it also seemed to provide the punishment that her guilt demanded for receiving more than she had been taught she deserved. At this point, it was impossible to separate psychological precursors of pain from physical ones.

M.A. By September, I was at the end of my rope. I was sent back to a neurologist who, in turn, referred me to the Chief of Psychiatry at the University. There was one alternative to try to help me; an admission to the Psychiatric Ward for evaluation, counseling, and testing. I reluctantly agreed and was admitted the next day. I was sure I was not psychotic and didn't understand the need for psychiatric care to cure my headaches. I felt like a stranger in no-man's land. The staff utilized hypnosis, biofeedback training, counseling, group therapy, and genuinely taught me to get in touch with myself.

Surprisingly enough, I discovered there were strengths and abilities deep down inside of me that I never imagined that I had. Having been brainwashed in my childhood, it was no small task to reverse my self-doubts and opinions and to think and act as a normal, well-adjusted, useful, intelligent human being. I had the support of the staff to nudge me up the ladder of self-esteem, one rung at a time, until I began to see myself as I really am. They spent hour after hour with me; listening, understanding, and offering suggestions on how to change. In retrospect, I must admit I wanted to give up and drift off into oblivion with a stiff boost of Demerol, knowing that I would awaken without the pain; but it was not to be that way.

Six days passed. There were times when the pain was so severe I could hardly breathe. During those early times I thought I'd die, wished I would, and was afraid I wouldn't. At last, the turning point came! I fell into an exhausted sleep that lasted about seven hours. When I awoke the pain wasn't gone but was miraculously lessened, and I felt as though I had conquered the world. It was almost incredible! I'd conquered a monster without the aid of drugs of any kind. It had taken courage. The pretty dark-haired nurse who had talked me through the harrowing severity of the throbbing, pulsating pain had been successful in teaching me how to breathe and relax, how to expect spasms of pain and ride them through. I was a survivor, a winner! I never dreamed it could possibly happen. For once in my life I said to myself, "I'm OK." A glimmer of hope shone and I felt that if I could do it once, I could do it again. I can never remember having felt so free and relieved.

Commentary

Now with her symptoms so intense, the patient required intensive treatment. It was on entry to University Hospital that the author was asked to develop a pain management program. At admission, psychological assessment confirmed a pattern of emotional isolation, constriction, and guilt indicative of internalization.

The patient's felt need for external nurturance and support was challenged by a program that both provided drug withdrawal and insisted that she confront her pain and fears. The attachment and support needs were also seen, however, in the quality of the treatment alliance developed with the nursing staff. She was compliant with instructions in spite of the difficulties described. With the support and nurturance provided by therapeutic staff officers, she was able to experience a sense of self-reliance and competence that was unfamiliar and new to her.

M.A. Winning once obviously didn't convince me the war was over. I'm not that naive. The war may never end, but I'd won a significant battle. Now I needed to learn more about causes and early signs so I could catch myself before the pain reached proportions that I couldn't handle again. This was learned slowly and with all the help I could muster. I was skeptical at first and of course scared. It didn't seem possible, but I was to come to the realization that these people weren't going to back down on their stand to have me see this through without drugs.

To start with, they armed me with a relaxation therapy tape. The contraction/relaxation exercise seemed to help me overall, not just in minimizing the headache. I felt less tense and uptight from the beginning. By feeling less tense I was more in tune with all my feelings and was able to deepen my understanding of why I was in pain as well as how to be "Boss" over it.

Here at last, at my disposal, were people who were more than pill pushers and bed makers. No misconception intended, the nurses and other medical personnel I've dealt with in the past were certainly not incompetents. It's just that this group helped me to explore the depths of my mind and, most important, they helped me begin to take a bold, glaring look at myself.

Commentary

The initial treatment focus was narrow band and internally focused, aiming particularly at the patient's subjective pain and anxiety. Concomitantly, however, support was required that centered around conflictual themes of attachment and nurturance. Acceptance and warmth were prerequisites to the establishment of a satisfactory treatment relationship.

Acknowledging and recognizing the emotional equivalents of M.A.'s sensations of pain were even more salient in the long run than her ability to cope with pain. Working with a psychiatric resident, a clinical psychology intern, and the nursing staff, a relaxation training program was developed that would later involve hypnosis and autogenic training (biofeedback was not found to be helpful).

M.A. I was still, after eight days of hospitalization, to meet the person who would provide even greater help in ridding me of some of the pain and teaching me how to live with the rest. My psychologist had a way about him that made me totally relaxed from the start. For probably the eleventeenth time, I sat through all the questions and queries about my background, upbringing, and childhood—plus gave as accurate as possible description of what my headaches were like, when they began, what I took for them, and how I coped with them. He listened attentively as I described the traumas I suffered as a child, and the frustrations and disappointments I encountered as an adult. He took notes and made suggestions. He taught me to rate my headaches and to relax via hypnosis. A psychology intern gave me several tapes and taught me various relaxation techniques. I found progressive relaxation, autogenics training, and visual imagery to be very helpful.

The therapy I was going through helped me dig into what makes me tick. As I relayed my not so pleasant upbringing, I began to see myself differently. My psychologist had the uncanny ability of making me spill my guts and, by getting out some of the old hostilities and deep-seated hang-ups, to see, accept, and understand why I am my own worst critic and harshest enemy. Even now, I haven't risen above all those idiosyncrasies, but I've sure come a long way.

Commentary

At the time my direct treatment with M.A. began, the primary focus was placed upon moving from the narrow band symptom orientation that had characterized the prior interventions to a treatment program that acknowledged the thematic characteristics of her interpersonal conflicts. The initial development of a treatment alliance was easily accomplished, and she was able to make the transition into a broad band psychotherapy mode relatively easily.

In the beginning, the treatment attempted to intervene at a medium level focus. Emphasis upon emotional awareness and escalation became dominant. Guided imagery and even implosion-like fantasies were invoked to stir up the many feelings that the patient had guarded herself from and that appeared to separate her from the experiences of loss, anger, and hurt. The patient's headaches escalated concomitantly with the experience of anger and hurt and decreased with visual imagery involving the acquisition of love and attachment. Relaxation training, autogenic training, and visual imagery were all used as preludes to a more systematic use of hypnosis and affective enhancement procedures.

M.A. Following the two-week stay on the Psychiatric Ward I was pleased to face the world, armed with a better self-understanding and NO medications. I had been through some of the worst migraines of my entire life, drug free. I felt like a new person. I never felt so positive of my ability and self-esteem. I agreed to go back to the psychologist on an outpatient basis and to follow whatever he had in mind to get control, keep control, and not slide back to my old ways.

I wrote pages and pages on end about my feelings and monitored my headaches every two hours. I brought him carbon copies of everything I wrote so he would know what I was going through in the real world of drug-free pain control. We were able, via the "monitoring notebook," to see a pattern to the pain. We decided to intervene at the beginning of each headache by taking a small amount of Tylenol and escaping to peace and quiet of the relaxation tapes. As I revealed more about the skeletons buried in my life's closet, I began letting them go and embarked on a more pain free life. I was finally finding happiness and freedom by accepting my own worth.

Commentary

The transition from affective enhancement and symptom control procedures to increasing emphasis upon insight and perceptual change is clear here. Exploration of automatic thoughts and directed change techniques were utilized at this point to assist the patient. Given her low level of reactance, the treatment strategies used were reliant upon the therapist's direction. Direct contact with the therapist, for example, was more effective than audiotape-assisted procedures for reducing stress. Hypnosis was particularly helpful both in controlling pain and in engendering improved self-regard.

M.A. I could now go on with living. What I had learned was priceless, invaluable. I was convinced I could go on forever, taking charge of my life and being in charge when a severe headache threatened to wage war. I cut down the frequency of visits with my psychologist. But, life is not all gravy. Three weeks later I was operated on to remove an ovarian cyst, ovary, and tube. I developed an infection and consequently suffered severe abdominal pain. I got my usual post-op migraines, and so I was back on the medication merry-go-round. When I was discharged from the hospital I was emotionally dependent on Stadol and went back to taking it for migraines.

A minor injury to my right knee sent me back to the hospital again several months later for surgery. I developed a blood clot in my right leg and didn't get home for nearly a month. The post-op headache remained. I was stuck on Stadol. I couldn't get away from it or the headache. I was holding onto the headache and had let go of the progress I'd made.

A second admission to the Psychiatric Ward became necessary. I was angry, depressed, and felt defeated. I did feel I could make it this time, though. The two weeks passed quickly, and I didn't miss having medication around, not physically or emotionally.

I went back to seeing my psychologist and our work continued in exploring the various areas of my life that caused me problems; marital difficulties, parental stresses, discouragement at being sick so much of the time. Though I felt that I had accepted Mom's death, I wasn't really free of the negative side of the relationship I had with her. I finally came to realize I wanted my smart, funny, loving, caring Mom alive, but wanted the sickness and irritability and sarcastic, temperamental, alcoholic sides of her to remain dead.

Commentary

The patient's patterned movement through pain and attachment can be observed in this section. Once observed, predicting this cycle sometimes helped her establish control. Even obtaining nurturance and relief in the context of therapy was dangerous, since it signaled the inevitability of abandonment. The recurrence of pain was often the first indication of M.A.'s fear of losing the relationship. The intense internalization of stress in the form of guilt and anxiety now was also a certain theme and required that the therapeutic focus be directed to the pattern of behavior from both a cognitive and an emotional perspective. Hypnosis and emotional awareness procedures that focused on dynamic themes were usefully employed.

M.A. My psychologist had taught me not to reward the headaches with drugs. I kept logs on the pain and wrote extensively on what I was experiencing as my therapy continued. It helps to monitor the pain. It's almost like saying, "Okay headache, you're messing up my day now, but I'll be checking on you in two hours." I began trying to predict how severe the pain would be in the next two hours. I always predicted it would be better. It's sort of like playing an important competitive event in which I HAVE to win.

Commentary

On each occasion of symptom redevelopment, focus was placed on retrenching the symptoms until they subsided. Then treatment moved back into a more dynamic focus. M.A.'s use of cognitive monitoring, mastery and cognitive instructional procedures is evident from this account. These continued to impact the pattern of emotional and behavioral interplay which was usually initiated with her needs for nurturance and ended with her guilt.

M.A. I've spent many hours in therapy but there does come a time to walk independently, to reduce therapy sessions, ease my way out of leaning on my psychologist, and live what I've learned. I realize that there will be setbacks. At first these setbacks upset me. My ever-patient psychologist helped me through several of these, and I learned that I am better armed than I used to be to go it alone.

In looking back over the therapy I've been involved in, it is difficult to draw a single conclusion. The single most important thing I learned is this. I am what I am. I am me. I will never be perfect and I must accept some inadequacies as human and normal, but I am OK. In the past year and a half I've never had to go through any struggle alone. People have helped me change my way of thinking and acting and, therefore, my life. They've stuck by me and listened and cared when I felt as low as low can go. Through it all I've emerged a better me. I understand me, my pain and know better how to live with it.

CONCLUSIONS

One sees in this patient the unique combination of low levels of reactance, a predominantly internalizing psychological coping strategy accompanied by psychophysiological symptoms, and a complex set of symptom patterns. The use of a broad band, internally oriented, and relatively directive treatment procedure was indicated.

An attachment seeking patient whose nurturance needs have been starved and frustrated benefits from a soft and warm therapeutic stance. Nonetheless, the therapist must be sensitive to the potential of developing undue dependency. It is important to gradually decrease the intensity of the therapeutic relationship and convey the awareness that warmth and support may remain even in the absence of weekly or daily contact. The door to therapy never closes in working with such patients, although the need for treatment becomes less intense as the basis for obtaining emotional support and nurturance is broadened.

Therapeutic Process

In working with patients like M.A., therapy moves between the poles of a broad and narrow band focus but always with an ultimate awareness of the core conflicts which represent the patient's approach to life. The intermediate goals of treatment, therefore, are for emotional awareness and perceptual change, selected for the band width required. Procedures designed to increase affective intensity are particularly useful early in treatment and relatively high levels of therapist directiveness can be employed. Directed fantasy and two-chair dialogues are most useful but always are implemented with an emphasis upon providing the patient with a sense of strength and self-regard.

As treatment proceeds, an increasingly insight-oriented focus is employed as an intermediate goal of therapy. Suggestions of directed behavior change take place later on in treatment and are designed both to expand the patient's basis of emotional attachments and to provide a means for asserting herself through the use of externalized rather than internalizing defenses.

16
Afterword

Three major considerations are involved in any delineation of eclectic psychotherapy. These include the appropriate match of patient and therapist, the adaptation of psychotherapeutic techniques to patient characteristics, and the patterning of psychotherapeutic interventions in time, both within and across therapy sessions. In this concluding chapter, certain important concepts that have been addressed in the previous pages will be underlined. Moreover, an attempt will be made to approach a number of salient issues which are still unresolved. Clinical expertise and research knowledge must be brought together in working toward answers to these questions.

IN RECAPITULATION

The relative impact of the patient–therapist relationship and technique variables to therapeutic outcome must be reconsidered and reemphasized before concluding this work. This book has often focused upon the techniques and procedural aspects of psychotherapy. This has been done with the full knowledge that such techniques account for relatively little therapeutic change. Indeed, it is the interaction of technique, therapist, patient, and therapy relationship that is psychotherapy. To separate therapeutic techniques from these nonspecific variables and to define these techniques alone as "psychotherapy" is to approach the treatment process with a disconcerting degree of myopia. Lambert and DeJulio (1978) have suggested that on the average less than 10% of the variance in outcome can be attributed to these technique variables. Psychotherapy cannot exert a treatment effect outside of a context that includes the therapist. Even when the treatment is automated and the therapist is not physically present, the patient may develop a variety of fantasies and expectations about the persons directing the treatment and then relate to these images in a way that must be considered in understanding the total context of the treatment. Psychotherapy is largely a process of persuasion and personal influence. The expectancy, hope, faith, and anticipation that are considered error variables in pharmacological treatments are active ingredients in psychotherapy. Psychotherapists are in the business of modifying these expectations, hopes, and faiths. This can only be done by retaining an awareness of the salience of the patient's images.

While patient variables, of themselves, probably bear the greatest weight in determining therapeutic outcome, research strongly suggests that the influence of even these variables is not immutable. If therapists are able and willing to change their approaches to fit the characteristics of their patients, increased benefit is potentiated. It is the interaction of therapeutic procedures within the patient-therapist relationship that constitutes psychotherapy.

The concept of psychotherapy as a persuasion process is not new. Therapies differ primarily in their views of emotional health, worthy life goals, and what constitutes appropriate or good adjustment. These are the same variables that distinguish psychotherapists, however. To the degree that a therapist can manage his interpersonal and contextual image, there is a strong probability that he can also render psychotherapy a powerful influence process. The ability to establish realistic and mutually agreed-upon expectations in the context of accepting and respecting the patient's dilemmas facilitates this process. Moreover, staying close to the patient's affect, addressing therapeutic issues from the context of the patient's experience, being willing to address both positive and negative feelings about the therapy relationship, and accommodating to changing therapeutic goals constitute powerful therapeutic ingredients. It is within this type of persuasive relationship that concerns arise with interpersonal compatibility, the applications of specific therapeutic techniques, and the patterning of interventions across time.

Patient and Therapist Compatibility

The major characteristic of a successful therapeutic relationship is a sense of collaboration in setting the direction and goals of the treatment process. This is a characteristic that seems to cross treatment settings, types, and relationships. To impose artificial, noncollaborative directions and therapeutic maneuvers on the process is to lose the most important ingredients of effective treatment. The therapist has the power to make patients worse as well as to assist them in the process of emotional healing. Sarcasm, criticism, negative expectations, gimmicks, and lack of faith in one's own therapeutic ability all serve to produce potentially damaging impacts upon those who seek psychotherapeutic services.

The therapist's impact is potentially much broader than that required for simple symptom alleviation or for inducing feelings of satisfaction. Through the course of psychotherapy, patients tend to acquire a wide variety of the personal viewpoints and values of their therapist. That is, changes in the patient's belief systems index movement that is ultimately defined as either improvement or worsening. In view of these facts, it is imperative to define the characteristics of one's belief systems and the attitudes that predicate the changes most beneficial to the treatment process. Values and attitudes that are involved with interpersonal styles of seeking attachment and separation and that, in turn, constitute life themes or conflictual struggles lie at the basis of much therapeutic change. These attitudes are appropriate contrast variables for facilitating the quality of the therapeutic alliance. That is, psychotherapy is a dissonance induction process wherein the patient gains by relating to a therapist whose interpersonal needs stand in contrast to his/her own.

In order for the therapeutic relationship to be maximally facilitated, however, the patient and therapist should also share certain perspectives. Shared humanistic and philosophical values also establish the basis for a positive relationship. It remains for the therapist to communicate the similarities and confront the discrepancies in order to assist the patient to readjust his/her life perspectives. Appropriate interpersonal compatibility combined with kind and genuine caring facilitate effective therapy.

Adopting Therapeutic Strategies to Fit Patient Variables

A number of variables have significance for predisposing the effectiveness of relatively specific treatments. To the degree that symptoms represent complex patterns of adjustment, for example, conflictual life themes rather than specific symptoms provide the most realistic treatment focus. It is change in these conflictual themes that predicates treatment benefit and satisfaction for these patients. If patients obtain a new view of these values and beliefs, they may view themselves and be viewed by others as having benefited from treatment.

While symptom complexity may dictate a broad or narrow band focus, sensitivity to threatened loss of freedom and dominant coping styles have relevance for the selection of more specific treatment strategies. A variety of treatments can be defined on the basis of shared intermediate objectives. These treatments vary in their focus and the degree of external control required for their implementation. In turn, these treatment dimensions interface with patients' coping styles and interpersonal reactance to allow the therapist to develop a prescriptive treatment strategy. While a patient's initial goals for psychotherapy may change over the course of time, the goal of conflict resolution or symptom removal provides the dark thread which welds and weaves a meaningful pattern from the multiple interventions utilized. By following this thread techniques can be selected that are likely to induce awareness of attitudinal dissonance and, thereby, maintain optimal levels of motivation producing arousal.

To compensate for the global generalities present in the proposed system, supplemental readings both on psychopathology and applications of psychotherapeutic techniques will be required. Interested readers may find that additional training experiences will be helpful in broadening their repertoire of applied knowledge.

Patterning Therapeutic Experiences

It is not enough to know the therapeutic procedures that are appropriate to implement at the initiation of treatment. Patient attitudes and behaviors change with time and treatment. Accordingly, the effective therapist will not only stay close to the patient's experience through the course of the therapeutic involvement but will systematically change therapeutic procedures in the process. While most therapists believe that they do precisely this, the best evidence available indicates that they are surprisingly unchanging from patient to patient (Strupp, 1981b). Therapists who are able to recognize their own behaviors and are willing to review their own therapy encounters are likely to improve their therapeutic flexibility. Therapy will be further facilitated by procedures that educate the patient to appropriate therapy roles before treatment begins.

Psychotherapy is primarily an interchange of persuasive influences. Both within and across therapeutic sessions there appears to be a maximally effective pattern of persuasive behaviors. This patterning of intervention includes establishing a collaborative atmosphere, maintaining the patient's cooperation, intensifying or reducing therapeutic arousal levels, underlining significant patterns as they are observed, and providing a mechanism for change.

Frequent feedback from both the patient and the therapist, a questioning attitude, a willingness to respond to the patient's needs and wants, and an understanding of the normal ebb and flow of feelings, are conducive to this therapeutic exchange. Early in the treatment process and within sessions, the ability to deepen the therapeutic experience and to draw the patient's awareness to current experiences that are associated with conflictual patterns sets the stage for therapeutic changes in the patient's perceptions, feelings and behaviors.

UNANSWERED QUESTIONS

What Is Therapeutic About Psychotherapy?

Numerous authors have observed that both maximally effective and ineffective therapists often share the same philosophy (Frank, 1981; Lieberman, Yalom & Miles, 1973). Nonspecific therapist characteristics outweigh the importance of treatment philosophies and techniques. While it is likely that a therapist can be taught to reliably apply philosophies and techniques, the degree to which he or she can be trained to have a therapeutic personality is still an unanswered issue. Indeed, some therapeutic qualities may be trained out of an individual over the course of academic experiences, and it is unlikely that the best of training institutions can "make a silk purse out of a sow's ear." Whether increased training or better selection criteria must be applied is a concern still to be addressed by the mental health fields. With the preoccupation on developing, teaching, and researching global treatment strategies rather than focusing upon the complexity and variety of how those strategies are applied within specific patient and therapist relationships, a satisfactory resolution to this question is not forthcoming.

Can Incompatibility Be Overcome With Technique?

We have emphasized the importance of a compatible belief and experiential system between patient and therapist. It is clear, however, that most clinical settings do not have an unlimited number of therapists with whom they can match the most appropriate patient. The problem is even more complex in private therapy where therapists are unlikely to refer patients out on the basis of incompatible belief systems, especially when their caseload is low and the rent is high. Yet we do not know the degree to which incompatible matches can be overcome through successful applications of techniques.

A related question is the degree to which successful matching between patient and therapist can compensate for inadequate technical application of treatment procedures. Current research suggests that successful matching of the patient and therapist, the establishment of a satisfactory and mutually supportive therapeutic alliance, and the development of trust within the relationship compensate for most negative influences created by sloppily applied treatment procedures.

What Is The Relationship Between Personality And Therapeutic Philosophy?

It is unlikely that therapists adopt a theoretical philosophy or apply treatment procedures randomly. Most therapists believe that their therapeutic procedures have evolved out of important issues in their personal development and constitute a reflection of their own personalities. In the most logical of worlds, therapeutic philosophy and techniques would be compatible with the therapist's personality. Indeed, it is enticing to think that the degree of compatibility between personality, personal attitudes, and theoretical philosophy might index effective therapists.

In spite of the persuasiveness of this argument, current literature does not support the belief that therapeutic procedures and philosophies evolve either out of personally meaningful experiences or personality traits. Therapists within any given school present a wide variety of personality styles and backgrounds. Research on the issue (e.g., Beutler & McNabb, 1981; Schwartz, 1978; Walton, 1978) suggests that the selection of therapeutic philosophy is more often based upon the type of training to which one has been exposed and an identification with a salient mentor. Therapists choose from those theoretical philosophies and techniques that they have been exposed to by charismatic teachers. Theoretically, then, one can increase one's repertoire of effective procedures by increasing the amount of exposure to powerful training experiences.

I am not so naive as to believe that most therapists will expend the energy, effort, and money required to develop the broad range of therapeutic procedures advocated. Until research can specify more clearly how expertise is developed, therapists will probably continue to employ a limited variety of treatment strategies on the assumption that these and only these are compatible with their own unique and correct views of the world.

Can Therapists Become Competent In Multiple Procedures?

An issue related to the foregoing question is the degree that the therapist can maintain high levels of competence in a wide variety of procedures. Thorne (1948) has advocated an eclectic psychotherapy in the model of the tradesman. He observes that no skilled craftsman would be expected to tackle a difficult task with only one tool. No carpenter can build a house with just a hammer, no matter how important the hammer may be. Few plumbers can repair a leak with just a wrench or screwdriver. This is not to minimize the importance of the tool but simply to emphasize the necessity of having a full repertoire of tools when approaching a task as complex as persuading the human mind. Research is needed, however, to investigate the degree to which competency in one set of procedures interrelates, facilitates, or inhibits competency in another. For example, can one be competent in both behavioral and experiential technologies, representing as they do, ostensibly conflicting theoretical bases? While numerous authors have attempted to interweave apparently discrepant therapeutic philosophies and procedures (e.g., Appelbaum, 1981; Wachtel, 1977), the success of this interweaving is still uncertain. Moreover, the degree to which such a theoretical amalgamation is reflected in one's technical applications is still undetermined.

A NOTE TO THE READER

This volume has attempted to address many issues related to a systematic application of eclectic psychotherapy. A model of person, context, relationship, and technique interactions has been proposed in this volume which includes speculations about the nature of the interface needed in order to effect psychotherapeutic gain. The reader is asked to keep in mind, however, that this is only a speculative model. It lacks the specificity that is desirable and, in many areas, supporting research. Clinicians will find much to criticize in this volume, and empirical research will undoubtedly prove many of the speculations invalid. The tentative nature of science and its slow progress must be kept in mind as one turns a critical eye to this conceptual system. To the degree that the foregoing material is controversial, future generations may be benefited. It would be worse if this or similar efforts to account for complex patient, system, therapist, and context interactions were to be ignored. Ultimately, the progress of the mental health fields will depend upon their willingness and ability to investigate not only the interventions they provide but both the context in which these interventions occur and the nature of the individuals applying them. The most difficult barrier of all is for the therapist to open up to inspection from others and to seek a critical appraisal of his/her own treatment effectiveness and the variables that contribute to it.

Finally, a word should be said about patient perceptions of the treatment process. One will observe in the preceding clinical examples that qualities of the therapeutic relationship are paramount to patients receiving the treatment. The inadequacies of treatment providers rather than the inadequacies of techniques form the basis for many patients' criticisms of the field. The descriptions of patients and their attributions of treatment success and failure are important areas for scientific investigation. It is imperative that we learn to listen and be responsive to the expressions of those whom we serve.

References

Abramowitz, C.V., Abramowitz, S.I., Roback, H.B., & Jackson, C. Differential effectiveness of directive and nondirective group therapies as a function of client internal-external control. *Journal of Consulting and Clinical Psychology*, 1974, **42**, 849–853.

Abramowitz, S.I. & Murray, J. Race effects in psychotherapy. In J. Murray and S.I. Abramson (Eds.), *Bias in Psychotherapy.* Los Angeles: University of California Press, in press.

Abramson, L.Y., Seligman, M.E.P., & Teasdale, J.D. Learned helplessness in humans: Critique and reformulation. *Journal of Abnormal Psychology*, 1978, **87**, 49–74.

Adler, A. *The Practice and Theory of Individual Psychology.* New York: Harcourt, Brace & World, 1927.

Alker, H.A., Tourangeau, R., & Staines, B. Facilitating personality changes with audiovisual self-confrontation and interviews. *Journal of Consulting and Clinical Psychology*, 1976, **44**, 720–728.

American Psychiatric Association, *Diagnostic and Statistical Manual of Mental Disorders*. (3rd ed.) Washington, D.C.: Author, 1980.

Amira, S. & Abramowitz, S.I. Therapeutic attraction as a function of therapist attire and office furnishings. *Journal of Consulting and Clinical Psychology*, 1979, **47**, 198–200.

Anderson, J.A.D., Basker, M.A., & Dalton, R. Migraine and hypnotherapy. *The International Journal of Clinical and Experimental Hypnosis*, 1975, **23**, 48–58.

Anderson, M.P. Imaginal Processes: Therapeutic applications and theoretical models. In M.J. Mahoney (Ed.), *Psychotherapy Process*. New York: Plenum, 1980.

Appelbaum, S.A. *Effecting Change in Psychotherapy.* New York: Jason Aronson, 1981.

Arizmendi, T.G. The effects of value similarity and client locus of control on convergence and improvement. Unpublished doctoral dissertation, University of Arizona, 1982.

Aronson, E., Turner, J.A., & Carlsmith, J.M. Communicator credibility and communication discrepancy as determiners of opinion change. *Journal of Abnormal Psychology*, 1963, **67**, 31–36.

Armstrong, S., Yasuna, A., & Hartley, D. Brief psychodynamic psychotherapy: Interrater agreement and reliability of individually specified outcomes. Paper presented at the 10th annual meeting of the Society for Psychotherapy Research, Oxford, England, July, 1979.

Ascher, L.M. & Efran, J. The use of paradoxical intention in cases of delayed sleep-onset insomnia. *Journal of Consulting and Clinical Psychology*, 1978, **8**, 547–550.

Atkinson, D.R., Brady, S., & Casas, J.M. Sexual preference similarity, attitude similarity and perceived counselor credibility and attractiveness. *Journal of Counseling Psychology*, 1981, **28**, 504–509.

Auerbach, A.H. & Johnson, M. Research on the therapist's level of experience. In A.S. Gurman and A.M. Razin (Eds.), *Effective Psychotherapy: Handbook of Research*. New York: Pergamon, 1977.

Ayllon, T. & Azrin, N. *The Token Economy: A motivational system for therapy and rehabilitation*. New York: Appleton-Century-Crofts, 1968.

Baer, P.E., Dunbar, P.W., Hamilton, J.E. II, & Beutler, L.E. Therapists' perceptions of the psychotherapeutic process: Development of a psychotherapy process inventory. *Psychological Reports*, 1980, **46**, 563–570.

Bailey, K.G. & Sowder, W.T., Jr. Audiotape and videotape self-confrontation in psychotherapy. *Psychological Bulletin*, 1970, **74**, 127–137.

Bakan, D. *On Method*. San Francisco: Jossey-Bass, 1967.

Baker, E.K. The relationship between locus of control and psychotherapy: A review of the literature. *Psychotherapy: Theory, Research and Practice*, 1979, **16**, 351–362.

Bandura, A. *Principles of Behavior Modification*. New York: Holt, Rinehart & Winston, 1969.

Bandura, A., Blanchard, E., & Ritter, B. The relative efficacy of desensitization and modeling treatment approaches for inducing affective, behavioral, and attitudinal changes. *Journal of Personality and Social Psychology*, 1969, **13**, 173–199.

Banks, W.M. The differential effects of race and social class in helping. *Journal of Clinical Psychology*, 1972, **28**, 90–92.

Barlow, D.H. On the relation of clinical research to clinical practice: Current issues, new directions. *Journal of Consulting and Clinical Psychology*, 1981, **49**, 147–155.

Bateson, G., Jackson, D.D., Haley, J., & Weakland, J. Toward a theory of schizophrenia. *Behavioral Science*, 1956, **1**, 251–264.

Beck, A.T., Rush, A.J., Shaw, B.F., & Emery, G. *Cognitive Therapy of Depression*. New York: Guilford, 1979.

Becker, J.F. & Munz, D.C. Extraversion and reciprocation of interviewer disclosures. *Journal of Consulting and Clinical Psychology*, 1975, **43**, 593.

Bednar, R.L. & Mobley, M.J. A–B therapist perceptions and preferences for schizophrenic and psychoneurotic clients. *Journal of Abnormal Psychology*, 1971, **78**, 192–197.

Beier, E.G., Rossi, A.M. & Garfield, R.L. Similarity plus dissimilarity of personality: Basis for friendship? *Psychological Reports*, 1961, **8**, 3–8.

Beigel, A. Psychiatric education at the crossroads: Issues and future directions. *American Journal of Psychiatry*, 1979, **136**, 1525–1529.

Benson, H. The *Relaxation Response*. New York: William Morrow & Co., 1976.

Berenson, B.G., Mitchell, K.M., & Laney, R. Level of therapist functioning, types of confrontation, and type of patient. *Journal of Clinical Psychology*, 1968, **24**, 111–114.

Berensen, B.G., Mitchell, K.M., & Moravec, J.A. Level of therapist functioning, type of confrontation, and patient depth of self-exploration. *Journal of Counseling Psychology*, 1968, **15**, 136–139.

Bergin, A.E. The effect of dissonant persuasive communications upon changes in a self-referring attitude. *Journal of Personality*, 1962, **30**, 423–438.

Bergin, A.E. The evaluation of therapeutic outcomes. In A.E. Bergin and S.L. Garfield (Eds.), *Handbook of Psychotherapy and Behavior Change*, (1st ed.) New York: John Wiley & Sons, 1971.

Bergin, A.E. Psychotherapy and religious values. *Journal of Consulting and Clinical Psychology*, 1980, **48**, 95–105.

Bergin, A.E. & Lambert, M.J. The evaluation of therapeutic outcome. In S.L. Garfield and A.E. Bergin (Eds.), *Handbook of Psychotherapy and Behavior Change*. (2nd ed.) New York: John Wiley & Sons, 1978.

Bergin, A.E. & Suinn, R.M. Individual psychotherapy and behavior therapy. *Annual Review of Psychology*, 1975, **26**, 509–556.

Berne, E. *Transactional Analysis in Psychotherapy*. New York: Grove Press, 1961.

Berzins, J.I. Sex roles in psychotherapy: New directions for theory and research. Paper presented at the Sixth Annual Meeting of the Society for Psychotherapy Research, Boston, June 1975.

Berzins, J.I. Therapist-patient matching. In A.S. Gurman and A.M. Razin (Eds.), *Effective Psychotherapy: A Handbook of Research*. New York: Pergamon, 1977.

Berzins, J.I., Seidman, E., & Welch, R.D. A–B therapist "Types" and responses to patient-communicated hostility: An analogue study. *Journal of Consulting and Clinical Psychology,* 1970, **34**, 27–32.

Bettinghaus, E. Operation of congruity in an oral communication setting. *Speech Monographs*, 1961, **28**, 131–142.

Beutler, L.E. Hearing loss effects on a procedural task sequence. *Journal of Motor Behavior,* 1970, **2**, 207–215.

Beutler, L.E. Predicting outcomes of psychotherapy: A comparison of predictions from two attitude theories. *Journal of Consulting and Clinical Psychology,* 1971, **37**, 411–416.

Beutler, L.E. More sources of variance: A reply to Cicchetti & Ryan. *Journal of Consulting and Clinical Psychology,* 1976, **44**, 860–861.

Beutler, L.E. Psychotherapy and persuasion. In L.E. Beutler and R. Greene (Eds.), *Special Problems in Child and Adolescent Behavior.* Westport, CT: Technomic, 1978.

Beutler, L.E. Toward specific psychological therapies for specific conditions. *Journal of Consulting and Clinical Psychology,* 1979, **47**, 882–892. (a)

Beutler, L.E. Values, beliefs, religion and the persuasive influence of psychotherapy. *Psychotherapy: Theory, Research and Practice*, 1979, **16**, 432–440. (b)

Beutler, L.E. Convergence in counseling and psychotherapy: A current look. *Clinical Psychology Review*, 1981, **1**, 79–101.

Beutler, L.E. & Anderson, L. Therapist characteristics in brief psychotherapy. *The Psychiatric Clinics of North America*, 1979, **2**, 125–138.

Beutler, L.E. & Crago, M. Self-report measures of psychotherapy outcome. In M.J. Lambert, E.R. Christensen and S. DeJulio (Eds.), *The Measurement of Psychotherapy Outcome in Research.* New York: John Wiley & Sons, in press.

Beutler, L.E., Dunbar, P.W., & Baer, P.E. Individual variation among therapists' perceptions of patients, therapy process and outcome. *Psychiatry,* 1980, **43**, 205–210.

Beutler, L.E. & Jobe, A.M. Evaluation of some psychological variables in the pharmacology of sleep. In R.L. Williams and I. Karacan (Eds.), *Pharmacology of Sleep*. New York: John Wiley & Sons, 1976.

Beutler, L.E., Jobe, A.M., & Elkins, D. Outcomes in group psychotherapy: Using persuasion theory to increase treatment efficiency. *Journal of Consulting and Clinical Psychology,* 1974, **42**, 547–553.

Beutler, L.E., Johnson, D.T., Neville, C.W., Jr., Elkins, D., & Jobe, A.M. Attitude similarity and therapist credibility as predictors of attitude change and improvement in psychotherapy. *Journal of Consulting and Clinical Psychology,* 1975, **43**, 90–91.

Beutler, L.E., Johnson, D.T., Neville, C.W., Jr., & Workman, S.N. Effort expended as a determiner of treatment evaluation and outcome: The honor of a prophet in his own country. *Journal of Consulting and Clinical Psychology,* 1972, **39**, 495–500.

Beutler, L.E., Johnson, D.T., Neville, C.W., Jr., & Workman, S.N. Some sources of variance in "accurate empathy" ratings. *Journal of Consulting and Clinical Psychology,* 1973, **40**, 167–169.

Beutler, L.E. & McNabb, C. Self-evaluation of the psychotherapist. In C.E. Walker (Ed.), *Clinical Practice of Psychology.* New York: Pergamon, 1981.

Beutler, L.E. & Mitchell, R. Psychotherapy outcome in depressed and impulsive patients as a function of analytic and experiential treatment procedures. *Psychiatry,* 1981, **44**, 297–306.

Beutler, L.E., Oro'-Beutler, M.E., & Mitchell, R. Systematic comparison of two parent training programs in child management. *Journal of Counseling Psychology,* 1979, **26**, 531–533.

Beutler, L.E., Pollack, S., & Jobe, A.M. "Acceptance," values, and therapeutic change. *Journal of Consulting and Clinical Psychology,* 1978, **46**, 198–199.

Beutler, L.E. & Thornby, J.I. Experiential, Psychoanalytic, and Cognitive-behavioral orientations and patient personality variables in psychotherapy. *Exceptional People Quarterly,* 1982, **1**, 258–284.

Biondo, J. & MacDonald, A.P., Jr. Internal-external locus of control and response to influence attempts. *Journal of Personality,* 1971, **39**, 407–419.

Biran, M. & Wilson, G.T. The treatment of phobic disorders using cognitive and exposure methods: A self-efficacy analysis. *Journal of Consulting and Clinical Psychology,* 1981, **49**, 886–899.

Brammer, L.M. & Shostrum, E.L. *Therapeutic Psychology.* Englewood Cliffs, N.J.: Prentice-Hall, 1960.

Brehm, J.W. *A Theory of Psychological Reactance.* New York: Academic Press, 1966.

Brehm, J.W. & Cohen, A.R. *Explorations in Cognitive Dissonance.* New York: John Wiley & Sons, 1962.

Brehm, S.S. *The Application of Social Psychology to Clinical Practice.* Washington, D.C.: Hemisphere, 1976.

Brehm, S.S. & Brehm, J.W. *Psychological Reactance: A Theory of Freedom and Control.* New York: Academic Press, 1981.

Brown, B.B. *Stress and the Art of Biofeedback.* New York: Harper and Row, 1977.

Bruch, H. Perils of behavior modification in treatment of anorexia nervosa. *Journal of the American Medical Association*, 1974, **230**, 1419–1422.

Bruch, H. *The Golden Cage: The Enigma of Anorexia Nervosa.* Cambridge, Mass.: Harvard University Press, 1978.

Bruner, J. From communication to language: A psychological perspective. *Cognition*, 1957, **3**, 255–287.

Brunink, S. & Schroeder, H. Verbal therapeutic behavior of expert psychoanalytically oriented, Gestalt and behavior therapists. *Journal of Consulting and Clinical Psychology,* 1979, **47**, 567–574.

Burger, J.M. Motivational biases in the attribution of responsibility for an accident: A meta-analysis of the defensive-attribution hypothesis. *Psychological Bulletin*, 1981, **90**, 496–512.

Butcher, J.N. & Koss, M.P. Research on brief and crisis-oriented therapy. In S.L. Garfield and A.E. Bergin (Eds.), *Handbook of Psychotherapy and Behavior Change.* (2nd ed.) New York: John Wiley & Sons, 1978.

Byrne, D. The repression-sensitization scale: Rationale, reliability, and validity. *Journal of Personality,* 1961, **29**, 334–349.

Byrne, D., Baskett, G.D., & Hodges, L. Behavioral indicators of interpersonal attraction. *Journal of Applied Social Psychology,* 1971, **1**, 137–149.

Byrne, K. & Stern, S.L. Antidepressant medication in the outpatient treatment of depression: Guide for nonmedical psychotherapists. *Professional Psychology,* 1981, **12**, 302–308.

Callahan, E.J. & Leitenberg, H. Aversion therapy for sexual deviation: Contingent shock and covert sensitization. *Journal of Abnormal Psychology,* 1973, **81**, 60–73.

Cartwright, D.S. Success in psychotherapy as a function of certain actuarial variables. *Journal of Consulting Psychology,* 1955, **19**, 357–363.

Cautela, J.R. Covert processes and behavior modification. *The Journal of Nervous and Mental Disease*, 1973, **157**, 27–35.

Cautela, J.R. Covert conditioning: Assumptions and procedures. *Journal of Mental Imagery,* 1977, **1**, 53–65.

Chittick, E. & Himelstein, P. Manipulation of self disclosure. *Journal of Psychology,* 1967, **65**, 117–121.

Claiborn, C.D., Ward, S.R., & Strong, S.R. Effects of congruence between counselor interpretations and client beliefs. *Journal of Counseling Psychology,* 1981, **28**, 101–109.

Cohen, J. & Twemlow, S.W. Psychological changes associated with guided imagery: A controlled study. *Psychotherapy: Theory, Research and Practice*, 1981, **18**, 259–265.

Cole, J.K. & Magnussen, M. Where the action is. *Journal of Consulting Psychology,* 1966, **30**, 539–543.

Comas-Diaz, L. Effects of cognitive and behavioral group treatment on the depressive symptomatology of Puerto Rican women. *Journal of Consulting and Clinical Psychology*, 1981, **49**, 627–632.

Cross, D.G., Sheehan, P.W. & Khan, J.A. Alternative advice and counsel in psychotherapy. *Journal of Consulting and Clinical Psychology*, 1980, **48**, 615–625.

Cryer, L. & Beutler, L.E. Group therapy: An alternative treatment approach for rape victims. *Journal of Sex and Marital Therapy*, 1980, **6**, 40–66.

Dahlstrom, W.G., Welsh, G.S. & Dahlstrom, L.E. *An MMPI Handbook: Volume 1: Clinical Interpretation*. Minneapolis: University of Minnesota Press, 1972.

Danieli, Y., Loew, C.A., & Grayson, H. Background and orientation. In C.A. Loew, H. Grayson and G.H. Loew (Eds.), *Three Psychotherapies*. New York: Brunner/Mazel, 1975.

Davanloo, H. *Basic Principles and Techniques of Short-term Dynamic Psychotherapy*. New York: Spectrum, 1978.

Davison, G.C., Tsujimoto, R.N., & Glaros, A.G. Attribution and the maintenance of behavior change in falling asleep. *Journal of Abnormal Psychology*, 1973, **82**, 124–133.

DeWitt, K., Kaltreider, N., Weiss, D., & Horowitz, M. Individual outcome assessment. Paper presented at the 11th annual meeting of the Society for Psychotherapy Research, Pacific Grove, California, June 1980.

Derogatis, L.R., Rickels, K., & Rock, A.F. The SCL-90 and the MMPI: A step in the validation of a new self-report scale. *British Journal of Psychiatry*, 1976, **128**, 280–289.

Doctor, R. Locus of control of reinforcement and responsiveness to social influence. *Journal of Personality*, 1971, **39**, 542–551.

Dollard, J. & Miller, N. *Personality and Psychotherapy*. New York: McGraw-Hill, 1950.

Dreikurs, R. *Children: The Challenge*. New York: Hawthorne Books, 1964.

Ekman, P. Body position, facial expression and verbal behavior during interviews. *Journal of Abnormal and Social Psychology*, 1964, **68**, 295–301.

Ekman, P. & Friesen, W. Nonverbal leakage and clues to deception. *Psychiatry*, 1969, **32**, 88–106.

Ellis, A. *Reason and Emotion in Psychotherapy*. New York: Lyle Stuart Press, 1962.

Ellis, A. & Harper, R.A. *A Guide to Rational Living*. Englewood Cliffs, N.J.: Prentice-Hall, 1961.

Ellsworth, P. & Carlsmith, J. Effects of eye contact and verbal content on affective response to a dyadic interaction. *Journal of Personality and Social Psychology*, 1968, **10**, 15–20.

Erickson, M.H. & Rossi, E.L. *Experiencing Hypnosis*. New York: Irvington, 1981.

Evans, G.W. & Howard, R.B. Personal space. *Psychological Bulletin*, 1973, **80**, 334–344.

Eysenck, H.G. The effects of psychotherapy: An evaluation. *Journal of Consulting Psychology*, 1952, **16**, 319–324.

Eysenck, H.G. & Eysenck, S.B.G. *Personality Structure and Measurement*. San Diego: Knapp Press, 1969.

Farina, A., Fisher, E.H., Sherman, S., Smith, W.T., Groh, T., & Mermin, P. Physical attractiveness and mental illness. *Journal of Abnormal Psychology*, 1977, **86**, 510–517.

Feldman, M.J. & Hersen, M. Attitudes toward death in nightmare subjects. *Journal of Abnormal Psychology*, 1967, **72**, 421–425.

Felipe, N. & Sommer, R. Invasions of personal space. *Social Problems*, 1966, **14**, 206–214.

Fenichel, O. *The Psychoanalytic Theory of Neurosis*. New York: Norton, 1945.

Festinger, L. *A Theory of Cognitive Dissonance*. Palo Alto: Stanford University Press, 1957.

Fey, W. Doctrine and experience: Their influence upon the psychotherapist. *Journal of Consulting Psychology*, 1958, **22**, 403–409.

Fiedler, F.E. The concept of an ideal therapeutic relationship. *Journal of Consulting Psychology*, 1950, **14**, 239–245.

Fiester, A.R. Client's perceptions of therapists with high attrition rates. *Journal of Consulting and Clinical Psychology*, 1977, **45**, 954–955.

Finch, A.J., Jr. & Kendall, P.C. Reflection-impulsivity: Implications and treatment strategies for child psychopathology. In L.E. Beutler and R. Greene (Eds.), *Special Problems in Child and Adolescent Behavior.* Westport, CT: Technomic, 1978.

Frances, A. & Clarkin, J.F. Differential therapeutics. *Hospital and Community Psychiatry,* 1981, **32**, 537–546. (a)

Frances, A. & Clarkin, J.F. No treatment as the prescription of choice. *Archives of General Psychiatry,* 1981, **38**, 542–545. (b)

Franco, E.A. & Kulberg, G.E. Content analysis of A & B males in a dyadic interaction. *Journal of Consulting and Clinical Psychology,* 1975, **43**, 345–349.

Frank, J.D. *Persuasion and Healing*. New York: Schocken Books, 1973.

Frank, J.D. The present status of outcome studies. *Journal of Consulting and Clinical Psychology,* 1979, **47**, 310–316.

Frank, J.D. Reply to Telch. *Journal of Consulting and Clinical Psychology,* 1981, **49**, 476–477.

Frank, J.D., Hoehn-Saric, R., Imber, S.D., Liberman, B.L., & Stone, A.R. (Eds.) *Effective Ingredients of Successful Psychotherapy.* New York: Brunner/Mazel, 1978.

Frankl, V.E. Paradoxical Intention: A Logotherapeutic Technique. *American Journal of Psychotherapy,* 1960, **14**, 520–535.

Freud, S. The interpretation of dreams. In *Standard Edition*. Vols. 4 & 5. London: Hogarth Press, 1953 (First German edition, 1900).

Freud, S. New introductory lectures on psycho-analysis. In *Standard Edition*, Vol. 22. London: Hogarth Press, 1964 (First German edition, 1933).

Freud, S. An outline of psychoanalysis. In *Standard Edition*, Vol. 23. London: Hogarth Press, 1974 (First German edition, 1939).

Fromm, E. & Shor, R.E. (Eds.) *Hypnosis: Developments in Research and New Perspectives*. (2nd ed.) New York: Aldine, 1979.

Garfield, S.L. Values: An issues in psychotherapy: Comments on a case study. *Journal of Abnormal Psychology,* 1974, **83**, 202–203.

Garfield, S.L. Some reflections on the nature of psychotherapy. Presidential address given at the eighth annual meeting of the Society for Psychotherapy Research, Madison, June 1977.

Garfield, S.L. *Psychotherapy: An Eclectic Approach*. New York: John Wiley & Sons, 1980.

Garfield, S.L. & Bergin, A.E. Personal therapy, outcome and some therapist variables. *Psychotherapy: Theory, Research and Practice*, 1971, **8**, 251–253.

Garfield, S.L. & Kurtz, R. A study of eclectic views. *Journal of Consulting and Clinical Psychology,* 1977, **45**, 78–83.

Garfield, S.L., Prager, R.A., & Bergin, A.E. Evaluation of outcome in psychotherapy. *Journal of Consulting and Clinical Psychology,* 1971, **37**, 307–313.

Gelder, M.G., Marks, I.M., Wolff, H.H., & Clarke, M. Desensitization and psychotherapy in the treatment of phobic states: A controlled inquiry. *British Journal of Psychiatry,* 1967, **113**, 53–73.

Geller, J.D. & Berzins, J.I. A–B distinction in a sample of prominent psychotherapists. *Journal of Consulting and Clinical Psychology,* 1976, **44**, 77–82.

Gendlin, E.T. Focusing. *Psychotherapy: Theory, Research and Practice*, 1969, **6**, 4–15.

Gibbs, L. & Flanagan, J. Prognostic indicators of alcoholism treatment outcome. *The International Journal of the Addictions*, 1977, **12**, 1097–1141.

Gillis, J.S. & Jessor, R. Effects of brief psychotherapy on belief in internal control: An exploratory study. *Psychotherapy: Theory, Research and Practice,* 1970, **7**, 135–136.

Gillis, J.S., Lipkin, M.D., & Moran, T.J. Drug therapy decisions: A social judgement analysis. *The Journal of Nervous and Mental Disease*, 1981, **169**, 439–447.

Gillis, J.S. & Moran, T.J. An analysis of drug decisions in a state psychiatric hospital. *Journal of Clinical Psychology,* 1981, **37**, 32–42.

Glad, D.D. *Operational Values in Psychotherapy.* New York: Oxford University Press, 1959.

Goldfried, M.R. Reduction of generalized anxiety through a variant of systematic desensitization. In M.R. Goldfried and M. Merbaum (Eds.), *Behavior Change Through Self-Control.* New York: Holt, Rinehart and Winston, 1973.

Goldfried, M.R. & Davison, G.C. *Clinical Behavior Therapy.* New York: Holt, Rinehart and Winston, 1976.

Goldstein, A.P. *Psychotherapeutic Attraction.* New York: Pergamon, 1971.

Goldstein, A.P. *Structured Learning Therapy: Toward a Psychotherapy for the Poor.* New York: Academic Press, 1973.

Goldstein, A.P., Heller, K., & Sechrest, L.B. *Psychotherapy and the Psychology of Behavior Change.* New York: John Wiley & Sons, 1966.

Goldstein, A.P. & Simonson, N.R. Social psychological approaches to psychotherapy research. In A.E. Bergin and S.L. Garfield (Eds.), *Handbook of Psychotherapy and Behavior Change.* (1st ed.) New York: John Wiley & Sons, 1971.

Goldstein, A.P. & Stein, N. *Prescriptive Psychotherapies.* New York: Pergamon, 1976.

Gomes-Schwartz, B. Effective ingredients in psychotherapy: Prediction of outcome from process variables. *Journal of Consulting and Clinical Psychology,* 1978, **46**, 1023–1035.

Gomes-Schwartz, B., Hadley, S.W., & Strupp, H.H. Individual psychotherapy and behavior therapy. *Annual Review of Psychology,* 1978, **29**, 435–471.

Gomes-Schwartz, B. & Schwartz, J.M. Psychotherapy process variables distinguishing the "inherently helpful" person from the professional psychotherapist. *Journal of Consulting and Clinical Psychology,* 1978, **46**, 196–197.

Goss, A.E. Verbal mediating response and concept formation. *Psychological Review,* 1961, **68**, 248–274.

Goulding, M.M. & Goulding, R.L. *Changing Lives Through Redecision Therapy.* New York: Brunner/Mazel, 1979.

Grant, E.C. An ethological description of non-verbal behavior during interviews. *British Journal of Medical Psychology,* 1968, **41**, 177–184.

Green, B.L., Gleser, G.C., Stone, W.N., & Seifert, R.F. Relationships among diverse measures of psychotherapy outcome. *Journal of Consulting and Clinical Psychology,* 1975, **43**, 689–699.

Greenberg, L.S. Resolving splits: Use of the two chair technique. *Psychotherapy: Theory, Research and Practice,* 1979, **16**, 316–324.

Greenberg, L.S. & Kahn, S.E. The stimulation phase in counseling. *Counselor Education and Supervision,* 1979, **19**, 137–145.

Greenwald, J.A. The ground rules of Gestalt Therapy. *Journal of Contemporary Psychotherapy,* 1972, **5**, 113–120.

Gurman, A.S. Instability of therapeutic conditions in psychotherapy. *Journal of Counseling Psychology,* 1973, **20**, 16–24.

Gurman, A.S. Therapist and patient factors influencing the patient's perception of facilitative therapeutic conditions. *Psychiatry,* 1977, **40**, 218–231.

Hall, E.T. Silent assumptions in social communication. *Disorders of Communication,* 1964, **42**, 41–55.

Hampson, R.B. & Tavormina, J.B. Relative effectiveness of behavioral and reflective group training with foster mothers. *Journal of Consulting and Clinical Psychology,* 1980, **48**, 294–295.

Harper, R.A. *Psychoanalysis and Psychotherapy: 36 Systems.* Englewood Cliffs, NJ: Prentice-Hall, 1963.

Harper, R.G., Wiens, A.N., & Matarazzo, J.D. *Non-verbal Communication: The State of the Art.* New York: John Wiley & Sons, 1978.

Harris, T. *I'm OK, You're OK.* New York: Harper & Row, 1967.

Heitler, J.B. Preparatory techniques in initiating expressive psychotherapy with lower-class, unsophisticated patients. *Psychological Bulletin,* 1976, **83**, 339–352.

Hersen, M. Personality characteristics of nightmare sufferers. *Journal of Nervous and Mental Disease,* 1971, **153**, 27–31.

Hill, J.A. Therapist goals, patient aims, and patient satisfaction in therapy. *Journal of Clinical Psychology,* 1969, **25**, 455–459.

Hobbs, N. Sources of gain in psychotherapy. *American Psychologist,* 1962, **17**, 741–747.

Hoehn-Saric, R., Frank, J.D., Imber, S.D., Nash, E.H., Stone, A.R., & Battle, C.C. Systematic preparation of patients for psychotherapy: I. Effects on therapy behavior and outcome. *Journal of Psychiatric Research*, 1964, **2**, 267–281.

Holzman, M.S. The significance of value systems of patient and therapist for outcome in psychotherapy. *Dissertation Abstracts*, 1962, **22**, 4073.

Hood, J., Moore, T.E., & Garner, D. Locus of control as a measure of ineffectiveness in anorexia nervosa. *Journal of Consulting and Clinical Psychology*, 1982, **50**, 3–13.

Horney, K. *New Ways in Psychoanalysis*. New York: Norton, 1939.

Horowitz, M.J. Spatial behavior and psychopathology. *Journal of Nervous and Mental Disease*, 1968, **146**, 24–35.

Houston, B.K. Control over stress, locus of control and response to stress. *Journal of Personality and Social Psychology*, 1972, **21**, 249–255.

Hovland, C. & Mandell, W. An experimental comparison of conclusion drawing by communicator and the audience. *Journal of Abnormal and Social Psychology*, 1952, **47**, 581–588.

Howell, R. & Jorgenson, E. Accuracy of judging emotional behavior in a natural setting: A replication. *Journal of Social Psychology*, 1970, **81**, 269–270.

Hoyt, M.F. Therapist and patient actions in "good" psychotherapy sessions. *Archives of General Psychiatry*, 1980, **37**, 159–161.

Hubble, M.A., Nobel, F.C., & Robinson, S.E. The effect of counselor touch in an initial counseling session. *Journal of Consulting and Clinical Psychology*, 1981, **28**, 533–535.

Janis, I. Effects of fear arousal on attitude change: Recent developments in theory and experimental research. In L. Berkowitz (Ed.), *Advances in Experimental Social Psychology*. Vol. 3. New York: Academic Press, 1967.

Janis, I. & Feshbach, S. Personality differences associated with responsiveness to fear arousing communications. *Journal of Personality*, 1954, **23**, 154–166.

Jennings, R.L. & Davis, C.S. Attraction-enhancing client behaviors: A structured learning approach for "non-YAVIS", *Journal of Consulting and Clinical Psychology*, 1977, **45**, 135–144.

Jesness, C.F. Comparative effectiveness of behavior modification and transactional analysis programs for delinquents. *Journal of Consulting and Clinical Psychology*, 1975, **43**, 758–779.

Johnson, D.W. & Matross, R.P. Attitude change methods. In F.H. Kanfer and A.P. Goldstein (Eds.), *Helping People Change*. New York: Pergamon, 1975.

Jones, E. Social class and psychotherapy: A critical review of research. *Psychiatry*, 1974, **37**, 307–320.

Jones, E.E. & Zoppel, C.L. Impact of client and therapist gender on psychotherapy process and outcome. *Journal of Consulting and Clinical Psychology*, 1982, **50**, 259–272.

Jourard, S.M. Effects of experimenter's self-disclosure in subjects' behavior. In C.D. Spielberger (Ed.), *Current Topics in Clinical and Community Psychology*. Vol. I. New York: Academic Press, 1969.

Kahn, M. Non-verbal communication as a factor in marital satisfaction. *Dissertation Abstracts International*, 1970, **30**, (10-B), 4794.

Kahn, M. & Baker, B. Desensitization with minimal therapist contact. *Journal of Abnormal Psychology*, 1968, **73**, 193–200.

Kaltreider, N., DeWitt, K., Lieberman, R., Horowitz, M., & Weiss, D. From individual outcome to generalized scales. Paper presented at the 11th annual meeting of the Society for Psychotherapy Research. Pacific Grove, California, June 1980.

Karon, B.P. & VandenBos, G.R. *Psychotherapy of Schizophrenia: The Treatment of Choice*. New York: Jason Aronson, 1981.

Katkin, E. & Murray, E. Instrumental conditioning of autonomically mediated behavior: Theoretical and methodological issues. *Psychological Bulletin*, 1968, **70**, 52–68.

Kazdin, A.E. Covert modeling and the reduction of avoidance behavior. *Journal of Abnormal Psychology*, 1973, **81**, 87–95.

Kazdin, A.E. Covert modeling, imagery assessment, and assertive behavior. *Journal of Consulting and Clinical Psychology,* 1975, **43**, 716–724.

Kazrin, A., Durac, J., & Agteros, T. Meta-meta analysis: A new method for evaluating therapy outcome. *Behavior Research and Therapy,* 1979, **17**, 397–399.

Kelly, F.S., Farina, A., & Mosher, D.L. Ability of schizophrenic women to create a favorable impression on an interviewer. *Journal of Consulting and Clinical Psychology,* 1971, **36**, 404–409.

Kelley, G. *The Psychology of Personal Constructs.* Volumes I and II. New York: Norton, 1955.

Kelman, H. Processes of opinion change. *Public Opinion Quarterly,* 1961, **25**, 57–78.

Kessel, P. & McBrearty, J.F. Values and psychotherapy: A review of the literature. *Perceptual and Motor Skills,* 1967, **25**, 669–690 (Monograph Suppl. no. 2-V25).

Kiesler, D.J. Experimental designs in psychotherapy research. In A.E. Bergin and S.L. Garfield (Eds.), *Handbook of Psychotherapy and Behavior Change.* (1st ed.) New York: John Wiley & Sons, 1971.

Kiesler, D.J. Some myths of psychotherapy research and the search for a paradigm. In A.P. Goldstein and N. Stein (Eds.), *Prescriptive Psychotherapies.* New York: Pergamon, 1976.

Kilmann, P.R. & Howell, R.J. Effects of structure of marathon group therapy and locus of control on therapeutic outcome. *Journal of Consulting and Clinical Psychology,* 1974, **42**, 912.

Kimball, C.P. Conceptual development in psychosomatic medicine: 1939–1969. *Annals of Internal Medicine,* 1970, **73**, 307–316.

Kipper, D.A. & Ginot, E. Accuracy of evaluating videotape feedback and defense mechanisms. *Journal of Consulting and Clinical Psychology,* 1979, **47**, 493–499.

Klein, N.C., Alexander, J.F., & Parson, B.V. Impact of family systems intervention on recidivism and sibling delinquency: A model of primary prevention and program evaluation. *Journal of Consulting and Clinical Psychology,* 1977, **45**, 469–474.

Kleinke, C.L., Staneski, R.A., & Berger, D.E. Evaluation of an interview as a function of interviewer gaze, reinforcement of subject gaze and interviewer attractiveness. *Journal of Personality and Social Psychology,* 1975, **31**, 115–122.

Klerman, G.L. & Weissman, M.M. Interpersonal psychotherapy: Theory and research. In J. Rush (Ed.), *Short Term Psychotherapies for Depression.* New York: Guilford, 1982.

Klinger, E. *The Structure and Functions of Fantasy.* New York: John Wiley & Sons, 1971.

Koffman, A. Locus of control and adjustment related to outcome of two treatments for insomnia. *Dissertation Abstracts International,* 1977, **38**, 178–179A.

Kolb, D. An examination of psychotherapy process and outcome: The roles of patient locus of control, perception of the quality of the therapeutic relationship and involvement in therapy. Unpublished doctoral dissertation, University of Iowa, 1981.

Kolb, L.C. *Noye's Modern Clinical Psychiatry.* Philadelphia: W.B. Saunders, 1968.

Koss, M.P. Length of psychotherapy for clients seen in private practice. *Journal of Consulting and Clinical Psychology,* 1979, **47**, 210–212.

Kozel, N. Perception of emotion: Race of expressor, sex of perceiver, and mode of presentation. *Proceedings of the 77th Annual Convention of the American Psychological Association,* 1969, **4**, 39–40. (Summary)

Kozel, N.J. & Gitter, A.G. Perception of emotion: Differences in mode of presentation, sex of perceiver, and race of expressor. *CRC Report,* (Whole No. 18), Boston University, 1968.

Kramer, E. Judgement of personal characteristics and emotions from nonverbal properties of speech. *Psychological Bulletin,* 1963, **60**, 408–420.

Lacey, J.I. Psychophysiological approaches to the evaluation of psychotherapeutic process and outcome. In A.E. Rubinstein and M.B. Parloff (Eds.), *Research in Psychotherapy.* Washington, D.C.: National Publishing, 1959.

Lambert, M.J., Christensen, E.R., & DeJulio, S.S. (Eds.) *The Measurement of Psychotherapy Outcome in Research.* New York: John Wiley & Sons, in press.

Lambert, M.J. & DeJulio, S.S. The relative importance of client, therapist, and technique variables as predictors of psychotherapy outcome: The place of therapist "nonspecific" factors. Paper presented at the annual mid-winter meeting of the Division of Psychotherapy, American Psychological Association, Scottsdale, March 1978.

LaPointe, K.A. & Rimm, D.C. Cognitive, assertive and insight-oriented group therapies in the treatment of reactive depression in women. *Psychotherapy: Theory, Research and Practice*, 1980, **17**, 312–321.

Larson, D.G. Therapeutic styles and schoolism: A national survey. *Journal of Humanistic Psychology*, 1980, **20**, 3–20.

Lazarus, A. Behavior rehearsal versus non-directive therapy versus advice in effecting behavior change. *Journal of Behavior Research and Therapy*, 1966, **4**, 209–212.

Leal, L.L., Baxter, E.G., Martin, J., & Marx, R.W. Cognitive modification and systematic desensitization with test anxious high school students. *Journal of Counseling Psychology*, 1981, **28**, 525–528.

LeCompte, W. & Rosenfeld, H. Effects of minimal eye contact in the instruction period on impressions of the experimenter. *Journal of Experimental and Social Psychology*, 1971, **7**, 211–220.

Lefcourt, H.M. *Locus on Control: Current Trends in Theory and Research*. New York: Lawrence Erlbaum Publ., 1976.

Levine, M. Scientific method and the adversary model: Some preliminary thoughts. *American Psychologist*, 1974, **29**, 661–677.

Levitsky, A. & Perls, F.S. The rules and games of Gestalt Therapy. In H.M. Ruitenbeck (Ed.), *Group Therapy Today*. New York: Atherton, 1969.

Lewinsohn, P.M. & Libet, J. Pleasant events, activity schedules and depressions. *Journal of Abnormal Psychology*, 1972, **79**, 291–295.

Lieberman, M.A., Yalom, I.D., & Miles, M.B. *Encounter Groups: First Facts*. New York: Basic Books, 1973.

Lipsky, M.J., Kassinove, H., & Miller, N.J. Effects of rational-emotive therapy, rational role reversal, and rational-emotive imagery on the emotional adjustment of community mental health center patients. *Journal of Consulting and Clinical Psychology*, 1980, **48**, 366–374.

Lohmann, J. The assessment of therapist acutal in-therapy behavior as perceived by the patient. Paper presented at the 10th annual meeting of the Society for Psychotherapy Research, Oxford, England, July 1979.

London, P. *The Modes and Morals of Psychotherapy*. New York: Holt, Rinehart & Winston, 1964.

Luborsky, L., Chandler, M., Auerbach, A.H., Cohen, J., & Bachrach, H.M. Factors influencing the outcome of psychotherapy: A review of quantitative research. *Psychological Bulletin*, 1971, **75**, 145–185.

Luborsky, L. & McLellan, A.T. Optimal matching of patients with types of psychotherapy: What is known and some designs for knowing more. In E. Gottheil, A.T. McLellan and K.A. Druley (Eds.), *Matching patient needs and treatment methods in alcoholism and drug abuse*. Chicago: Charles C. Thomas, 1981.

Luborsky, L., Mintz, J., Auerbach, A., Christoph, P., Bachrach, H., Todd, T., Johnson, M., Cohen, M., & O'Brien, C.P. Predicting the outcomes of psychotherapy: Findings of the Penn Psychotherapy Project. *Archives of General Psychiatry*, 1980, **37**, 471–481.

Luborsky, L., Singer, B., & Luborsky, L. Comparative studies of psychotherapies. *Archives of General Psychiatry*, 1975, **32**, 995–1008.

Luborsky, L., Woody, G.E., McLellan, A.T., O'Brien, C.P., & Rosenzweig, J. Can independent judges recognize different psychotherapies? An experience with manual-guided therapies. *Journal of Consulting and Clinical Psychology*, 1982, **50**, 49–62.

Luthe, W. & Schultz, J.H. *Autogenic Therapy: Applications in Psychotherapy*. New York: Grune & Stratton, 1970.

Mahoney, M.J. Psychotherapy and the structure of personal revolutions. In M.J. Mahoney (Ed.), *Psychotherapy Process: Current Issues and Future Directions*. New York: Plenum, 1980.

Malan, D.H. The most important development since the discovery of the unconscious. In H. Davanloo (Ed.), *Short-term Dynamic Psychotherapy.* New York: Aronson, 1980.

Malan, D.H. *Toward the Validation of Dynamic Psychotherapy.* New York: Plenum, 1976.

Malkiewich, L.E. & Merluzzi, T.V. Rational restructuring versus desensitization with clients of diverse conceptual levels: A test of a client-treatment matching model. *Journal of Counseling Psychology,* 1980, **27**, 453–561.

Marks, I.M. Exposure treatments: Clinical applications. In S. Argas (Ed.), *Behavior Modification: Principles and Clinical Applications.* (2nd ed.) Boston: Little-Brown, 1978.

Marks, I.M. & Gelder, M.G. A controlled retrospective study of behavior therapy in phobic patients. *British Journal of Psychiatry,* 1965, **111**, 561–573.

Marziali, E., Marmar, C., & Krupnick, J. Therapeutic alliance scales: Development and relationship to psychotherapy outcome. *American Journal of Psychiatry,* 1981, **138**, 361–364.

McAllister, A. & Kiesler, D.J. Interviewer disclosure as a function of interpersonal trust, task, modeling and interviewer self disclosure. *Journal of Consulting and Clinical Psychology,* 1975, **43**, 428.

McCarron, L.T. & Appel, V.H. Categories of therapist verbalizations and patient-therapist autonomic response. *Journal of Consulting and Clinical Psychology,* 1971, **37**, 123–134.

McLachlan, J.C. Benefit from group therapy as a function of patient-therapist match on conceptual level. *Psychotherapy: Theory, Research and Practice,* 1972, **9**, 317–323.

Meara, N.M., Pepinsky, H.B., Shannon, J.W., & Murray, W.A. Semantic communication and expectations for counseling across three theoretical orientations. *Journal of Counseling Psychology,* 1981, **28**, 110–118.

Meehl, P.E. The cognitive activity of the clinician. *American Psychologist,* 1960, **15**, 19–27.

Mehrabian, A. *Nonverbal Communication.* Chicago: Aldine-Atherton, 1972.

Mehrabian, A. & Williams, M. Nonverbal communication of perceived and intended persuasiveness. *Journal of Personality and Social Psychology,* 1969, **13**, 37–58.

Meichenbaum, D. *Cognitive-Behavior Modification: An Integrated Approach.* New York: Plenum, 1977.

Meichenbaum, D. & Cameron, R. Training schizophrenics to talk to themselves: A means of developing attentional controls. *Behavior Therapy,* 1973, **4**, 515–534.

Meichenbaum, D., Gilmore, B., & Fedoravicius, A. Group insight vs. group desensitization in treating speech anxiety. *Journal of Consulting and Clinical Psychology,* 1971, **36**, 410–421.

Meichenbaum, D. & Goodman, J. Training impulsive children to talk to themselves: A means of developing self-control. *Journal of Abnormal Psychology,* 1971, **77**, 115–126.

Messer, S.B. & Meinster, M.O. Interactional effects of internal vs external locus of control and directive vs nondirective therapy: Fact or fiction. *Journal of Clinical Psychology,* 1980, **36**, 283–288.

Middlebrook, P.N. *Social Psychology and Modern Life.* New York: Alfred A. Knopf, 1974.

Miller, I.W., III & Norman, W.H. Effects of attributions for success on the alleviation of learned helplessness and depression. *Journal of Abnormal Psychology,* 1981, **90**, 113–124.

Millon, T. *Modern Psychopathology.* Philadelphia: W.B. Saunders, 1969.

Mintz, J. Measuring outcome in psychodynamic psychotherapy. *Archives of General Psychiatry,* 1981, **38**, 503–506.

Mintz, J., Auerbach, A.H., Luborsky, L., & Johnson, M. Patient's, therapist's, and observers' views of psychotherapy: A "Rashomon" experience or a reasonable concensus? *British Journal of Medical Psychology,* 1973, **46**, 83–89.

Mitchell, K.M., Truax, C.B., Bozarth, J.D., & Krauft, C.C. Antecedents to psychotherapeutic outcome. Paper presented at the 20th annual meeting of the Southeastern Psychological Association, Hollywood, FL, May 1974.

Montagu, A. *Touching.* New York: Perennial Library, 1971.

Moreno, J.L. *Psychodrama.* New York: Beacon, 1946.

Mueller, W.J. & Dilling, C.A. Therapist-client interview behavior and personality characteristics of therapists. *Journal of Projective Techniques and Personality Assessment*, 1968, **32**, 281–288.

Nash, E., Hoehn-Saric, R., Battle, C., Stone, A., Imber, S.D., & Frank, J.D. Systematic preparation of patients for short-term psychotherapy: II. Relation to characteristics of patients, therapist and the psychotherapeutic process. *Journal to Nervous and Mental Disease*, 1965, **140**, 374–383.

Neuhaus, E. & Astwood, W. *Practicing Psychotherapy.* New York: Human Sciences Press, 1980.

Nierenberg, G. & Calero, H. *How to Read a Person Like a Book*. New York: Hawthorne Books, 1971.

Norcross, J.C. & Prochaska, J.O. A National survey of clinical psychologists: Characteristics and activities. *The Clinical Psychologist*, 1982, **35**, 2, 1–8.

Ollendick, T.H. & Murphy, M.J. Differential effectiveness of muscular and cognitive relaxation as a function of locus of control. *Journal of Behavior Therapy and Experimental Psychiatry*, 1977, **8**, 223–228.

Olson, R.P., Ganley, R., Devine, V.T., & Dorsey, G.C., Jr. Long-term effects of behavioral versus insight oriented therapy with inpatient alcoholics. *Journal of Consulting and Clinical Psychology*, 1981, **49**, 866–877.

Omer, H. Paradoxical treatments: A unified concept. *Psychotherapy: Theory, Research and Practice*, 1981, **18**, 320–324.

Orlinsky, D.E. & Howard, K.I. The good therapy hour. *Archives of General Psychiatry*, 1967, **16**, 621–632.

Orlinsky, D.E. & Howard, K.I. The relation of process to outcome in psychotherapy. In S.L. Garfield and A.E. Bergin (Eds.), *Handbook of Psychotherapy and Behavior Change*. (2nd ed.) New York: John Wiley & Sons, 1978.

Orlinsky, D.E. & Howard, K.I. *Varieties of Psychotherapeutic Experience*. New York: Teachers College Press, 1975.

Orne, M.T. The nature of hypnosis: Artifact and essence. *Journal of Abnormal and Social Psychology*, 1959, **58**, 277–299.

Osborn, K. Validation of the Psychotherapy Preference Questionnaire: A Measure of expectancy and preference for directive vs. nondirective psychotherapy format. Unpublished doctoral dissertation, Virginia Polytechnic Institute and State University, 1981.

Overall, J.E. & Gorham, D.R. The Brief Psychiatric Scale. *Psychological Reports*, 1962, **10**, 799–812.

Parloff, M.B. Untitled. Presidential Address presented at the ninth annual meeting of the Society for Psychotherapy Research, Toronto, June 1978.

Parloff, M.B. Psychotherapy and research: An anaclitic depression. Frieda Fromm-Reichman Memorial Lecture, Washington School of Psychiatry, April 1980.

Paul, G.L. & Lentz, R.J. *Psychosocial Treatment of Chronic Mental Patients*. Cambridge, Mass.: Harvard University Press, 1977.

Paulson, M.J. & Lin, T.T. Predicting WAIS IQ From Shipley-Hartford Scores. *Journal of Clinical Psychology*, 1970, **26**, 453–461.

Perls, F.S. Dream seminars. In J. Fagan and I.L. Shepherd (Eds.), *Gestalt Therapy Now*. Palo Alto: Science and Behavior, 1970.

Perls, F.S. *Gestalt Therapy Verbatim*. Moab, Utah: Real People Press, 1969.

Perls, F.S., Hefferline, R.F., & Goodman, P. *Gestalt Therapy.* New York: Julian Press, 1951.

Phillis, J.A. Children's judgements of personality on the basis of voice quality. *Developmental Psychology*, 1970, **3**, 411.

Pilowsky, I. Abnormal illness behavior. *British Journal of Medical Psychology*, 1969, **42**, 347–351.

Polster, E. & Polster, M. *Gestalt Therapy Integrated*. New York: Brunner/Mazel, 1973.

Pope, B. *The Mental Health Interview: Research and Application*. New York: Pergamon, 1979.

Qualls, P.J. & Sheehan, P.W. Electromyograph biofeedback as a relaxation technique: A critical appraisal and reassessment. *Psychological Bulletin*, 1981, **90**, 21–42.

Quinlan, D.M. & Janis, I. Optimal level of contact in counselor-client dyads. Paper presented at the 6th Annual Meeting of the Society for Psychotherapy Research, Boston, June 1975.

Raush, H.L. Research, practice and accountability. *American Psychologist*, 1974, **29**, 678–681.

Ricks, D.F. Supershrink: Methods of a therapist judged successful on the basis of adult outcomes of adolescent patients. In D.F. Ricks, M. Roff and A. Thomas (Eds.), *Life History Research in Psychopathology.* Minneapolis: University of Minnesota Press, 1974.

Rock, N.L., Shipley, T.E., & Campbell, C. Hypnosis with untrained nonvolunteer patients in labor. *The International Journal of Clinical and Experimental Hypnosis*, 1969, **17**, 25–36.

Roessler, R. Personality, psychophysiology and performance. *Psychophysiology*, 1973, **10**, 315–327.

Rogers, C.R. *Client-centered Therapy.* Boston: Houghton-Mifflin, 1951.

Rogers, C.R. The necessary and sufficient conditions of therapeutic personality changes. *Journal of Consulting Psychology*, 1957, **21**, 95–103.

Rokeach, M. *The Nature of Human Values*. New York: Free Press, 1973.

Rokeach, M. *The Three Christs of Ypsilanti*. New York: Vintage, 1964.

Rosen, G.M., Glasgow, R.E., & Barrera, M., Jr. A controlled study to assess the clinical efficacy of totally self-administered systematic desensitization. *Journal of Consulting and Clinical Psychology*, 1976, **44**, 208–217.

Rosenhan, D.L. On being sane in insane places. *Science*, 1973, **179**, 250–258.

Rosenthal, D. Changes in some moral values following psychotherapy. *Journal of Consulting Psychology*, 1955, **19**, 431–436.

Rotter, J.B. Generalized expectancies for internal versus external control of reinforcement. *Psychological Monographs*, 1966, **80**, (1, Whole No. 609).

Rotter, J.B. *Social Learning and Clinical Psychology.* Englewood Cliffs, NJ: Prentice-Hall, 1954.

Rowe, C.J. *An Outline of Psychiatry.* Dubuque, Iowa: Wm. C. Brown, 1980.

Rush, A.J., Beck, A.T., Kovacs, M., & Hollon, S.D. Comparative efficacy of cognitive therapy and pharmacotherapy in the treatment of depressed outpatients. *Cognitive Therapy and Research*, 1977, **1**, 17–38.

Rush, A.J., Hollon, S.D., Beck, A.T., & Kovacs, M. Depression: Must pharmacotherapy fail for cognitive therapy to succeed? *Cognitive Therapy and Research*, 1978, **2**, 199–206.

Russell, R.L. & Stiles, W.B. Categories for classifying language in psychotherapy. *Psychological Bulletin*, 1979, **86**, 404–419.

Sarbin, T.R. & Slagle, R.W. Hypnosis and psychophysiological outcomes. In E. Fromm and R.E. Shor (Eds.), *Hypnosis: Developments in Research and New Perspectives*. (2nd ed.) New York: Aldine, 1979.

Satir, V. *Conjoint Family Therapy.* Palo Alto: Science and Behavior Books, 1964.

Sattler, J.M. The effects of therapist-client racial similarity. In A.S. Gurman and A.M. Razin (Eds.), *Effective Psychotherapy: A Handbook of Research*, New York: Pergamon, 1977.

Scheidler, T. Use of fantasy as a therapeutic agent in latency-age groups. *Psychotherapy: Theory, Research and Practice*, 1972, **9**, 299–302.

Scherer, D. Attribution of personality from voice: A cross cultural study of interpersonal perception. *Proceedings of the 79th Annual Convention of the American Psychological Association*, 1971, **6**, 351–352. (Summary)

Schlamowitz, K.E., Beutler, L.E., Scott, F.B., Karacan, I., & Ware, C. Reactions to the implantation of of an inflatable penile prosthesis among psychogenically and organically impotent males. *The Journal of Urology*, in press.

Schmidt, L.D. & Strong, S.R. Attractiveness and influence in counseling. *Journal of Counseling Psychology*, 1971, **18**, 348–351.

Schofield, W. *Psychotherapy, the Purchase of Friendship*. Englewood Cliffs, N.J.: Prentice Hall, 1964.

Schramski, T.G. The persistence of therapeutic change. Unpublished doctoral dissertation, University of Arizona, 1981.

Schwartz, B.D. The initial versus subsequent theoretical positions: Does the psychotherapist's personality make a difference? *Psychotherapy: Theory, Research and Practice*, 1978, **15**, 344–349.

Schwartz, R.D. & Higgins, R.L. Differential outcomes from automated assertion training as a function of locus of control. *Journal of Consulting and Clinical Psychology*, 1979, **47**, 686–694.

Sherif, M. & Hovland, C.I. *Social Judgement*. New Haven: Yale University, 1961.

Shipley, W.C. A self-administering scale for measuring intellectual impairment and deterioration. *Journal of Psychology*, 1940, **9**, 371–377.

Shorr, J.E. *Psychotherapy Through Imagery*. New York: Intercontinental Medical Corp., 1974.

Shows, W.D. & Carson, R.C. The A–B therapist "type" distinction and spatial orientation: Replication and extension. *The Journal of Nervous and Mental Disease*, 1966, **141**, 456–462.

Sifneos, P.E. *Short-term Dynamic Psychotherapy: Evaluation and Technique*. New York: Plenum Press, 1979.

Simonton, B.C., Simonton, S.M., & Creighton, J. *Getting Well Again*. Los Angeles: J.P. Tacher, 1978.

Skinner, B.F. *Science and Human Behavior*. New York: MacMillan, 1953.

Sloane, R.B., Staples, F.R., Cristol, A.H., Yorkston, N.J., & Whipple, K. *Psychotherapy Versus Behavior Therapy*. Cambridge: Harvard University Press, 1975.

Smith, E.W.L. Postural and gestural communication of A and B "therapist types" during dyadic interviews. *Journal of Consulting and Clinical Psychology*, 1972, **39**, 29–36.

Smith, M.B. *Social Psychology and Human Values*. Chicago: Aldine, 1969.

Smith, M.L., Glass, G.V., & Miller, T.I. *The Benefits of Psychotherapy*. Baltimore: Johns Hopkins, 1980.

Snyder, C.R. & Fromkin, H.L. *Uniqueness: The Human Pursuit of Difference*. New York: Plenum, 1980.

Sommer, R. *Personal Space: The Behavioral Basis of Design*. Englewood Cliffs, NJ: Prentice-Hall, 1969.

Spiegel, J.P. & Machotka, P. *Messages of the Body*. New York: Free Press, 1974.

Spinetta, J.J., Rigler, D., & Karon, M. Personal space as a measure of a dying child's sense of isolation. *Journal of Consulting and Clinical Psychology*, 1974, **42**, 751–756.

Stambaugh, E.E. & House, A.E. Multimodality treatment of migraine headache: A case study utilizing biofeedback, relaxation, autogenic and hypnotic treatments. *The American Journal of Clinical Hypnosis*, 1977, **19**, 235–240.

Stampfl, T.G. & Levis, D.J. Essentials of Implosive Therapy: A learning-theory-based psychodynamic behavioral therapy. *Journal of Abnormal Psychology*, 1967, **72**, 496–503.

Staples, F.R., Sloane, R.B., Whipple, K., Cristol, A.H., & Yorkston, N.J. Process and outcome in psychotherapy and behavior therapy. *Journal of Consulting and Clinical Psychology*, 1976, **44**, 340–350.

Stein, D.M. The effectiveness of paratherapists: An integration of empirical research. Unpublished doctoral dissertation, Brigham Young University, 1982.

Steiner, I. Perceived freedom. In L. Berkowitz (Ed.), *Advances in Experimental Social Psychology*. Vol. 5. New York: Academic Press, 1970.

Stiles, W.B. Psychotherapy recapitulates ontogeny: The epigenesis of intensive interpersonal relationships. *Psychotherapy: Theory, Research and Practice*, 1979, **16**, 391–404.

Storr, A. *The Art of Psychotherapy*. New York: Methuen, 1980.

Stroebel, C.F. *Biofeedback Procedures*. New York: Biomonitoring Application, 1978.

Strong, S.R. Counseling: An interpersonal influence process. *Journal of Counseling Psychology*, 1968, **15**, 215–224.

Strong, S.R. & Dixon, D.N. Expertness, attractiveness and influence in counseling. *Journal of Counseling Psychology*, 1971, **18**, 562–570.

Strong, S.R. & Schmidt, L.D. Trustworthiness and influence in counseling. *Journal of Counseling Psychology*, 1970, **17**, 197–204.

Strupp, H.H. An objective comparison of Rogerian and psychoanalytic techniques. *Journal of Consulting Psychology*, 1955, **19**, 1–7.

Strupp, H.H. The performance of psychoanalytic and client-centered therapists in an initial interview. *Journal of Consulting Psychology*, 1958, **22**, 265–274.

Strupp, H.H. On the basic ingredients of psychotherapy. *Journal of Consulting and Clinical Psychology*, 1973, **41**, 1–8.

Strupp, H.H. Some observations on the fallacy of value-free psychotherapy and the empty organism: Comments on a case study. *Journal of Abnormal Psychology*, 1974, **83**, 199–201.

Strupp, H.H. The therapist's theoretical orientation: An overrated variable. *Psychotherapy: Theory, Research and Practice*, 1978, **15**, 314–317.

Strupp, H.H. Clinical research, practice and the crisis of confidence. *Journal of Consulting and Clinical Psychology*, 1981, **49**, 216–219. (a)

Strupp, H.H. Toward the refinement of time-limited dynamic psychotherapy. In S.H. Budman (Ed.), *Forms of Brief Therapy*. New York: Guilford Press, 1981. (b)

Strupp, H.H. & Bloxum, A.L. Preparing lower class patients for group psychotherapy: Development and evaluation of a role-induction film. *Journal of Consulting and Clinical Psychology*, 1973, **41**, 373–384.

Strupp, H.H. & Hadley, S.W. A tripartite model of mental health and therapeutic outcomes. *American Psychologist*, 1977, **32**, 187–196.

Strupp, H.H. & Hadley, S.W. Specific vs. nonspecific factors in psychotherapy: A controlled study of outcome. *Archives of General Psychiatry*, 1979, **36**, 1125–1136.

Strupp, H.H., Hadley, S.W., & Gomes-Schwartz, B. *Psychotherapy for Better or Worse: The Problem of Negative Effects*. New York: Jason Aronson Inc., 1977.

Stuart, R.B. Behavioral contracting within the families of delinquents. *Journal of Behavior Therapy and Experimental Psychiatry*, 1971, **2**, 1–11.

Sullivan, H.S. *The Interpersonal Theory of Psychiatry*. New York: Norton, 1953.

Sundland, D.M. Theoretical orientation: A multi-professional American sample. Paper presented at the eighth annual Meeting of the Society for Psychotherapy Research, Madison, June 1977.

Sundland, D.M. & Barker, E.N. The orientation of psychotherapists. *Journal of Consulting Psychology*, 1962, **26**, 201–212.

Szasz, T.S. The myth of mental illness. *American Psychologist*, 1960, **15**, 113–118.

Tankard, J.W. Effects of eye position on person perception. *Perceptual and Motor Skills*, 1970, **31**, 883–893.

Taylor, J.W. Relationship of success and length in psychotherapy. *Journal of Consulting Psychology*, 1956, **5**, 232.

Tennen, H., Rohrbaugh, M., Press, S., & White, L. Reactance theory and therapeutic paradox: A compliance-defiance model. *Psychotherapy: Theory, Research and Practice*, 1981, **18**, 14–22.

Thompson, T. & Dockens, W.S. (Eds.) *Applications of Behavior Modification*. New York: Academic Press, 1975.

Thorne, F.C. Principles of directive counseling and psychotherapy. *American Psychologist*, 1948, **3**, 160–165.

Tolor, A. & Reznikoff, M. Relation between insight, repression-sensitization, internal-external control and death anxiety. *Journal of Abnormal Psychology*, 1967, **72**, 426–430.

Townsend, R.E., House, J.F., & Addario, D. A comparison of biofeedback-mediated relaxation and group therapy in the treatment of chronic anxiety. *American Journal of Psychiatry*, 1975, **132**, 598–601.

Truax, C.B. & Mitchell, K.M. Research on certain therapist interpersonal skills in relation to process and outcome. In A.E. Bergin and S.L. Garfield (Eds.), *Handbook of Psychotherapy and Behavior Change*. (1st ed.) New York: John Wiley & Sons, 1971.

Truax, C.B., Silber, L.D., & Wargo, D.G. Training and change in psychotherapeutic skills. Unpublished manuscript, University of Arkansas, 1966.

Turner, S.M., Calhoun, K.S., & Adams, H.E. (Eds.) *Handbook of Clinical Behavior Therapy.* New York: John Wiley & Sons, 1981.

Ullmann, L.P. & Krasner, L. (Eds.) *Case Studies in Behavior Modification.* New York: Holt, Rinehart & Winston, 1965.

Ullmann, L.P. & Krasner, L. *A Psychological Approach to Abnormal Behavior.* Englewood Cliffs, NJ: Prentice-Hall, 1969.

Valiant, G.E. Theoretical hierarchy of adaptive ego mechanisms. *Archives of General Psychiatry.* 1971, **24**, 107–118.

VandenBos, G.R. & Karon, B.P. Pathogenesis: A new therapist personality dimension related to therapeutic effectiveness: *Journal of Personality Assessment*, 1971, **35**, 252–260.

Verplanck, W.S. The control of content of conversation: Reinforcement of statements of opinion. *Journal of Abnormal and Social Psychology,* 1955, **51**, 668–676.

Wachtel, P.L. *Psychoanalysis and Behavior Therapy.* New York: Basic Books, 1977.

Wadden, T.A. & Anderson, C.H. The clinical use of hypnosis. *Psychological Bulletin*, 1982, **91**, 215–243.

Wallach, M.S. & Strupp, H.H. Dimensions of psychotherapists' activity. *Journal of Consulting Psychology,* 1964, **28**, 120–125.

Walton, D.E. An exploratory study: Personality factors and theoretical orientations of therapists. *Psychotherapy: Theory, Research and Practice*, 1978, **15**, 390–395.

Warren, N.C. & Rice, L.N. Structuring and stabilizing psychotherapy for low-prognosis clients. *Journal of Consulting and Clinical Psychology,* 1972, **39**, 173–181.

Waskow, I.E. & Parloff, M.B. (Eds.) *Psychotherapy Change Measures.* (Publication No. 74-120) Rockville, Maryland: National Institute of Mental Health, 1975.

Watson, D.L. & Tharp, R.G. *Self-Directed Behavior: Self-Modification for Personal Adjustment.* Monterey, CA: Brooks/Cole, 1972.

Weakland, J.H., Fisch, R., Watzlawich, P., & Brodin, A.M. Brief therapy: Focused problem resolution. *Family Process*, 1974, **13**, 141–168.

Weathers, L. & Liberman, R.P. Contingency contracting with families of delinquent adolescents. *Behavior Therapy,* 1975, **6**, 356–366.

Weekes, C. *Simple, Effective Treatment of Agoraphobia.* New York: Hawthorne, 1976.

Weeks, G.R. & L'Abate, L. *Paradoxical Psychotherapy: Theory and Practice With Individuals, Couples, and Families.* New York: Brunner/Mazel, 1982.

Weissman, M.M. & Paykel, E.S. *The Depressed Woman: A Study of Social Relationships.* Chicago: University of Chicago Press, 1974.

Welkowitz, J. & Kuc, M. Interrelationships among warmth, genuineness, empathy, and temporal speech patterns in interpersonal interaction. *Journal of Consulting and Clinical Psychology,* 1973, **41**, 472–473.

Welsh, G.S. An anxiety index and an internalization ratio for the MMPI. *Journal of Consulting Psychology,* 1952, **16**, 65–72.

Widman, J.C. Effects of therapist personality characteristics on client locus of control as measured by the Rotter Internal-external Locus of Control Scale. *Dissertation Abstracts International*, 1978, **39**, 685–686A.

Wilkins, G., Epting, F., & VandeRiet, H. Relationships between repression-sensitization and interpersonal cognitive complexity. *Journal of Consulting and Clinical Psychology,* 1972, **39**, 448–450.

Wilson, W. & Miller, H. Repetition, order of presentation and timing of arguments and measures as determiners of opinion change. *Journal of Personality and Social Psychology,* 1968, **9**, 184–188.

Wolfe, B.E. Moral transformations in psychotherapy. *Counseling and Values*, 1978, **23**, 43–48.

Wolpe, J. *The Practice of Behavior Therapy.* New York: Pergamon, 1973.

Wolpe, J., Brady, J.P., Serber, M., Agras, W.S., & Liberman, R.P. The current status of systematic desensitization. *American Journal of Psychiatry*, 1973, **130**, 961–965.

Wolpe, J. & Lazarus, A. *Behavior Therapy Techniques: A Guide to the Treatment of Neuroses*. Oxford: Pergamon Press, 1966.

Yates, A. *Biofeedback and the Modification of Behavior*. New York: Plenum, 1980.

Zillman, D. Rhetorical elicitation of agreement in persuasion. *Journal of Personality and Social Psychology*, 1972, **21**, 159–165.

Zimbardo, P.G. (Ed.) *The Cognitive Control of Motivation: The Consequences of Choice and Dissonance*. Glenview, Ill.: Scott, Foresman & Co., 1969.

Zimmer, J.M. & Pepyne, E.W. A descriptive and comparative study of dimensions of counselor response. *Journal of Counseling Psychology*, 1971, **18**, 441–447.

AUTHOR INDEX

SUBJECT INDEX

About the Author

Larry E. Beutler, Ph.D., is professor of psychiatry and psychology at the University of Arizona, College of Medicine. He received B.A. and M.S. degrees from Utah State University in Logan, Utah. His Ph.D. was obtained in clinical psychology from the University of Nebraska-Lincoln, in 1970. He served on the faculties of Duke University Medical Center (Highland Hospital Division), Stephen F. Austin State University, and Baylor College of Medicine before taking his current position.

Dr. Beutler is a Diplomate of the American Board of Professional Psychology in Clinical Psychology and has been active both as a clinical practitioner, educator, and psychotherapy researcher. He has authored or coauthored approximately 200 papers, journal articles, and book chapters on psychotherapy, psychopathology, sexual dysfunctions, sleep disorders and clinical training. In addition to the current book, he has coedited a book entitled, *Special Problems in Child and Adolescent Behavior.*

Dr. Beutler is currently President of the Section on Continuing Professional Development for the American Psychological Association's Division of Clinical Psychology. He has served in numerous capacities for national, state, and local professional organizations. He is currently on the editorial board for the *Journal of Consulting and Clinical Psychology,* the *Journal of Social and Clinical Psychology,* and *Exceptional People Quarterly.* He also serves as an ad hoc review editor for numerous other journals.

Dr. Beutler currently lives in Tucson, Arizona where he is Chief of Clinical Psychology and Director of Clinical Research within the Department of Psychiatry at the University of Arizona.